Edward D. (Edward Dafydd) Morris

Ecclesiology

A Treatise on the Church and Kingdom of God on Earth

Edward D. (Edward Dafydd) Morris
Ecclesiology
A Treatise on the Church and Kingdom of God on Earth
ISBN/EAN: 9783337144302
Printed in Europe, USA, Canada, Australia, Japan
Cover: Foto ©Lupo / pixelio.de

More available books at **www.hansebooks.com**

THE CHRISTIAN DOCTRINE IN OUTLINE

ECCLESIOLOGY

A TREATISE ON

THE CHURCH AND KINGDOM OF GOD ON EARTH

BY

EDWARD D. MORRIS, D.D.
PROFESSOR OF SYSTEMATIC THEOLOGY IN LANE THEOLOGICAL SEMINARY

Εἰς μίαν, ἁγίαν, καθολικὴν καὶ ἀποστολικὴν Ἐκκλησίαν.
—*Symbolum Nicaeno Const.*

NEW YORK
CHARLES SCRIBNER'S SONS
1885

PREFATORY.

The following pages contain a condensed summary of a series of Lectures delivered during the past seventeen years to the students of this Institution, in this department of Christian Doctrine. In the effort to prepare a succinct treatise, available for practical uses, rather than an elaborate dissertation, it has been deemed desirable to omit all extended discussion of controverted points, and simply to incorporate, with the briefest statement of grounds and reasons, such conclusions as have justified themselves to the author after careful investigation. Minor divisions and notations, employed in the class-room, have for the most part been omitted; only such authorities as are easily accessible, are mentioned by way of reference.

Prepared originally for the benefit of theological students, this brief volume—the fruit of many happy studies in this interesting field—is now, with some hesitation, sent forth from its seclusion here, in the hope that it may prove useful in wider circles. The fact that there is in present circulation, hardly any work of the same class, and covering the same ground, seems in part at least to justify such hope. And if the perusal of this treatise should help any single mind into clearer, broader, more irenic conceptions of the Church, or should contribute in the slightest measure toward the harmonizing of opinion and action among Christian men around this one divine Institution on whose growth and efficiency the interests of spiritual Christianity, the world over, seem now so vitally dependent, that hope will have gained its largest realization.

E. D. M.

Lane Theological Seminary:
January, 1885.

CONTENTS.

INTRODUCTION. 5–13

I. Ecclesiology: The Term Defined, . . 5
II. Relation to other Divisions of Doctrine, 7
III. Biblical Basis of the Doctrine, . . 8
IV. Sketch of Opinions in Ecclesiology, 9
V. Importance of the Proposed Inquiry, 11

CHAPTER FIRST.

THE CHURCH IN THE DIVINE PLAN.

THE IDEA, THE HISTORY, AND THE JUSTIFICATION. 13–41

I. Definition of the Term, Church: Various Uses, . 13
II. Analysis of the Term:
    Association, Piety, Constitution, Object, Permanence, . 16
III. Historic Unfolding of this Conception, 19
IV. The Church Patriarchal: First Division, 20
V. The Church Patriarchal: Second Division:
    The Abrahamic Church, ... 22
VI. The Church Hebraic: Preliminary Remarks, . . 23
VII. The Church Hebraic: Special Characteristics:
    Doctrine, Law, Ritual, Priesthood, Seal, . . 24
VIII. The Church Hebraic: Historic Development:
    The Theocratic, the Royal, the Prophetic Eras, 27
IX. The Church as Constituted by Christ: Preliminary, . 29
X. Its Identity with Patriarchal and Hebraic Churches:
    In Foundation, in Conditions, in Aim and Destiny, 31
XI. Important Points of Contrast Noted, . 32
XII. General Argument For The Church: . . 33
    1. It lies constructively in the Religious Nature, . 34
    2. Required by Religion as an Experience, . . . 36
    3. Religion perpetuated and advanced through the Church, 38
    4. The Divine Glory manifested through it, . 39

CHAPTER SECOND.

THE IMPERSONAL CONSTITUENTS OF THE CHURCH:

ITS DOCTRINES, ITS SACRAMENTS, ITS ORDINANCES.   41–79

I. DOCTRINES DEFINED: CHURCH CREEDS DESCRIBED, . 42
II. CHURCH CREEDS: REASONS FOR THEIR EXISTENCE, . 43
III. OBJECTIONS TO CREEDS: LIMITATIONS OF CREEDS, . . 44
IV. SACRAMENTS DEFINED: NUMBER OF SACRAMENTS, . . 46
V. BAPTISM DEFINED: GENERAL SCRIPTURAL WARRANT, . 48
VI. BAPTISM: ITS NATURE AND DESIGN, . . . 50
VII. BAPTISM: MODES OF ADMINISTRATION:
    Further Questions as to Usage, . 52
VIII. BAPTISM: SUBJECTS OR RECIPIENTS, . 56
IX. SCRIPTURE WITNESS TO INFANT BAPTISM, . 59
X. THE LORD'S SUPPER: WARRANT AND NATURE, . 62
XI. THE LORD'S SUPPER: DESIGN AND PARTICIPANTS, . 65
XII. THE LORD'S SUPPER: INFUENCE AND WORTH:
    Other kindred Observances, ... 67
XIII. ORDINANCES DEFINED: POSITIVE INSTITUTIONS, 70
XIV. THE SABBATH—A SACRED TIME:
    1. Its triple Institution, . . . 71
    2. Its threefold Design, . . 72
    3. Its perpetual Obligation, . . 73
    4. The Change of Day justified, . 74
    5. Manner and Spirit of Observance, . 74
XV. THREE ASSOCIATED ORDINANCES:
    1. The Sanctuary—a Sacred Place, . 75
    2. The Means of Grace—a Sacred Cultus, . 77
    3. The Ministry—a Sacred Service, . . . 78

CHAPTER THIRD.

THE PERSONAL CONSTITUENTS OF THE CHURCH:

ITS MEMBERS, ITS OFFICERS.   80–111

I. THE PERSONAL ELEMENT SUPREME, . . . 80
II. CHURCH MEMBERSHIP: PRELIMINARY VIEW, . 82
III. MEMBERSHIP IN THE PRIMITIVE CHURCH, . . 83

IV. GREEK AND PAPAL VIEW OF MEMBERSHIP, . . . 85
V. PROTESTANT VIEW AFTER THE REFORMATION, . . . 87
VI. CURRENT PROTESTANT OPINION: THE FORMAL VIEW, . 89
VII. CURRENT PROTESTANT OPINION: THE SPIRITUAL VIEW, . . 91
VIII. MEMBERSHIP IN THE PARTICULAR CHURCH:
 Four specific Conditions requisite, . . . 94
IX. MEMBERSHIP OF THE CHILDREN OF BELIEVERS, . 96
X. THE CHURCH AN ORGANIZATION:
 Offices and Officers requisite, . . . 98
XI. TEMPORARY CHURCH OFFICES:
 1. The Prophetical Office, . 100
 2. The Apostolical Office, . 100
 3. The Evangelistic Office, . 102
XII. PERMANENT CHURCH OFFICES:
 1. The Office of Instruction, . . 104
 2. The Office of Government, . . 105
 3. The Office of Administration, . . 106
XIII. OFFICERS REQUISITE IN THE CHURCH:
 The Ministry—call and functions, . . . 107
XIV. CHURCH OFFICERS: FURTHER QUESTIONS:
 Investiture, Authority, Limitations in Tenure, . 110

CHAPTER FOURTH.

THE CHURCH AS A DIVINE KINGDOM:

GOVERNMENT, POLITIES, DISCIPLINE.   112–151

I. THE CHURCH AS A STRUCTURE: GENERAL CONCEPTION, . 112
II. CHURCH GOVERNMENT DEFINED AND JUSTIFIED, . . 114
III. CHURCH GOVERNMENT IN SCRIPTURE. 117
IV. VARIETIES IN CHURCH GOVERNMENT: DIVERSE POLITIES, . . 118
V. THE PAPAL POLITY: ITS POSITION AND CLAIM, . . . 121
VI. THE PAPAL POLITY CONSIDERED, ... 124
VII. THE PRELATIC POLITY: ITS CLAIM OUTLINED, . . 127
VIII. PRELATISM EXAMINED, ... 129
IX. INDEPENDENCY: ITS GENERAL POSITION, . . 132
X. THE CLAIM OF INDEPENDENCY REVIEWED, . . . 135
XI. THE REPRESENTATIVE POLITY STATED AND JUSTIFIED: . 137
 1. Derived from the Jewish synagogue system, . 139

2. Developed gradually under apostolic guidance, . . 140
3. Designed to secure efficiency in government, . 141
4. Represented church fellowship and unity, . . 142
5. Justified by Scripture and experience, . 143
XII. CARDINAL PRINCIPLES IN ADMINISTRATION:
  Headship of Christ: Supremacy of Scripture, . 143
XIII. PRACTICAL ADMINISTRATION:
  Authority and Obedience, . . . 146
XIV. DISCIPLINE AS A CHURCH FUNCTION:
  Warrant, Aims, Spirit, Methods, Extent, . 148

CHAPTER FIFTH.

THE CHURCH IN HUMAN SOCIETY:

ITS UNITY, ITS GROWTH, ITS RELATIONS.

I. PRESENT CHURCH DIVISIONS: FORMS AND CAUSES, . 151
II. CHURCH DIVISIONS: GOOD AND EVIL FRUITS, . 154
III. ORGANIC ONENESS: THE PAPAL VIEW, . . 156
IV. SPIRITUAL UNITY: THE PROTESTANT VIEW, . . . 158
V. THE CHRISTIAN CHURCH A GROWTH: GENERAL CONCEPTION, . 160
VI. INTERNAL LAW OF CHURCH GROWTH:
  Spiritual Propagation, ... 162
VII. EXTERNAL LAW OF CHURCH GROWTH:
  Spiritual Conquest, ... 165
VIII. ILLICIT PROCESSES OF CHURCH GROWTH, ... 167
IX. THE CHURCH IN HUMAN SOCIETY: GENERAL VIEW, . . 169
X. THE CHURCH AND HUMAN SIN, ... 171
XI. THE CHURCH AND HUMAN INSTITUTIONS:
  Church and the Family: Church and State, . . 174
XII. THE CHURCH AND EDUCATION: CHURCH AND CULTURE, . . 177
XIII. THE CHURCH AND MORALITY: CHURCH AND REFORM, . . 181
XIV. THE CHURCH AND CIVILIZATION:
  Consummation of Humanity through the Church, . 183

ECCLESIOLOGY:

THE CHURCH AND KINGDOM OF GOD ON EARTH.

INTRODUCTION.

I. ECCLESIOLOGY: THE TERM DEFINED.—The work of Salvation begins with the individual soul. In its exterior form, it is a redemption of the sinner from the judicial grasp of divine law, and from the penal issues of his sin. In its interior substance, it is a spiritual deliverance from sin itself, and a restoration of the sinner to holiness, and to everlasting life. This personal salvation, wrought out externally through the redemptive work of the Son of God, and internally through the regenerative and sanctifying ministries of the Spirit of God, must antedate in time and become the substantial basis of all social or generic changes effected among mankind through the Gospel. The personal result is always and of necessity primary. The general aim and methods of the Gospel, the historic labors of our Lord for individual souls, the registered activities of the Holy Ghost, the peculiar type of character developed in and through these divine instrumentalities, all illustrate this great antecedent and most practical truth: Salvation must begin with the individual man.

Yet Christianity is also social and generic in both its idea and its manifestation. It contemplates man in the aggregate; it seeks the restoration of human society: its gracious purpose can be consummated only in the salvation of Humanity. As sin has passed through the individual man into the family, corrupting and destroying the household life, the salutary power of the Gospel must enter into the family circle to transform it by the same gracious processes through which the individual is both justified and sanctified before God. As sin has passed in like manner into the state, this divine religion must also enter into the political life of man, to arrest the sway of evil, purify social principle and practice, restore true civil order, and in a word renew the state as well as the family. More broadly still, as sin has penetrated and infected our humanity in the aggregate, working everywhere organic as well as particular devastation, Christianity must aim at nothing less than the regeneration of that humanity in every aspect and every relation,—the restoration on the earth of that social as well as individual Paradise which sin has both forfeited and destroyed. The failure to recognize these generic aims and issues of Christianity, originating in a false or defective Anthropology, leads on directly to much narrow or erroneous teaching respecting the sublime ministry of the Christian faith in the world. The purely individualistic view of salvation is one against which, therefore, the devout student should be ever on his guard: Our Gospel is a Gospel for humanity as well as for the individual man.

In this comprehensive social work, the chief agent or instrument employed is the Church,—a divine organism set up among men for the purpose of affecting humanity savingly through the Gospel, and endowed with all the capabilities requisite to this high function. Regarded as an organism, the Church receives and enjoys the same gracious influences which produce and develop the Christian life in the individual soul. It is established by Christ, founded on His Word, sustained by His Spirit, quickened through grace, and divinely commissioned for its special work. Regarded as an instrumentality, the Church is vested with divine efficiency adequate to this peculiar mission: the power of Christianity to penetrate and restore human society is specially embodied in it. It is true that this gracious mission is entrusted immediately to each and every disciple,—in virtue of his renewed nature each believer is directly sent forth by Christ to do his specific part in the restoration of our lost humanity to holiness and to God. It is true that God also utilizes the family and the state, in the consummation of His gracious purpose; for whenever salvation enters a family, renewing the inmates individually through His Word and Spirit, He not only raises the family inwardly into a new life, but transforms it at once into a new regenerative force in human society,—as truly an agent in the spiritual restoration of humanity, though in a subordinate sphere, as the Church itself. So when the world comes somewhere in the future to see the sublime spectacle of a thoroughly Christianized state, it will be made to realize as we can not now realize, what a mighty instrumentality for the diffusion and perpetuation of the true religion such a state may be. Yet it is to the Church, as at once the family of God and the kingdom of God among men, that this great task is primarily entrusted: it is through the Church as a divine organism and instrumentality that these results are mainly to be attained.[1]

---

[1] "What is given objectively in Christ, is to be appropriated by Humanity. But Humanity is designed, by such appropriation, to become the Church, or Community of Faith. As the center of the Kingdom of God, the Church is the final aim which Christ proposes to His activity." DORNER, *Theol.*, Vol. IV: 154. Also, NEANDER, *Planting and Training*, etc., pp. 417, *seq.*

Hence ECCLESIOLOGY, which may be defined as *the doctrine of Scripture respecting the Church*, in the broadest sense of this phrase, is an essential and conspicuous division of Christian Theology. As a complete theological system can not pause with the contemplation of the work of grace wrought in the individual man, but must proceed to consider that work as wrought out more extensively in the heart of humanity, such a system must include a full account of that divine agency through which this broader work is mainly accomplished. It must thoughtfully study and describe the Church, not merely in its historic manifestations, but also in its nature and constituents, in its constitution and spirit and capabilities, and in its authorized relations to the salvation of mankind. To such an investigation, conducted on the simple basis of Scripture, in loyalty to the divine Word, and in the temper of loving appreciation, attention will here be given.

II. RELATION TO OTHER DIVISIONS OF CHRISTIAN DOCTRINE.—It is important at the outset, that this division of sacred doctrine should be set in proper relations to the other main departments of Christian theology. Clear and sound views of Revelation, for example, alone can furnish adequate protection against the error of regarding the Church, with its organization and ordinances, as a human institution merely; or against the equally mischievous error of going beyond what the Bible teaches, and claiming divine warrant for what are merely the churchly contrivances or appointments of men. In like manner, an erroneous Anthropology, especially on the point of human sinfulness and guilt and peril, will lead on at once to pernicious theories respecting the real need or the proper field and functions of this divine organism. Nor can any sound conception of the Church, especially in its great providential mission in the world, be gained by one who cherishes serious error respecting the divine Paternity,—the being and providence and moral administration and gracious purpose of God the Father, as related to human life and human destiny. Still more obvious is it, that just and deep views of the person and work of Christ and of the Holy Spirit (Soteriology and Pneumatology) and especially of salvation itself contemplated as a personal experience and possession, must furnish an essential basis for sound teaching as to that peculiar instrumentality through which salvation is primarily to be diffused and perpetuated among men. And finally, no small part of the error into which many fall, respecting the future of humanity on earth, the coming and reign of Christ among men, the ultimate supremacy of true religion, the article of death, the intermediate estate, and even the resurrection and judgment and the life to come, has its origin in the failure to appreciate the essential elements, the true significance, of a thoroughly biblical Ecclesiology.

Two general tendencies to error are especially recognizable here. The first is the tendency so disastrously illustrated in the Papal, and in some affiliated communions,—the tendency to lift the doctrine of the Church out of its proper relation to other departments of doctrine, and to give it an undue prominence in the Christian scheme: to exalt sacraments and ordinances unduly, to carry legitimate authority out into tyrannical applications, and even to make the Church an agent coördinate with Christ himself in the bestowment of salvation. The second is the tendency, almost equally disastrous among Protestants, to decry churchly authority, to undervalue churchly teaching, to regard sacraments and ordinances and constitutions as insignificant, and even to pronounce the Church a human organization merely, void of supernatural efficiency, and without distinctive mission among men. Against all such perversion a comprehensive Ecclesiology, constructed purely from the Scripture and received and maintained in its proper relations, in the temper of true faith, furnishes the only adequate protection.

III. BIBLICAL BASIS OF THE DOCTRINE.—The cardinal principle in construction here is to be found in strict adherence to the teaching and warrants of the Word of God respecting the Church. For the obvious fact is that the Church in its idea is a purely biblical conception—as supernatural as the scheme of salvation itself. Analogies may be derived from other sources: the family or the state, for example, may furnish illustrations with which to make this conception more vivid or more practical. Men may legitimately reason in detail from the principles biblically given: applying these more specifically, or drawing inferences from them for use in ecclesiastical organization or administration. But the idea of the Church is found in the Bible alone: nature does not furnish, nor did human wisdom produce it. All the essential principles, all the main elements, all the real authority in the case must be derived from the written Word, and be accepted because the written Word declares them.

That this biblical conception is clear, extensive, adequate, will become fully apparent on closer examination. How large a place the Church has occupied from the beginning in the economy of grace, every student of the Old Testament readily perceives. The construction and organizing and government of the Church, and the utilizing of the Church as a factor in the development of piety even in the Patriarchal, and still more distinctly throughout the Mosaic or Hebraic era, constitute in fact a very large part of the revealed accounts of that introductory dispensation. In a way still more marked, the New Testament, after its biographic records concerning our Lord himself, is occupied very largely with the origin and formation, the constitution and laws and practice, the prerogatives and duties, and the historic development and final victory of the Church. We see the divine idea, introduced in the earlier dispensation, further expanded and justified by our Lord and by His apostles, until at length, as in a vision, we discern the living Church standing in the very center of the Christion scheme,—the explaining and consummating element in a vital, progressive, conquering Gospel. Nor is this conception to be viewed as Pauline simply: for while the apostle to the Gentiles gave form and method largely to the earlier churches, especially on Gentile ground, yet the proper warrant for such construction, and the essential principles to be regarded in it, were first carefully defined by Christ Himself. It is also obvious from the narrative in the Acts, and from his own epistles, that Peter shared conspicuously with Paul in the task of primitive church organization. Other apostles, as is evident, were associated with these leaders in that great task; and in fact, under apostolic direction the Church went as an essential product wherever the Gospel went, whether on Gentile or on Jewish soil, until it came finally to be regarded everywhere as the representative institution of Christianity. Throughout the New Testament, and increasing in prominence as this later volume of Revelation progresses, the doctrine of the Church is thus extensively and adequately revealed. While the minor applications, details of organization and administration, are not given, the Holy Spirit has thus taken pains to set forth every essential element,—to place the Divine Idea distinctly and impressively before the eye of faith.

It is obvious, therefore, that this biblical disclosure should thoroughly regulate all inquiry in this department. There is indeed always room for the question whether any given sacrament or ordinance, any specific office or form of constitution, is clearly revealed in Scripture. There is always room for the further question, whether any particular church rules or usages or judgments, not directly prescribed in the Word of God, are sustained by the more general principles laid down in that Word. But the cardinal principle to be insisted upon in all ecclesiastical inquiry, broad or minute, is the supremacy of Scripture,—a principle involving prime obligation not merely to receive all that the Scripture teaches, but also to pause where the Scripture pauses, and to claim divine warrant for nothing beyond what the Scripture, faithfully interpreted, makes clear.

IV. SKETCH OF OPINIONS IN ECCLESIOLOGY.—Departure from this principle has manifestly been the chief occasion of those numerous controversies and conflicts, running through the centuries, which have made the history of Ecclesiology one of the saddest sections in the history of Christian Doctrine. From the first deviation from the biblical simplicity of the Apostolic Age down to our own time, Christendom has been incessantly convulsed by antagonistic theories of the Church,—divided into conflicting organizations severally claiming on scriptural authority to be the authorized household of faith. During the three or four centuries succeeding the Apostolic, we discern the progressive growth of a tendency, earthly and human rather than biblical, to materialize the Church, especially under the form of the episcopate. Discontent with the simple principles and methods laid down in the Bible combined easily with a natural longing for a religious organism that should resemble more closely such a vast, massive, regnant structure as the Roman State. Hence offices were gradually multiplied; official distinctions and prerogatives were pressed into prominence; the clergy became not only a separate, but a dominating class; the structure of the Church throughout grew to be more elaborate, and its worship more stately and spectacular, and its authority more imperial. The entire process, beautiful in some aspects, but in its spiritual influence widely disastrous, must be regarded as a departure throughout from the written Word, and its result was a dislocation of the Church from its true position in the Christian scheme, and the introduction of the more extensive errors, the grosser corruptions, of the Papacy.

For ten or twelve centuries we find this unscriptural development maintaining its control, and subordinating the biblical doctrine to the opinions and ambitions of men. The Church becomes less and less a divine family—grows to be more and more a spiritual empire. With one infallible head as king, with a vast array of princely cardinals, bishops and minor ecclesiastics, with a superinduced mass of precedents and usages unwarranted by the divine Word, the simple institution which Christ and His apostles founded, changes into an organism wholly at variance with both the letter and spirit of Scripture. That organism becomes at length the central and the controlling factor in Christianity. Doctrines become authoritative only as it announces them; sacraments are transmuted into gaudy and spiritless forms; the priesthood grow more arrogant and more corrupt as their prominence is increased. Even Christ and His grace become at length subordinate to the control of the Church, and salvation is as truly its gift as His. Such were some of the results of that process of departure from the clear teaching of Scripture, which it was one of the primary aims of the Reformation to arrest.

But while the Reformation was largely effectual in uprooting this false conception on which the Church of Rome was founded, Protestantism was unable to provide a substitute in which all could be agreed. Breaking off violently from the Papal system, the Reformers were prevented by many differences, doctrinal and otherwise, from framing to their own satisfaction any antithetic conception of the Church. Old views, usages, standards, stood in the way: questions respecting the sacraments, respecting the divine right of government, respecting the proper interpretation of certain texts of Scripture, impeded their course. Presbyterianism of various types and shades shared the field with Episcopacy on one side, and Independency on the other. Hence by degrees arose those divergent and antagonistic organizations, which gave point to the famous taunt of Bossuet,[1] and which still furnish to both the papist and the skeptic their chief weapon of assault upon evangelical Protestantism. Hence it is that Ecclesiology is even now, as it has been called, the undeveloped and obscure element in the Christian scheme of doctrine. Like the correlative department of Pneumatology, this lies as yet largely in the shadow of those great truths respecting Christ and His objective work in human redemption, which it was the providential mission of the Reformation to bring into the foreground of Christian belief. What the Protestantism of our time clearly needs, next to a deeper insight into the personality and work of the Holy Spirit, is substantial agreement concerning what the Bible teaches as to the Church, and a concurrent purpose to pause where the Bible pauses, and to rest all church organization on its authority alone.

V. IMPORTANCE OF THE PROPOSED INQUIRY: METHOD OF DISCUSSION.—These historic glimpses make obvious the importance of careful study of this department in Christian Doctrine. As an eminent writer has recently declared, there is in this domain still far too often a perfect Babel of tongues. After generations, even centuries, of fierce conflict, many grave questions in that domain are still unsolved. Even the proper conception of the Church has hardly yet been framed; its antiquity and historic unity and justifying grounds have not been made clear; its coming development and its final future are still matter of strenuous debate. Neither the meaning nor the numbers nor the relations of the sacraments have been satisfactorily determined: the Sabbath, the various means of grace, the right conception of worship, the orders of the ministry, are still in issue. The various sects and schools of Christendom are still very far from agreement respecting polity, government, discipline; and the final unification of that Christendom in the one holy, catholic and apostolic Church of which the earliest creeds speak in such glowing terms, seems to human view rather a fabled dream than even a remote possibility. And yet such church questions

---

[1] BOSSUET: *Variations of the Protestant Churches.* "Let them therefore do what they think fit, and whatsoever God shall suffer them to do—in respect to these vain projects of agreement: they will be eternally the mutual punishment and grievance of each other; they will bear eternal testimony against each other, how unhappily they usurped the title of *Reformers:* and that the method they took for the correction of abuses, could tend to nothing but the subversion of Christianity."—*Appendix to Book XIV.*

are in our age continually pressing to the front for solution. Vaticanism, foiled in the effort to retain temporal power, is endeavoring all the more urgently to secure spiritual supremacy through its theory of the Church, and to make it clear to the world that Protestantism is a vast, mischievous, guilty schism. Meanwhile Protestants, although naturally less affected by church questions, are being led to see how mutually destructive their positions are, and to blush in view of the painful contradictions as to the Church within their various communions. Urgent as the demand of the age is for the immediate proclamation of the Gospel to all mankind, and urgent as is the kindred demand for closer and higher application of the principles of that Gospel to human life in lands already Christianized, yet thoughtful Protestants are more and more realizing that one essential preliminary to the attainment of these ends must be found in deeper, broader, more harmonious and more inspiring views of what the Church of Christ is, as the divinely chosen instrument to be employed in securing such results. Moreover, at the other extreme from Romanism, stands a thoughtless indifferentism, which neither appreciates what the Bible teaches concerning the Church, nor contributes in any way to make that Church the incomparable social and evangelizing force it ought to be. Rationalism generally goes still further, regarding the Church as a human organization merely, which came into existence at a certain stage in the development of Christianity, and is destined at a more mature stage in that development to pass away. What is needful on all sides as a corrective to such tendencies, is a thoughtful return to the biblical conception of this divine and gracious organism, with full purpose to know and appropriate all that God has taught us respecting it in His unerring Word.

In the endeavor to unfold this biblical conception, the first aim will be to set forth the divine idea of the Church as given in Scripture,—to sketch in outline the historic manifestation of this idea, and to suggest the general argument for the existence of such an organization as a factor in the scheme of redemption. The next aim will be to present with some degree of fullness what may be styled the impersonal elements or constituents of the Church; its doctrines and confessions, its sacraments, and its ordinances. An examination of the personal constituents or factors in the Church will follow, including especially the proper theory of church membership, and the true view respecting church officers, and the nature and scope of church authority. The Church as organized under some visible form of government will next be considered, with some reference to the existing varieties of such government, and to the general principles to be recognized in church administration and especially in church discipline. The whole discussion will be concluded with some consideration of practical topics bearing upon the internal unity of the

Church, and upon its vital relations to human society and to human progress, as the true kingdom of God among men.

In these investigations the supreme purpose will be to state simply what is plainly taught in the Divine Word, and to maintain nothing which is not by direct inference clearly deducible from this biblical teaching. Against an irreverent indifference, which regards ecclesiological inquiry as of small import, and counts the Church as chiefly a human construction, no one who enters on such studies, can too carefully guard himself. And on the other hand, the student should be carefully protected against the influences of an insidious ecclesiasticism which too often confounds with divine truth the fancies and commandments of men, and which inevitably, if indulged, transforms the disciple into an ecclesiastical partizan, alike unwilling and unable to discern just what and only what God in His Word has set forth as of final authority on this great theme. If both of these errors be sedulously shunned, diligent and prayerful study will surely find enough in this broad field both to compensate for toil and to guide in duty and in service within that Holy Church, whose shelter and whose privilege all believers are alike entitled to share.

CHAPTER I.

THE CHURCH IN THE DIVINE PLAN:

THE IDEA, THE HISTORY, AND THE JUSTIFICATION.

The first step in the attaining of a truly biblical Ecclesiology, is to define the term Church, and to ascertain analytically the contents of that term, as these are indicated in Scripture. This may properly be followed by a brief sketch of the historic unfolding of this conception in the economy of grace, as seen in the Patriarchal, the Hebraic and the Christian dispensations. The chapter will be concluded with a succinct account of the general argument for such an organization, as an essential factor in the scheme of human salvation.

I. DEFINITION OF THE TERM, CHURCH: VARIOUS USES.—The term Church, (German, *kirche;* Scotch, *kirk;* and the Teutonic and Scandinavian languages generally) is derived from the Greek word, κυριακός,—

a derivative from κύριος. It was sometimes applied in the earlier English to the Jewish, or even to a pagan place of worship. It signified primarily a house in which the Lord especially dwelt—more broadly, a building consecrated to religion. The Greek derivative was in some cases used (Liddell, Robinson, *in loc*) with reference to the Sabbath, or to other periods of time consecrated specially to the Lord and His service. It came, however, to be employed at an early date to designate the religious organization inhabiting such a building, and engaging statedly in such joint devotions; and this is the use and meaning here to be retained. The term ἐκκλησία (Welsh, *eglwys*; French, *eglise*; Italian, *chiesa*; and the other Romanic languages) illustrates the same transition in signification. Applied in classic Greek to any assembly of persons called out, or called together, for any specific purpose (in which sense it is employed in the New Test.: Acts 19: 32, 39), this term came early to designate a religious or a Christian assembly, and such an assembly, not as convened on a single occasion, but rather as in some way organized and having permanent existence. The same transition appears in the parallel word, συναγωγή, often employed in the Sept. like ἐκκλησία, to describe not merely the place of assembling, but a company of persons brought together for religious, and even in some instances for secular purposes,—thus gradually coming to indicate a permanent religious congregation. It is applied by our Lord to the Jewish synagogue, Matt. 18: 17; and in two instances, Acts 7: 38, Heb. 2: 12, to the Israelites, regarded as a religious body. The Hebrew terms, עֵדָה (assembly in general) and קָהָל (assembly for worship; see Lev. 4: 13–14, where both words are used), convey essentially the same meaning; they find their nearest parallel under the Gospel in the term Church. It is to the New Test. however, rather than the Old, that we are to look for complete definition and for more precise terminology. The Church at first lived chiefly in the family, or dwelt in and with the state; it was the special work of Christ and His apostles both to disengage it from such connections, and to give it distinct place and form, and, therefore, more exact appellatives.

This primary signification gradually broadens out in the New Test. into three separate meanings, which need to be carefully noted in both their affiliations and their contrasts. The first of these refers to a particular congregation, assembling in any consecrated place for worship and fellowship, such as the church at Rome or Colosse, or the church in the house of Philemon; Rom. 16: 5, Coll. 4: 15, Philemon 1: 2. These were individual companies of believers, convened habitually in certain private residences or places for religious service and communion. The second of these meanings refers to a group, more or less extensive, of such particular churches located in a given district or region, and drawn together through the consciousness of a common faith into some form of voluntary compact; as the churches of Galatia or of Asia, 1 Cor. 16: 1, 19. If there were several congregations in such cities as Jerusalem or Antioch or Ephesus or Rome, they are in most cases described in apostolic usage as the church in each of those cities,—a fact which strongly suggests the existence of some form of organization binding together particular congregations in given localities even from the earliest times. The third meaning refers to the collective body of those who professed to receive the Gospel, or to the complete company of those who were truly united in heart to Christ, as their Lord and Master; Eph. 5: 25, 1 Tim. 3: 15. In this general sense, the term sometimes included, not merely those who had received the historic Christ, but also all those who from the earliest periods, and in the dim light of the Mosaic or the Patriarchal dispensation, had seen and trusted in Him as their promised Redeemer; Col. 1: 18. It comprehended in some cases the whole family of God, not only on earth, but also in heaven, nor merely those who had lived or were then living, but all who to the end of time should believe in Him; Eph. 1: 10–12. The distinction between a visible profession of such faith, and its actual exercise as manifested in a truly Christian life,—between the church actual and the church ideal, is expressed by the theological rather than biblical terms, visible and invisible.[1]

The metaphors employed, especially in the New Test. to describe the Church, are worthy of notice in this connection. The Church in whatever form is the house or habitation of God, 1 Peter 2: 5; the temple of God, or of the Holy Ghost, 1 Cor. 3: 16; the city of God, Rev. 21: 2. The Church is the flesh of Christ, Eph. 5: 30; the body of Christ, 1 Cor. 12: 27; the bride of Christ, Eph. 5: 31-2. The Church embodies in itself the fullness of its divine Redeemer, Eph. 1: 22; represents His grace and His glory, Eph. 5: 27; is the pillar and ground of His saving truth, 1 Tim. 3: 15; and is in its membership, the salt of the earth, and the light of the world, Matt. 5: 13-14. And what is thus declared to be true respecting the Church as organized under the Gospel, may be seen to be true from the Old Test. delineations of the Church, under the Hebraic dispensation, and even in the Patriarchal ages. Dear as the apple of His eye, graven as a holy name on the palms of His hands, infinitely precious in His sight, embodying always His love and His grace, the Church under whatever form is to the Triune Deity ever an object of fathomless interest. Subordinately to the Lord Himself, it may justly be viewed as the embodied brightness of

---

[1] On the various uses of the term, Church, see SMITH. J. PYE. *First Lines of Christ, Theol.*, p. 617 *seq.*

the divine glory, and the express image or representation of the divine personality among men.

II. ANALYSIS OF THE TERM.—Passing from this general view to the analysis of the term, church, we may discover five distinct elements or characteristics. Of these, the first is *association;* a church is always a community or an organization. This association is not based on natural relationship, or instituted through involuntary connections, like the family or the state. The relationship is voluntary rather than natural; those who enter into it step out in a manner more or less marked from their natural connections, and are joined together on a distinctively spiritual basis. This is true even where the church rests within a single household, like that of Noah, or in affiliation with a single nation like the Hebrews. Still more obviously is this true under the Gospel, where the ties of kindred or of nationality are entirely ignored by those who come together within the communion of the church. Here the community or organization is simply and wholly religious.[1]

More distinctively, the inward principle and bond by which the church is held together is *piety*. Every such association is a company of persons who believe in God, and, under the Christian economy, in Christ, and who are devoted to the divine service. There may be persons within its visible communion who have no such qualification for membership,—who merely profess such piety. There are entire churches, or even extensive sections of nominal Christendom, in which this qualification is hardly apparent, and to which we can not properly apply the honorable phrase of Scripture, the church of the living God. We recognize also a species of inherited connection—a constructive membership by anticipation—enjoyed by the children of believers, before they have attained to what is termed personal religion. Yet the general fact remains that the uniting bond in the church, under all dispensations, is a spiritual bond, instituted and sustained through the exercise of personal faith. The degree and the forms of such faith doubtless vary in different stages and eras, but the essential principle is ever one and the same. Piety, piety alone, is the conclusive test of membership; all other tests and qualifications are at best subordinate.

The third element in the conception is a definite form of *constitution*,—certain rules of fellowship, involving responsibility to a common authority, and controlling within prescribed limits the individual life and activity. A church may indeed exist in some sense without a written code—without formal regulations, visibly administered and visibly shaping the organization. The beautiful picture given in the earlier

---

[1] "Where the Holy Spirit unites the hearts, there a *community* must exist, from which will soon proceed a *communion* distinct from every other."—VAN OOSTERZEE: *Dogm*. Sec. 128.

chapters of the Acts of the Apostles—where simple piety manifested in peculiar forms of faith and love and devotion pervades the entire community as a celestial inspiration, higher than all written or visible law—exhibits the church in such comparatively unorganized condition. During the millenial era, a similar elevation of the church may be enjoyed, superseding all formal laws and constitutions through the sovereign potencies of a perfected spiritual life. But these are exceptional conditions rather than the normal and permanent state of the church on earth. As we read on in the history, we soon discover in the apostolic church the growth of more definite organization, the exhibition of recognized authority, an administration of law, which shows us more exactly what is the divine purpose as to the permanent estate. This characteristic is certainly less distinct at times, as in the Patriarchal era: the form of constitution divinely prescribed is not always the same. But the Church of God is at all times and everywhere a kingdom, existing under law.

As this divine communion has in all ages a distinct constitution, and one animating principle, so it has in all ages but one appointed and definite end,—an end in harmony with the divine idea and purpose. This end is embodied in the two words, worship and testimony. Worship is the expression before God, in suitable forms, such as praise or prayer, of the holy sentiments which dwell habitually in the breasts of all who truly know and believe in Him. Such expression is due to Him, in virtue even of the primary or natural relations which we discover ourselves to sustain towards Him as His creatures, and His subjects and children. It is more eminently due to Him, in virtue of the spiritual relations into which He permits us through faith to enter; it is the spontaneous manifestation of the truly filial and loving spirit here, as it is an instinctive occupation and joy of angels in the heavenly state. But God desires not merely individual worship, or the adoration of the consecrated household; He desires also the public, organized, swelling chorus of praise ascending from the great congregation of those who love Him. Hence the culture of believers in the sacred art of worship is one of the distinctive functions of the church, and the offering of such worship before God in times and ways appointed by Him, is her primary, her highest work. —Kindred to this is the function of testimony,—the bearing of organized and permanent witness to the divine existence and character, to spiritual truth however revealed, and especially to the love and grace of God as manifested in the plan of salvation. He designs His church to be in this sense a reflection of Himself; the expositor of His law, and the representative of His grace. The church reveals and exhibits His glory, as no individual, or aggregate of individual believers standing apart, could ever do.—Nor are these two functions conflicting or separate. The church testifies most impressively while engaged in truly spiritual worship; in a deep sense, it worships while it is engaged in bearing witness before men.

The final characteristic of the church of God on earth is permanence; it is endowed with *an enduring life*. As an association or community, it has the crowning element of perpetuity: though voluntary rather than natural, it is not temporary, but abiding as an organization. Its piety may be exhibited under various forms, and in various measures, but the inward spirit will abide, unchanged and unchangeable. The forms of its constitution may vary, and its laws be from time to time modified; but it will never cease to be a Πολιτεία. Its methods of worship or of testimony may change with the ages, but its testimony is to be as enduring as the sun, and the flames of its worship are to ascend as long as the earth endures. Particular churches may dwindle or pass into decay; the whole church may appear at certain stages in its peculiar history to be well nigh extinguished. Yet an enduring life is the distinguishing feature of the Church of God through all ages, all dispensations. It is so rooted in the religious nature of men, as well as in the divine purpose—is so adjusted to the abiding needs and instincts of holy souls, and to the permanent necessities of mankind, and sustains so vital a place in the great scheme of salvation, that it can not perish while the work of saving men goes on. It began with the first crude groupings of human society; it has lived on through all subsequent variations in the condition or experience of humanity; it still retains in undiminished volume its essential life and vigor. We may justly infer that an enduring life, continuing while the world lasts, is one of its essential qualities.

Bringing together the five characteristics named, and ignoring what is peculiar to any given age or dispensation, we may in general define a church as an organization of those who love God, existing permanently under some prescribed constitution, for the purpose of worship and testimony concerning Him. More broadly, the Church of God on earth is the company or community of the pious, separated spiritually from the rest of mankind, and existing organically through all time, in order to bear witness to His person, authority, truth and grace, and to worship and glorify Him before the world. If the definition be limited to the church as visible, still the association can be composed only of those who profess piety, and who avow themselves to be consecrated to these spiritual ends. The question respecting the constructive or anticipatory connection of the children of believers with the church, will be considered at a later stage. What is desired here is simply to supply a general definition, which shall include the Church of the Old Testament, as well as the Church of Christ under the Gospel. See definition, Westminster Conf., Chap. XXV: Form of Gov., Chap. II.[1]

III. HISTORIC UNFOLDING OF THIS GENERIC CONCEPTION.—Accepting this general definition and analysis of the term, we may next note in brief the historic development of the remarkable institution thus described. For, the introduction of this spiritual organism was coëval with the earliest manifestations of the religious nature in man; it was imbedded in that nature as truly as the family was imbedded in the domestic, or the state in the political nature of humanity. The formal structure which all varieties of natural religion, even the crudest, assume at certain stages in their development, is evidence that such a tendency exists in the religious nature of man. So far as the true faith is concerned, the evidence is conclusive. Not merely in the New Testament, under the Christian dispensation, but just as truly in the Old Testament, under the Hebraic dispensation, do we find this divine organism springing into existence. Nor did the Church assume its first definite form under the shaping hand of Moses, or grow into distinctness and power in the succeeding age of Samuel or David, or the prophets. We may go back to the patriarchal period, and in the families of Jacob and Isaac and Abraham, and in the primitive household of Noah, find traces of its presence. We may follow up still further the earlier lines of this gracious development, and obtain proofs that, as soon as men even before the deluge became conscious of their spiritual life and relations, they began to be associated together in what were the primeval forms of the Church of God on earth. While these introductory revelations are of necessity too brief to be made the basis of much speculative reasoning, it still is interesting and important to discern this divine institution appearing thus at the very origin of the religious life in humanity.

What we are to sketch is therefore not a series of churches following one another in a divinely ordered succession, each tributary to its successor, yet substantially independent of it, but rather a single organism assuming a variety of outward form and existing under diversified

---

[1] The *marks* or *notes* of the Church Invisible, according to the New Test., are catholicity or universality, sanctity or piety, and infallibility—in the sense of a continuous and supreme guidance through the Holy Spirit, such as befits the earthly body of Christ. Romanism rejects the conception of an invisible, as distinct from the visible Church; and demands for the latter, as its distinguishing marks or notes.—to quote from Bellarmine—profession of the true faith, communion in the sacraments, and submission to a legitimate head, the Roman pontiff. Calvin, for all the Reformers, held that any church is a true church in which are found belief in the Gospel, the preaching of the Word, and due administration of the sacraments: *Institutes*, Book IV: Chap. 1. So the Reformed Confessions generally: for summary, see HODGE, *Theol.*, I: 135-137.

earthly conditions, still retaining in all dispensations the same essential characteristics, and aiming to subserve always one and the same spiritual end. This true, interior, indestructible unity is to be held as an indispensable element in our investigation. Protestantism has sometimes surrendered this cardinal doctrine of unity, under the pressure of some specific inference as to sacrament or belief or order, but always at far greater cost than advantage. That the Church of God on earth has from the beginning been, is now, and is to be until the close of the Gospel economy, one Church, is a fundamental proposition in the Christian scheme.[1] We may, however, trace at least three distinct forms under which this one Church has existed, three varieties of condition in which it has been set, three types of relation which it has sustained to humanity. These may be classed as the Patriarchal, the Hebraic, and the Christian.

IV. THE CHURCH PATRIARCHAL: FIRST DIVISION.—In tracing the course of the Church Patriarchal, we may properly consider the subject under two main divisions: the Church prior to Abraham, and the Church Abrahamic.—It is not without reason that the historic allusions in Gen. 4: 26, and Gen. 6: 2, are viewed as descriptive of a religious distinction already established among men. Thus early the pious called upon the name of the Lord, and were—as many commentators suggest—called by the name of the Lord; they were the recognized sons of God in contrast with the sons and daughters of men.[2] Have we not warrant for believing also that the institution of sacrifices which existed as a personal rite in the age of Abel, became early a public as well as private mode of worship? Was not the Sabbath, even from the creation, a time consecrated to associated as well as individual devotion? May not the first Messianic promise (Gen. 3: 14-19), brief and indistinct though it may have appeared, have been from the beginning a sufficient basis, not merely for personal faith, but also for religious combination and fellowship, in the presence of a world extensively verging toward unbelief? It is also to be remembered that while the first of these historic references relates to a time comparatively contiguous to the Fall, the second follows a period of fourteen centuries during which the earth was rapidly filling with population, and human society had, at least in other respects, assumed definite and permanent form. Moreover, it is certain that during this long period God com-

---
[1] On the Unity and Perpetuity of the Church, HODGE, *Church Polity*, p. 67-88.

[2] "The religious thought it necessary to attach to themselves the title of Sons or Worshipers of God, in distinction from the sons of men."—JAHN, *Archæology*, p. 378. "They took upon themselves the title of the Sons of God; considering themselves as His children by adoption, in distinction from wicked men, who were the children of God by creation only."—DWIGHT, *Serm.*, 149. See Delitzsch is LANGE, Genesis, *in loc;* especially the Dissertation, *Bene Elohim*.

muned habitually with individual saints, such as Enoch and Lamech (Gen. 5: 22, 29), and that household piety existed in primitive simplicity at many points, in the presence of abounding sin. And surely it is no unwarrantable inference from such premises that, although we may learn nothing respecting its actual structure, a living and visible Church had existence among men from century to century, down to the diluvian age.

It was a fearful declension among the sons of God thus set apart, as well as the outbreaking wickedness among the sons and daughters of men, which brought on the retribution of the deluge. The Church had apparently been compressed by surrounding sin within the narrow limits of a single family; Gen. 6: 8–9. The general condition of the race is fearfully sketched by our Lord Himself; Matt. 24: 36–39. But household religion still survived. Notwithstanding the offense of Noah, the narrative concerning him, studied in the light of later allusions, justifies the belief that he possessed the piety requisite to true church membership, and that he had trained his family, prior to the great catastrophe, to the exercise of like faith, and to the forms of public worship. His first act after the deluge (Gen. 8: 20–22) was to erect an altar, and to offer sacrifices thereon, in the presence of his household—a religious usage doubtless derived from his devout ancestry, and indicating of itself an established mode of social devotion. The gift to him of the second Messianic promise (Gen. 9: 25–27) is further assurance that he was a sincere believer in the first promise; and we are assured that this second promise became to him, and to his family, the basis of an enlarged spiritual union and fellowship. Is it too much to assume on these evidences that the Church of God really existed within this sanctified household, and that this Church in the form it assumed after the deluge, with altar and sacrifice, was the fit reproduction and succession of the Church which God had instituted in the very beginning of human history? From the deluge to the calling of Abraham—a period of four centuries—no distinct record of the Church remains. The story of the attempt to rear the tower of Babel (Gen. 11: 1–9) shows us how disastrously sin had become diffused among the teeming populations which sprang from the three-fold stock of Noah, exhibiting itself at length in open rebellion against God, and in guilty fear of His providence and of His wrath. Cities had meanwhile been builded; nations had been founded; lands and territories had been divided. Humanity had grown a second time into maturity; and of that maturity, as in the earlier era, sin was the crowning characteristic. Yet there are evidences that religion still survived, as a social element as well as a personal experience. There were still devout households like those of Terah and Haran, in which the deposit of grace yet dwelt in safety; Gen. 11: 27-29. The traditions of an earlier age, especially the Messianic promises, were preserved in memory; the traditional modes of worship survived, and the Church still lived.

V. THE CHURCH PATRIARCHAL: SECOND DIVISION.—Descending in the order of time to the Church Abrahamic, we find that, in the phrase of Luther, God for the third time begins the history of the Church with a new family. That history opens with the third Messianic promise (Gen. 12: 1-3), in which the salvation to come was directly associated with the household of Abraham, as in the second it had been associated with the name of Shem, his ancestor. The special covenant with Abraham recorded in Gen. 17: with its specific ordinance of circumcision, and its special assurances as to the land of Canaan, must be interpreted in the light of this antecedent promise. The spiritual experience of the earlier patriarchs was also reproduced in Abraham, with clearer recognition of the divine will as the law of life, with higher phases of feeling and purpose, and with a more distinct engrafting of religion upon his household, and through him upon the family life of mankind. Especially on its material side, this third promise was repeated successively to Isaac and to Jacob, among the posterity of Abraham (Gen. 26: 24, 28: 13-15, 35: 9-12), with such exactness of language, and such carefulness of application, as to leave no room for doubt that they were the lineal inheritors of the Church, with all its attendant blessings. Religion flourished in their households, in the same forms, under the same spiritual conditions, and distinguished by the same initiatory and typical rite, as before in the family of Abraham. Notwithstanding the degeneracy and idolatry prevalent around them, and even among their own kindred in the country of Haran, these religious families thus became repositories of the true faith,—the home and refuge of the divinely constituted Church.

This association of the churchly with the domestic life of man—this combination of the church with the family, preparatory to its assumption of the tribal type, is further illustrated in conjunction with the fourth Messianic promise, referring to Judah, among the sons of Jacob, as the elect ancestor of the Savior to come; Gen. 49: 8-12.[1] Though Judah was made chief, there can be no question that all of the sons of Jacob shared in the spiritual hope which sprang directly from that promise, or that their households were drawn and held together by the consciousness of religious life which that promise justified. The anticipated Shiloh shed his unifying influence on all alike; inspiring them to a common worship, leading them to observe the same religious ceremonial, and giving to each a recognized place and name within the one household of faith.

---

[1] HENGSTENBERG, *Christology*: Vol. I. *Messianic Prophecies in the Pentateuch.*

From the descent of the twelve consecrated families into Egypt to the deliverance under Moses—a period of two centuries, or more—we are left to incidental allusions, such as the one recorded in Ex. 2: 23-25, in which the traditional preservation of the ancestral religion and the continued trust of the Hebrews in the ancient promises are made manifest. The descendants of Abraham unquestionably bore with them into their Egyptian exile the cardinal elements of the patriarchal faith, and continued to observe the religious rites in which they had been trained in Canaan. As they clung to the covenant of their fathers, we may believe that they endeavored to comply with the spiritual conditions which that covenant imposed. One interesting reference (Ex. 16: 22-30) to their recognition of the Sabbath, after the Exodus but prior to the Sinaitic command, may be regarded, notwithstanding the objection urged by Paley, as clearly revealing not merely a tradition, but also an habitual observance. But a Sabbath as clearly presupposes public sacrifices, and other acts of social worship, and is strongly suggestive of a recognized church life, as existing throughout this disciplinary period in the Hebraic history. It is no empty presumption therefore that the ancestral faith still survived, and that Moses, in the reconstruction that followed, was mainly enunciating afresh and with more direct authority from God, religious institutions and forms of organization whose fruitful germs had thus been graciously preserved in the heart of the chosen people.

VI. THE CHURCH HEBRAIC: TWO PRELIMINARY REMARKS.—Following the exodus, occurs not merely the organization of a more strictly national life—the twelve tribes passing consciously and freely into the one Hebrew state, but also the constituting of the Church in a corresponding form as representative not of family devotion or tribal faith, but of the religion of the nation. We may glance first at the specific modifications which that transformation induced, and then at the history of the organization thus instituted. Two introductory considerations should be noted at the outset:

The divine selection of the Hebrew nation to be for fifteen centuries the particular home and safeguard of the Church, is often misapprehended by those who suppose themselves to see in this selection an injustice to other tribes and races of men. But was it not inevitable that religion, beginning as it must with individual souls, should pass first into the household, and from the family into the tribe, by a natural and healthful process of diffusion, until the time came when it could pass further, as it did, from the tribe into the nation, and so become at length a corporate factor in the national life? And was it not as inevitable that the true religion should tarry awhile in the nation, as it had before done in the pious household, until the appointed day when it might successfully pass beyond all national boundaries, and enter as a controlling power into the life of mankind,—pervading all countries and races with its hallowing influences, and sanctifying our humanity in the aggregate? In fact, the divine election of individuals or families, tribes or nations, has always been the introductory step to a larger good, in which others were finally to share equally with the first recipients. And properly viewed, the Hebraic Church, like the Patriarchal, will be seen to be but a temporary, yet indispensable preparation for the Church Universal.

The other explanatory remark relates to the peculiar combination between the Church Hebraic and the Hebrew state. The reasons for that combination are largely of the class just suggested. Was not a political organization indispensable to the safety and growth of the spiritual organism so intimately associated with it? As the state unified the twelve tribes, retiring their differences in the presence of one national constitution, and binding them together by the consciousness of common interests and destiny, so it tended to consolidate their religious beliefs, to harmonize their spiritual experiences, and to make their worship one and the same. Moreover, the state was itself a theocracy, controlled mainly by religious rule and obligation, and therefore in many of its appointments a species of religious culture. While the state gave form and strength to the Church, the Church in turn penetrated, ruled, sanctified the state. This fact was especially obvious after the entrance into Canaan, during the period of the Judges, and eminently in the royal era before the national rupture. The reason for the combination doubtless lay in the stage of development which the Church at that juncture had attained; when the reason ceased, the relationship ceased also, and the Church lived on in higher form, while the nation as a nation died. A proper understanding of these relations between the Hebrew Church and the Hebrew state, it should be added, is of vital importance in the solution of numerous ecclesiastical issues,—such as some of those between Romanism and Protestantism,—which the Christian thought of our time is especially called upon to consider.[1]

VII. THE CHURCH HEBRAIC: ITS SPECIAL CHARACTERISTICS.—As compared with its predecessor, the Hebrew Church was marked by the following distinctive features. First of all, we find a marked development of doctrine,—an enlargement in both the quantity of religious truth known, and the degree of clearness with which truth was appre-

---

[1] Authors to be consulted on the general subject: MICHAELIS, *Commentaries on the Laws of Moses:* WARBURTON, *Divine Legation of Moses:* Book IV, especially. HENGSTENBERG, *Kingdom of God in the Old Test.* KURTZ, *Hist. of Old Covenant.* Also, OEHLER, *Theol. of Old Test.*

hended. The existence and general attributes of God, recognized and believed in from the first, were made far more distinct; the power and sovereignty of God were greatly emphasized by the experiences in Egypt and at Sinai, and through the providential interpositions of the wilderness, and the triumphal advent into the promised land; the moral qualities of the Deity, such as justice and purity and holiness and grace, were brought out into peculiar light. The divine grace, revealed before in promises, was now shadowed forth in new suggestive ceremonies, and affirmed by further direct revelations. In the aggregate this larger treasure of sacred doctrine constituted a marked peculiarity of the Hebraic, as distinguished from the Patriarchal Church.—A more definite and comprehensive law was another of these distinguishing features. It is not important here to consider the question whether, in the economy of grace, there was any divine provision for what has been termed a progressive morality. But the fact should be noted that the great principles of morality, stamped on the moral constitution of man and obligatory on men in all anterior ages, were here explained, expanded, applied, and made as never before the recognized basis of church life. The substance of the Decalogue, for illustration, had always been obligatory: the shedding of blood was murder, slander was sinful, even from the days of Abel. The enactments at Sinai were but fresh declarations, in more distinct and impressive form, of what men had known and had been bound always to observe. Yet this Sinaitic law, with its wider and closer application, marked a new era in the moral history of mankind, and especially in the career of the Church on which its requisitions were, amid such awful demonstrations of divine authority, specifically imposed. Henceforth, that authority was to be more directly acknowledged; both the outward life and the disposition and the heart of believers were to be more closely regulated and tested. Law was to enter in more impressive aspect into the religious life of the Church, in order that at length grace might the more abound.[1]

In conjunction with an expanded doctrine and a more definite law, we discover a prescribed ritual. Whether we regard sacrifices as originating in some profound instinct of human nature, or as already directly enjoined by Jehovah upon the patriarchs, we discover the institution here assuming complete form, and becoming the type and vehicle of a scheme of redemptive grace. The prescribed ceremonials of the Hebrew Church were far in advance of the observances that had preceded them, in respect to their variety and elaborateness, their power to impress the soul, and their authoritativeness. They were not only fitted to induce and cultivate a new, better type of religious ex-

---
[1] WINES. *Laws of the Ancient Hebrews*, especially, Book I; Chap. I: II.

perience; they were also fitted to prepare the way peculiarly for the advent of a still higher economy of redemption. Both of these ends were sought in that remarkable ritual; and the degree of spiritual vitality attained under its influence is conclusive proof of its value as a feature in the Hebrew Church.—With this should be associated the tributary institution of the priesthood, the construction of the sanctuary, and the direct regulations as to the Sabbath,—all designed to assist in the culture of such an enlarged type of religious experience among the chosen people. Aforetime, the head of each household, the patriarch of each tribe, had filled the priestly office. In that mysterious personage, Melchisedec, priest and king at once in a wider relation (Gen. 14: 18–20, Heb. 7: 1–16), we discern the first hint of that broader official priesthood afterwards realized in Aaron and his descendants, and more remotely in our Lord himself. Such a consecrated order needed a tabernacle or temple, with its ark and tables and altars, as a suitable place, and also the Sabbath and an ordained series of holy occasions as suitable times wherein they might adequately discharge their priestly functions in behalf of the people. The relation of these persons, places, times, as accessories to the Church into which they were authoritatively introduced, can not be too carefully studied, especially in the light of their subsequent reproduction, in more spiritual forms, under the higher economy of the Gospel.

It should also be observed that the patriarchal seal of membership was preserved and made obligatory under the new dispensation. The devout Hebrew was not only to believe in the larger truth revealed, to submit himself to the more comprehensive and spiritual law, to conform to the elaborated ritual with its special observances and adjuncts, but also to signify his full acceptance and submission by receiving in his own person and in his offspring the distinguishing mark by which the true Hebrew was to be set apart perpetually from all other men. This was not a national mark merely; it was a religious seal also, expressing the same spiritual truths as when it was first imposed upon Abraham (Gen. 17: 9–14), and assuring its recipients of the same covenanted grace. And in the instituting of this sacramental observance, the constitution of the Hebraic Church became complete.—In closing this survey, it is important to note here both the resemblances to the Church of the patriarchs, and the contrasts apparent at each of these five points. While we see essentially the same doctrine, rule, ceremony and seal, we see these set always in fresh relations, and invested with added meaning and dignity. The contrast becomes as marked almost as the resemblance; it is sometimes so misapprehended as to lead to the false notion of another and different Church. But closer examination reveals an essential identity, in which the Church Patriarchal is the living germ and the Church Hebraic the developed plant, fragrant with larger grace and larger blessing.

VIII. THE HEBRAIC CHURCH: ITS HISTORIC DEVELOPMENT: THREE ERAS.—From this cursory view of the essential features or characteristics of the Hebraic Church, we may turn to note its history in brief, with special reference to its preparatory relation to the more glorious Church afterwards to be established under Christ.[1] For twenty-five centuries from the Fall, and nearly fifteen centuries from the new organization of mankind in the household of Noah, the Church had lived substantially within the family. For fifteen centuries more it was to exist in this national form, dwelling within the territory of a single people, and separated by certain broad lines from contact with the rest of the race. Both the first and the second of these remarkable arrangements should be interpreted in the light of the principle already stated: the seclusion and segregation were always in order to and suggestive of an ultimate expansion and universality. The families of the earth were to be blessed through the family of faithful Abraham; the nations of the earth were to be blessed through the Hebrew nation, thus elevated and sanctified through the presence of this indwelling faith and this organized Church. Three distinct eras are traceable in its career: the theocratic, the royal, the prophetic.

The theocratic era extends from the Exodus to the crowning of Saul; B. C. 1491—B. C. 1095, according to the received chronology. It includes the final formulation of the Mosaic ceremonial, the settlement and unification of the nation in the promised land, the irregular domination of the Judges, and the peculiar viceroyalty of Samuel,—a period in which the people were governed by direct theocratic revelations, coming chiefly through the priesthood. We behold the singular spectacle of a nation among whom the Church and the state seem coterminous, and civil and religious law are identical in their claim: among whom divine authority is recognized as supreme, and religion is enthroned as the chief social principle. The people are seen to move and act as a manifested Providence directs them; God is enthroned as their chosen and only King, and His revealed will is their only accepted rule, whether in the state, the household, or the individual soul. Far as they seem often to fall below this ideal, especially during the confused era of the Judges, the ideal survives, and continues to be as truly their guide and inspiration as was the pillar of cloud and of fire during the Exodus. Yet this condition was designed to be temporary rather than permanent. As the tabernacle so carefully constructed

---

[1] BUNSEN: *Hist. of the people of Israel.* STANLEY: *Hist. of the Jewish Church.* See also, references to Hengstenberg, Kurtz, Oehler.

in the wilderness, and so faithfully carried with them during their wanderings, was to give way at length to the more glorious temple, so this introductory stage in the national experience was to be succeeded by another of greater volume and of higher significance.

The royal era, extending from the crowning of Saul to the downfall of the Jewish monarchy (B. C. 1095—B. C. 588) was such a period. It was not simply the selection of a human king, and the introduction of the splendid age of David and Solomon, which distinguished this era. The human element becomes indeed more prominent, but the divine supremacy survives in undiminished force. The tabernacle disappears in order that the temple may rise into view on Mount Zion. Jerusalem becomes both the political and the religious capital. The Mosaic ritual, which had fallen partly into disuse during the troublous times preceding, is revived and enforced, with far greater elaborateness and splendor. As the nation rose into power and influence, the Church rose with it—still the controlling factor in the Hebrew life. Visions of the salvation to come became more distinct with the advancing centuries, and the Messianic promises inherited from patriarchal times found fit succession in the Messianic predictions of men like David and Isaiah, and some among the minor prophets. Even after the fatal rupture between the tribes, and the withdrawal of Ephraim from Judah, the national faith and worship remained; the church lived still as the organizing center of both the northern and the southern confederation.

The prophetic era, reaching from the captivities to the birth of Christ, presents the singular phenomenon of a religion surviving amid the decline of all other elements in the Hebrew life—of a Church abiding, and even increasing in spiritual quality and influence, while the state that had hitherto nourished and protected it was passing into decay. For some centuries prior to the carrying of Zedekiah and his people to Babylon, while the power of the ritual and the priest were waning, God had been raising up a succession of prophets to whom the care of this church was to be specially entrusted, and by whom the church was to be trained into higher ethical experiences, and prepared for the more spiritual economy that was to follow. It was not the divine plan that the church should die out with the nation; rather was it planned that the nation as a containing vessel should be broken into fragments, in order that the church might strike out its roots into surrounding soil, and might grow into its predestined universality. The peculiar function of the prophets was not merely to enforce the ritualistic cultus represented by the priesthood; it was to bring out more fully the spiritual truths and duties which that cultus typified. It was to preserve and mature the religious principle in a better form; to enforce obligation more thoroughly and widely—to bring the soul nearer to God through deeper experience. They were also to reveal more distinctly the coming redemption, and to describe in clearer terms the approaching Redeemer; and thus to bring in, amid the overthrow of earthly interests and hopes, the strong inspiration to be derived from this new manifestation of the Christ by whom life and immortality were to be brought to light. It is an error therefore to regard the prophetic era as a descent from the elevation which the Hebrew faith had attained under David and Solomon. The Hebraic dispensation was in no sense a failure. Closer study reveals the interesting fact of a steady advance, along the lines of a truly spiritual development, from Mount Sinai to Mount Zion, from the tabernacle to the temple, from the splendors of an external worship to the better experiences flowing from a deepened religious life, and from the priestly and the kingly down to and through the prophetic discipline. The theocratic era prepared the way for the royal, and this in turn prepared the way for the period during which the outer shell of faith fell off, and the essential principle of faith germinated into form and beauty, by way of preparation for the advent of a Savior and a religion wherein the Patriarchal and the Hebraic churches were to find their final and perfect realization.

IX. THE CHURCH AS CONSTITUTED BY CHRIST: PRELIMINARY REMARKS.—As the religious life flows gradually through the individual into the family, the tribe and the nation—as the discipline of the theocracy introduces the further development of the royal era, and prepares the way for the riper experience of prophetical times, so the entire history of the Church from its earliest beginnings, and during all its varied forms, must be regarded as a vast divine preparation for the church that was to follow,—the Church Universal, constituted by our Lord Himself. The rites and ceremonies, regulations and duties imposed during these antecedent stages were not only fitted to develop true piety in those who observed them; they were also designed to be typical of the more thorough spiritual culture which the Gospel was to introduce. They were so many seeds divinely planted, that in due season they might spring forth into maturity under the fairer light of the new economy—the economy of the Immanuel. As every thing that was permanently valuable in the patriarchal period was carried over into the Hebrew discipline, so all of permanent spiritual value in Hebraism passed naturally, after a sanctifying process, into the better, broader, spiritual organism that was to succeed it.

The comparative silence of Christ respecting the constitution, the forms and usages, of the Church which it was a part of His mission to found, is significant. While He announces the fact that such a Church was to be a direct outgrowth of His redemptive work, its particular construction seems to be to his view incidental. He indeed endorses or institutes the two great Christian sacraments; He points out certain essential principles in church fellowship and church discipline; He indicates the foundations of divine doctrine on which the Church must be built—Himself the chief corner-stone. Beyond this He is silent. How is that sacred silence to be explained, excepting on the hypothesis that He foresaw on one side, that mere forms or constitutions, however rigidly enjoined, would avail nothing apart from true piety dwelling in the heart; and on the other side, that such piety, awakened and matured through Him, would be sure to lead the Church into appropriate rules and usages, and would make it prosperous and fruitful under whatever mode of organization? To introduce such a gracious economy as He came to establish, by planting everywhere another Church in avowed rivalry with the existing Judaism, would have frustrated His supreme purpose; to bring in His Church through the antecedent processes involved in the new life He imparted, letting the organization follow after the piety that required it, was both profoundly philosophic in itself, and a sure pledge of ultimate success.

The same divine principle clearly regulates the Apostolic teaching. In the minds of those who organized the new Church under the guidance of the Spirit, particular rules and usages, methods of organization, varieties of constitution, seem to have had but secondary place. They, like their Master, dwelt most upon individual piety; they sought most the cultivation of those holy graces, of which Christian fellowship, Christian communion, were to be the certain outgrowth. Religion was first, and the Church was in order to religion; the Church never became prior in their scheme of development. Nor did they organize the Church according to their own opinions; every thing was carefully subordinated to the teaching of Christ, and to the supreme direction of His Spirit. The impression that Paul rather than Christ was the founder of the Christian Church, and the kindred impression that Paul and Peter or James were at variance in their theories of organization, and therefore founded Pauline churches on Gentile, and Petrine or Jacobean churches on Jewish soil—thus introducing antagonism into the very structure of primitive Christianity, can not be justified by any clear evidence drawn either from the apostolic writings or from the records of the apostolic age. Nor can it be affirmed that one rigid form was agreed upon by those who laid the foundations of the Church, to be exactly followed through the long and complex process, continued during the first century, of planting particular organizations of believers in the various portions of the known world. What degree of special warrant for any variety of such organization above another, can be derived from the New Testament, may be shown hereafter; for the present, it is important simply to recognize the general fact here stated.

X. ITS IDENTITY WITH THE PATRIARCHAL AND HEBRAIC CHURCHES. —It is essential to note in brief the several points of identity between the Church thus founded by Christ and His apostles, and the Churches Patriarchal and Hebraic—especially the latter. To regard these as independent organizations, having only certain general relations and resemblances, is to misapprehend entirely their true affinity—to ignore their essential oneness. This oneness is repeatedly declared in the New Testament; both by our Lord, as in Luke 1: 32–33, Matt. 22: 43–45; and by the apostles, as in Rom. 11: 17–26, Eph. 2: 11–22, 3: 4–6. To use the metaphor of Paul, the Christian Church was grafted upon the Jewish, in such a sense that both the original stock and the growing graft became one and the same tree. This oneness is further indicated in the fact that prophecies given to the Church in its earlier stages are realized only under the Gospel, such as those which brighten so singularly the latest chapters of Isaiah. And by the kindred fact that promises made to the people of God under the earlier dispensation are fulfilled only after Christ had wrought out His redemptive work; illustrations may be seen in Acts 2: 16–18, 39, Gal. 3: 7–9, 28–29. The O. T. prophecies nowhere suggested the ultimate destruction of the Hebraic Church, but rather its expansion through the admission of the Gentiles, in exact harmony with the event. We have also abundant evidence that the Hebrew Church rested, like the Christian, on Christ Himself as its true corner-stone; Rom. 4: 9–25, Gal. 3: 16. The Messianic assurances which had sustained believers even from the times of Noah or of Adam, and which had been inherited by the children of Israel, and interpreted through the Mosaic ceremonial system, all found their final key and fulfillment in Him. Moreover, as the foundation was essentially the same, the uniting bond of faith, loyalty, devotion, was substantially one in the antediluvian patriarch, in the Jewish saint, and in the Christian disciple. Piety is but one divine growth, under whatever sky; and piety varying in grade and manifestation, but the same in substance, was in all dispensations the one animating principle. More specifically, there are many constitutional as well as spiritual lineaments, wherein this essential unity may be traced and illustrated; studying the old, we see the new imbedded in it—studying the new, we discern at many points the familiar features of the old.

This identity is sometimes urged and sometimes questioned, for the special reason that it is supposed to justify—if it be established—the baptism of children under the Gospel, as a counterpart to circumcision under the Mosaic economy. The same tendency is manifested in connection with certain questions at issue between Romanists and Protestants, and among Protestants themselves, respecting church organization. But whatever may be judged to be the bearings of the general fact on any particular issue such as these, is it not clear that no Christian can afford to deny or to disparage this sacred oneness? The practical alternative is to regard the first and second forms of church life as failures, whereas in fact both are taken up and spiritualized, and made essential parts of the perfected Church under the Gospel. The economy of redemption is successful at each stage, and the transition from stage to stage is to be viewed only as a gracious development,—first the blade, then the ear, and finally the full corn in the ear. All believers are alike bound to hold and teach, whatever its bearing on specific issues, that the Church of God on earth is but One Church; the Bible justifies no other judgment.

XI. IMPORTANT POINTS OF CONTRAST NOTED.—But while Scripture teaches this essential oneness, it also brings into view some counterbalancing contrasts by which the Christian organization is forever broadly distinguished from its predecessors. First of all, we behold in Christ and His mediatorial work the fulfillment of the types, promises, prophecies, given to the earlier Church,—a fulfillment which involves the retirement forever of what was typical and introductory in these antecedent dispensations. There was no longer a Savior to come, to be contemplated through the glass of prophecy, and to be hoped for and prayed for by believing souls. Type and prediction were gloriously fulfilled in a present Shiloh, a present Christ.—In like manner, the sacrifices of patriarchs, the entire ceremonial cultus of the Hebrews, precious though they had been as aids to personal faith, were of no further spiritual value, since the great offering had once for all been made. In the presence of the Gospel, Mosaism was no longer needful, and was therefore finally retired; the schoolmaster had led men to the historic Christ, and his mission was therefore ended. Law was not to be abrogated; it was rather to be taken up into the higher economy of grace, and to become a law of life rather than a commandment unto death. In every prominent aspect, the peculiarities of the antecedent discipline of the people of God were thus to be transmuted by the touch of Christ, and made available and efficacious in conjunction with His scheme of saving grace.

It is obvious also that personal religion, in forms more spiritual and exalted—a type or measure of piety such as the Hebrew had but dimly known, and such as our Lord himself came in part to illustrate, was to be a distinguishing feature of the Christian Church. It was indeed the faith of Abraham which the disciple of Christ was to cherish; but it was the Abrahamic faith, broadened in its range, far more powerful in its action, and more controlling and spiritualizing in its effect on character. While the same principle of obedience was to be recognized, that obedience was to be ennobled throughout by the mighty impulses of holy love enkindled by personal contact with a living Redeemer. The Christian manhood was to be of a higher type, having a completer structure and efficiency, than the patriarchal or the Jewish. And in conjunction with this fresh development of gracious character, all domestic, tribal, national barriers were to be broken down, and the Church of God, thus endowed inwardly, was to go forth on a mission to all tribes and races—to preach this perfected Gospel to every creature. The set time had now come for a world-wide development. The Messiah had come to humanity; and His Church was to be made universal. The restrictions of Judaism were no longer needful, and were therefore thrown aside. The true religion had now taken on its final form; and the way was open for its implantation in all lands.

The student of Ecclesiology can not too carefully consider this gracious evolution, as it goes on from stage to stage until it attains its present degree of completeness. Close examination will show him how compactly joined together the divine process is at each historic transition;—it will reveal to him the true relationship of much that may otherwise seem fragmentary or extraneous; it will give new meaning to the older Scriptures at a thousand points, and serve to bind the Old Testament and the New, the various ceremonies, the complex aggregate of type and ritual and promise, into one superhuman and sublime unity. He will find the incarnate Christ not only explaining and illuminating all the past, even from the antediluvian or the Mosaic era, but giving meaning and grandeur to all that the Christian Church is, or is to become. That Church is the complete Body, of which this historic Christ is ever the divine and glorious Head.[1]

XII. GENERAL ARGUMENT FOR THE CHURCH: SEVERAL SECTIONS. —This brief outline of the divine idea of the Church, as that idea has been unfolded in history, furnishes of itself a distinct justification of the remarkable organism thus sketched. The simple existence of such an organism, through so long a period, in such varied and impressive forms, and in such relations to religion, becomes a sufficient explanation and defence. Yet it may be of service to note, at this stage, the general lines of argument by which such a divine construction as this is justified. Let it be observed that the question here suggested has no reference to the inquiry whether any specific church or denomination has a right to exist, or whether either of these three economic forms described as Patriarchal or Hebraic or Christian, can show just grounds for its particular existence. The present inquiry relates only to the one

---

[1] VAN OOSTERZEE: *Theol. of the New Test.*, Sect. 41. BERNARD, *Progress of Doct. in N. T.*: pp. 203–207.

Church of God on earth, whether past or present or future. Is this singular organism a human or a divine construction—does it exist by human or divine authority?[1] Is it some temporary adjunct of religion, of relatively slight importance, and likely to be outgrown with time; or has it a permanent place in the very structure of the true religion, and therefore an enduring life, and a full justification both in the human needs to which it ministers, and in the nature of the divine faith to which it is made accessory?

In asking whether the Church of God ought to be, we contemplate something more than the Church invisible—the spiritual body of Christ, made up of all who have ever believed on Him, and unified by the possession of religious life through Him, yet held together by no external constitution. This invisible Church has always tended to assume visible forms, and has existed in the world at every stage within some species of outward organization. It is therefore the visible Church as thus organized, standing out in the life of humanity as distinctly as the family or the state,—the Church of God, clad in these visibilities, and acting organically under divine commission upon the religious nature and destinies of man—concerning which the present inquiry is proposed. Four lines of evidence, separate in form, but cumulative in their pressure and result, may be considered:

1. *The Church constructively in the religious Nature.*—The Church, as thus defined, lies constructively in the very nature of man as a religious being. We recognize it as a valid plea for the existence of the family and the state, that the nature of man, domestic on the one side and social or political on the other, demands them. These two primordial institutions have their foundations in the universal needs of the race; man can not reach the proper consummation of his being and his happiness without their aid. There may be defects or blemishes in the domestic life of individual men, which render the particular household inadequate to satisfy this personal want; there may be communities or tribes in which the family tie is not duly honored or enjoyed; yet the family as an institution survives through all such adverse experiences, as something no less enduring than humanity. In like manner, though governments often fail to meet their appointed ends, and though revolutions sometimes subvert constitutions or dynasties, still the state survives, the world over, as an indispensable adjunct of healthful civilization. Like the family, it lives on through all changes of form,

---

[1] "I define a Church to be a company of men, professing the Christian religion, united in the person of one sovereign, at whose command they ought to assemble, and without whose authority they ought not to assemble." HOBBES, *Leviathan*, Part III. *Of a Christian Commonwealth; Ch. XXIX.*

because it is demanded by one of the deepest, most pervasive and most powerful instincts of mankind.

That man has a religious as well as a domestic or a social or political nature, will not be questioned by any thoughtful student. The universality of religion in the world, the number and variety of the natural faiths, the multiplied modes of worship, the costly sacrifices and temples, the priestly orders, the struggles of sects and schools, the rivalries of beliefs, the conflicts of men and nations around religious issues, and other like phenomena, leave no room for doubt on this point. Nor can it be questioned that the religious instinct in mankind is as powerful as it is universal; in fact, it stands well-nigh first among the most potential impulses at work in the experience and life of the race. But religion, even in its natural forms, is always a social and associating instinct. Though faiths visibly opposite sometimes lead men into bitter antagonism, adherents of the same faith are always spontaneously drawn together by their conscious unity in belief. While nothing segregates more quickly than religion, nothing more quickly associates, affiliates, unifies. Even where geographic or other natural lines of distinction would keep men separate, this sense of oneness in the gratification of so profound a principle brings them together above all differences, in conscious and even loving communion. And this is eminently true of that type of religious life which God Himself has directly implanted among men. There are defective conceptions or modes of piety which lead individuals to separate themselves from their fellows, as in monastic seclusion; but a healthful piety of the biblical type tends spontaneously to fellowship—it finds its best nutrition and strength and blessedness in communion. The history of the true people of God in all ages illustrates this proposition.

Hence the existence in all lands and times of religious associations, representing this deep yearning of human nature. In connection with even the lowest types of natural religion, we discern what may properly be described as crude suggestions or imitations of what we behold in its fullness in the Church. Family union, tribal fellowship, even national organization of this sort, spring up freely as by some universal law wherever religion in any form exists. As these faiths become more complex and elaborate, and are more widely diffused, this power to combine their adherents in visible association becomes more and more effective. And wherever biblical piety exists, this tendency manifests itself with peculiar intensity. Family altars are builded; households and tribes are welded together by spiritual as well as natural affinities; organizations spring into being, and visible membership becomes a personal badge and privilege. The sense of religious affiliation becomes an informing principle, a controlling law, expressing itself in visible communion and in enduring association. The Church, in a word, is the direct outgrowth of this vital tendency; it lies constructively in the very nature of man as a religious being. And wherever scriptural piety prevails, the Church springs consequently into existence by a necessity as real as that which creates everywhere the state or the family.[1]

2. *Religion as an experience requires the Church.*—The nature of religion, viewed as an experience, requires such an organization in order to its proper development. As an experience, religion in the biblical sense may be contemplated in this connection as both an inspiration and a discipline or cultus. On the one side, piety enters into the soul of man as a sublime force, awakening new thoughts and convictions, stirring the spiritual sensibilities into action, impelling the will to fresh activity along higher lines, and filling the moral nature throughout with a nobler, grander life. The true religion infuses another spirit into him who receives it, makes him a new man in respect to all moral quality and relation, is enthroned in him henceforth as a heavenly inspiration. And in that inspiration the central element is love,—love to God, and love to man, supplanting all selfish isolation or discord, and uniting its possessor in dear and everlasting union with all who truly cherish the same holy feeling.—On the other side, piety comes into the soul as a new and higher law—a more effective moral regimen or cultus. The inspiration it first imparts, it immediately begins to regulate and control for useful ends. It sets itself up as a holy principle, to be henceforth obeyed—obeyed absolutely and for evermore. It enters at once into the practical life of man; it places an intelligent, rectified will on the throne, and aims to bring all the spiritualized activities into conformity with the behests of duty. As love is the inspiring principle, obedience is the regulating rule. Hence religion becomes a holy cultus, a blessed discipline throughout, whereby the soul is brought at length into that perfect union with God which the very term so happily suggests.

Is it not easy to see how essential at many points the Church is, as a help in the development and culture of a true religious inspiration? We may take the central element of love as an illustration here. It is a familiar law of our emotional nature, that positive sensibility can thrive within the soul only through the aid of appropriate spheres and modes of expression. The affection of the mother requires a child, on which it can grow strong by lavishing itself; the sentiment of patriotism can not exist in one who was born and lives solely on the ocean.

---

[1] "The religious principle, when sound and living, has in itself an assimilating and associating character (quality). It binds not merely man to God; but also men to each other."—VAN OOSTERZEE, *Christian Dogm.*, Sec. 128.

Thus, pious love, as cherished toward God, both recognizes Him as its object, and grows into vigor only as it expresses itself in affectionate allegiance and worship. Holy devotion, loyal service, are the primary forms in which such love finds voice and volume. But the disposition to worship and to serve is not an isolating tendency. It blooms most freely under the stimulations of holy example and holy fellowship. Herein lies the value of family religion, of social religious activities, and of the combined and swelling chorus of adoration in the sanctuary. And the Church, in a word, fills just here a special, an indispensable place in the religious life; it furnishes a broad sphere in which this sentiment of love toward God, expressed in both worship and service, can act itself out most effectively.

In like manner the Church supplies the external conditions essential to the full development of love toward man. Viewed in relation to the world, this divine organism becomes the living embodiment of the sentiment of brotherhood—the fine sense of humanity. It is the chief agency through which Christian love can reach and help the sinful, the suffering, the lost. It is the appropriate center of all holy activities which have for their object the spiritual, and even the temporal welfare of mankind. Considering on the other hand, the relation of believers to each other, we see at once that the sacred *Caritas* of the Gospel could not well exist without such provision, sphere, opportunity, as the Church supplies. If there were no such thing as practical fellowship within this hallowed circle—no mutual friendships, no companionship in labor, no sympathy in trial or sorrow,—how dwarfed the sentiment of brotherhood in Christ would become, and how much narrower would be the range alike of Christian enjoyment, and of Christian growth!

What is true respecting religion as an inspiration, is no less apparent if we regard it as a holy cultus or discipline. How obviously does the principle of obedience, like the sentiment of love, need just such sphere and occasion as the Church supplies! In how many beautiful ways within the household of faith, is the soul trained to service and drilled in duty! What higher, more practical incentives are brought to bear upon it there, to make it more prompt, more ardent, more effective, in the discharge of religious obligation! How much are the sense of loyalty, the principle of service, the capacity and disposition of the disciple to be useful, increased through the influence of such examples as the Church produces! In a word, we have abundant evidence that religion as an experience could not be matured either as a glowing inspiration or as a divine discipline, if there were no such organism as this to supply it sphere and culture. And while the Church answers, as we have seen, to the instinctive demands of human nature viewed as religious, it also justifies its peculiar place in history by these unique ministrations to the religious life. What the devout nature needs, the holy life in the pious soul still further demands.

3. *Religion perpetuated and advanced through the Church.*—Contemplating the Church more broadly as the representative of piety in human society, we discover still further reason for its continuous existence.— First of all, it is through this divine organism that religion is chiefly perpetuated in the world. Believers die out from life; and so far as they are concerned, apart from the memory of their faith, religion dies with them. Generations perish; and the piety of one generation can live in the next only as it is by some appropriate means transmitted. And in such transmission the force of parental example, the influence of a godly ancestry, though inestimably precious, are not sufficient. God therefore does not rely exclusively on the law of perpetuation through personal or through social influence. In order that religion may abide permanently in the earth, He prefers to crystallize it in institutions, such as the pious family and eminently the devout Church. In other words, He organizes piety within His chosen household of faith, and thus enables it to maintain its place and power imperishably among men. In His great purpose, the Church thus stands forth, age after age, as one of the indestructible things in human life; and while the Church thus stands, the religion which the Church represents, must survive, even down to millennial times.[1]

This divine organism sustains a like relation to the diffusion and advancement of piety among men. If the true faith is yet to be received by all mankind—if the world is to become holy, as Scripture definitely teaches, we readily perceive that this mighty task must be carried forward through the most effective agencies which God Himself can command. Such a work can not be safely left to individual effort, or to the joint activities of any single generation, even under the impulse of an inspiring, comprehensive charity. It is a work which transient individuals, evanescent generations, left to themselves, could never prosecute efficiently; it is a work which God only can properly conduct and consummate, through such instrumentalities as He only can provide. To this end therefore He has constituted and endowed the Church; assigning to it directly this vast task of discipling the nations. The commission is not given to His people individually or

---

[1] "If religion had not some external institution, it would not have a manifestation among men as a distinct, substantive, all-important thing,—it would appear like a matter of private opinion,—its nature and evidence could scarcely be made sensible, still less prominent, in the eyes of mankind at large; and the grand benefits to be derived from social instruction and worship would be lost." —SMITH J. PYE, *Christ. Theol.*, p. 616.

even collectively; it is given to them organically, as one which can be fulfilled only through their compacted endeavor. And it is not difficult to see in how many ways the organized Church is specially fitted for such service. Its ordinances and worship, its creeds and testimonies, its spiritual vitalities, its capacities for aggressive operation, all qualify it peculiarly for such diffusion as well as preservation of the Gospel. Is it not difficult indeed to see how even divine wisdom could have devised a more effective method—a more capable instrumentality? Is it not obvious also that the great end in view is actually secured, in ever enlarging measure, through the efficiencies of this peculiar organism? And have we not clear testimony in Scripture, that as the world is finally brought to Christ, the relations of the Church to that glorious consummation, will become more and more sublimely apparent?

4. *The Divine Glory revealed through the Church.*—Still further argument may be derived from the supreme relations of the Church, as the accredited representative of the divine glory in the earth.—It is a familiar fact that even pagan altars and temples were erected, not merely as convenient places for sacrifice or worship, but rather as permanent memorials, ever witnessing to the deities to whom they were devoted. The grand temple at Ephesus was an enduring monument to that Diana whom the Ephesians and the world were agreed in worshiping. The Jewish tabernacle, and afterward the temple, were erected largely for a like purpose. They stood enduringly before the people as places where God especially dwelt, and in which His glory was especially revealed. So, from the earliest times, has the Church been erected and set up on high among men, not only that it might afford quickening and culture to the religious principle, and contribute to the preservation and advancement of that principle in the world, but also that it might be through all ages an organic witness and memorial for God. There are two forms in which the Church thus becomes a representative of the divine glory, worship and testimony:

God is glorified in the assembly of His saints in a form and degree beyond what is possible in the single life or within the pious household. The single life indeed glorifies Him in its own especial measure; and it is the highest attainment and privilege of the believer to be thus known and read of all as one who bears the image of God. The pious household glorifies God in its sphere, as often as the flames of devotion are seen to arise from the family altar, and men catch the passing fragrance of domestic sacrifice and consecration. But there is something in the worship of the sanctuary, in the joint adoration of the Church, higher and even more precious in the sight of heaven. The spectacle of the whole vast household of faith throughout the world, turned toward God, and expressing its trust and love in the forms peculiar to itself, is the sublimest image of heaven which our earth produces; it is the representative here, under narrower measures and yet in essential likeness, of that unending adoration which John in his vision describes as the crowning glory of the heavenly state.—God is also glorified by the testimony which His Church is ever bearing, not only to the intrinsic worth and blessedness of religion, but also to the infinite glory of Him in whom true religion finds both its source and its consummation. The individual disciple and the pious house alike testify to God, and alike make His glory manifest. Blessed be His grace for the convincing witness which is thus continually uttering itself in holy lives, in consecrated homes! But the testimony of a devout Church is both more diffusive in its quality, and more enduring in its effect. It is more than the aggregated declaration of the saints who compose that witnessing household. An added strength, a reverberating conclusiveness, comes from the combination of so many concurrent voices within the one organism; and what the Church thus declares, through its creeds, its sacraments, its teaching and life, the world can not well refrain from hearing. And is not this one among the special considerations which combine to justify the existence of that Church;—must not an organization which secures such an end so efficiently, have divine warrant, and be entitled to an enduring place in the world?

5. *Conclusion: The Church is of God.*—Grouping these lines of evidence around the common conclusion toward which they point, we are led to believe that the Church is not a fabric originating in human superstition, or a contrivance of the priesthood, or a construction of the state, as Hobbes affirmed. As an historic problem simply, it is impossible to account for its existence on any such hypothesis. Nor is it an accident or incident in the development of piety in the world— some temporary expedient divinely introduced for a specific end, but destined to pass away with the particular exigency that gave it birth. The ends which the Church was appointed to secure are as universal and enduring as are the demands of the religious nature—as enduring and universal as religious experience. The Church exists also, as we have seen, because the perpetuation and advancement of religion in human society require such an instrumentality, and because the declarative glory of God is made through its devotion and its testimony more luminous and more convincing. On these grounds the place which the Church holds in the Bible is fully explained, and the long and intricate history of the Church is made clear as the day. Unbelief can not question the right of such an organism to be.[1]

The obligation to sustain this divine institution holds therefore a high place among religious duties. The right of the Church to claim visible

---
[1] LUTHARDT, *The Church*, p. 66. Also PALMER, *Church of Christ*, Vol. 1: p. 7.

and hearty allegiance from all pious souls, and to command their support in every practicable way, is placed beyond question. The opposition in which inconsiderate or willful minds indulge, is sinful. Indifference to this fundamental claim, or to any of the particular services implied in it, is hardly less sinful in the sight of Him by whom the Church has been in every age and dispensation maintained as one of the three primordial institutions in human life. The special duty of sustaining this sacred institution by our gifts as well as by active effort in its behalf, is clearly enjoined in Scripture. The contributions received from the Israelites for the erection of the tabernacle (Ex. 35: 20–30, Numb. 7:) and afterwards of the temple (1 Chron. 29: 6–9) and the tithing required for the support of the priesthood (Numb. 18: 20–24, Heb. 7: 5,) in addition to the large expenditures involved in the maintenance of the sacrificial system, as illustrated in 1 Kings 8: 62–66, 2 Chron. 7: 5–7, all show how decisively this duty was enforced under the Mosaic economy. Under the Gospel the same obligation is enjoined in many ways; not only in contributions to the needy saints, or in the sharing of goods in common, and the devotion of property to the benefit of the Church, but also in the special support of those called to fill the ministerial, or any other kindred office. The earnest claim of Paul, as to his support of himself at a certain period in his apostolate (1 Cor. 9: 7-18) is itself strong proof of the recognition among the churches of this general obligation. Furthermore, we may see in the vast expenditure for temples, sacrifices, priests, required by some of the great natural religions, a distinct though it be erroneous illustration of the broad principle incorporated thus in the true faith; that the maintenance of the Church, in the discharge of its vital functions in the sphere of religion, is a duty as distinct, comprehensive, vital, as the diligent support of the family or loyal devotion to the state.

CHAPTER II.

THE IMPERSONAL CONSTITUENTS OF THE CHURCH:

ITS DOCTRINES, ITS SACRAMENTS, ITS ORDINANCES.

Having gained analytically and historically a distinct conception of the Church of God on earth, and having discovered a proper justification of the existence of this remarkable organization, we are now prepared to enter upon closer examination of its constituents—its component elements. These are of two classes, the impersonal and the personal. The impersonal elements, to be considered in the present chapter, are three: Doctrines, Sacraments and Ordinances.

I. DOCTRINE DEFINED: CHURCH CREEDS DESCRIBED.—A doctrine may be defined as any truth derived from Scripture, and essential to the Christian system, so expressed and described as to guard against unscriptural error.[1] Doctrines are to be carefully distinguished from both opinion and dogma. An opinion is the judgment of an individual, or of a class or school, on some element or aspect of revealed truth,—a judgment only probable in itself, obligatory upon no one beyond the holder, and liable to frequent fluctuation. A dogma is an opinion which has acquired some species of external authority, and is enforced upon others, without adequate justification in the judgment or conviction of those who receive it. Doctrines are rather those truths which stand forth as central in the Scripture, which become authoritative through their own inherent evidence and force, and which are widely accepted by believers as essential elements in the Christian scheme. The doctrines of grace are the cardinal truths directly declared and taught in the Bible, in order to human salvation, expressed in words so as to be understood, and commending themselves authoritatively to our faith.

When such cardinal truths are brought together under some unifying principle into a system —especially when they are thrown into authoritative form by the Church, and imposed upon its members as articles of belief, the term Doctrine assumes a new significance. A fresh investiture of authority, drawn not from that Scripture which declares, but from the organized Church which affirms it, then surrounds such doctrine. The truths so grouped become at once a Creed or Confession, representing the common conviction of the body that proclaims it, whether for edification or for defence. The statements given contain the authorized teaching of the body, and constitute a Rule of Faith, or in ancient phrase, a Canon of Belief.

Apart from all question respecting doctrine in the form of creeds, there can be no real debate as to the need of doctrine within the Church. If it be said that the simple language of Scripture is sufficient, without such additional human statements, it may be replied that since truth is not definitively described at any point in the Bible, but is spread diffusively through it, it becomes both a necessity and a privilege for the sanctified mind to gather up this scattered teaching, and to bring

---

[1] SMITH, H. B., *Introduction to Christ. Theol.*, p. 56.

it into definite form, and into logical coherence. This is indispensable also to that function of the Church as a teacher of men—to that mission of the Church as a messenger of truth to mankind, on which Protestantism insists as one of the essential marks of the true household of faith. Moreover, such transmutation of Scripture into doctrine is a healthful and invigorating exercise; the Church has always been both most vigorous in itself, and most zealous as a public teacher, when it has thus held the cardinal truths of the Gospel in most distinct, collected, potential form. In a word, doctrine in some shape seems indispensable to spiritual Christianity; it sets forth that Christianity, apart from all formalized perversions of it such as the Papacy has introduced, and exalts it immeasurably above the great natural faiths such as the Asiatic, in which no such invigorating and inspiriting element appears.[1]

II. CHURCH CREEDS: REASONS FOR THEIR EXISTENCE.—Reverting to the question whether Christian doctrine should ever assume the form of creed or confession, we may observe that the Church has existed, as it did in the apostolic age, or may exist again as in the millennial age, without any such authoritative symbol. Wherever there is known agreement respecting the truth held, or wherever there is no error or heresy at work subverting the truth, the embodiment of doctrine in a creed may be a needless task. Such, for illustration, were the convictions and belief of the early disciples, and so free was the Gospel at that stage from the encroachments of false opinion, or the assaults of opposing faiths, that believers were not impelled to do more than verbally to testify to what they believed. But the general position of the Church is different, and in its ordinary estate more formal creeds are born of a distinct necessity, and are obviously essential to its most effectual life and work. This necessity is twofold—external and internal:

The external necessity may be seen in the various relations which the several divisions of the Church sustain to each other, or which the Church as a whole sustains to opposing heresies or false faiths, or to the unbelieving world. It is obvious that in the divided state into which Protestantism has fallen, suspicions may often be quieted, discords healed, unity and confidence secured, and the general interest promoted, by the enunciation of a clear, strong, spiritual creed. The symbols of

---

[1] "The doctrines that center in Him, are not mere theories, abstract opinions, but they express the essential facts about His person and work. The Church can no more thrive without them, than morality can prosper without precepts and prohibitions. The attempt to separate Christian doctrine from the Christian life is vain. The two are as vitally connected as are the principle of life and the formative principle in the case of every seed or embryo."—SMITH, H. B., *Christ. Theology*, p. 593.

the Reformation originated chiefly in such a demand; they were largely the voices of church calling to church, in attestation of what each maintained as essential truth. The presence of heresy respecting cardinal doctrine, has been another frequent occasion for such attestation. The œcumenical creeds of the fourth and fifth centuries had their rise primarily in exigencies of this class; it is to Arius and Pelagius and their disciples, that we owe these monumental declarations of Christian belief. To Romanism, to the Greek Church, to Mohammedanism, and even to those great natural religions which from the beginning have stood over against spiritual Christianity, a similar debt is due. Even the great varieties of unbelief, especially the modern forms of skepticism, have suggested the need of earnest, united declaration by the Church of those great doctrines to which these types of error have been opposed. In a word, is it not manifest that, were such confessions in no sense essential to the Church inwardly, their existence is fully justified by these great exterior uses to which history shows them to have been so decisively subservient?

But the Church needs such creeds to meet its own interior needs; they sustain many important relations to its inward condition, experience and growth. As a bond of union, the Westminster Symbols, for illustration, have been of incalculable value not merely to the particular churches associated together under the Presbyterian order, but to the general interests of Presbyterianism throughout the world. As regulative guides to those who teach or who hold office within the Church, such statements of belief are vastly helpful, on one side as a confirmation of their teaching, and on the other as a guarantee against error in such teaching. As helps in the indoctrination of believers, they are—especially in the catechetical form—of possibly greater service. They supply clear definitions, explain what is obscure, guide and stimulate inquiry, and in the aggregate furnish to the private member a special and effectual education in the doctrines of grace. In the aggregate, the influence which such confessions exert on the thought and conduct of those who are brought under their training, though often silent and unobserved, is far more effective than most persons suppose. A comparison of creedless denominations with those that possess strong, positive creeds, will abundantly confirm this estimate.

III. OBJECTIONS TO CREEDS: PROPER LIMITATIONS.—Most of the objections urged against this doctrinal or confessional constituent of the Church, rest rather on the deficiencies of creeds, or on the perversion of them for wrong ends, than on either doctrines or confessions in themselves. To object that the Bible is sufficient as it stands, or that Christian life is something higher and more conclusive than all creeds, or that such doctrinal or confessional constructions are human merely, and therefore unimportant, is really to say but little to the purpose. To object that creeds are too voluminous or too minute, as they sometimes are; or that they represent rather the differences than the agreements of believers, as is too frequently the case, is simply to suggest, not their abrogation, but their improvement. It is indeed quite obvious that the primary function of a Christian confession is not to incorporate all minor points of belief, as might be done in a system of theology, but rather to embody in definite form those central elements of faith which lie at the basis of all true church life. No less obvious is it, that it can never be the main office of such a confession to spread out differences, and stand forth as divisive standards around which partisans may rally, but rather to draw together and so far as possible to unify all who hold to the common Gospel. Most of all is it obvious that the great historic confessions, whether of the earlier Church, or of the era of the Reformation, were never intended primarily to be used tyrannically by churchly authorities as instruments to arrest freedom of inquiry, or to bind the household of faith in unwilling allegiance to opinion or dogma. This objection might in like manner be urged against all theology, or even the Gospel itself, since now as in the age of Paul there are those who pervert that Gospel to illicit and injurious uses. As a further answer, it should be held constantly in view that the Church which frames a creed, has the right at any moment to revise it wherever it is defective—to modify, expand, abbreviate, change the document itself, and also to regulate at all times the use or abuse made of it by ecclesiastical authorities. Such a prerogative is certainly to be exercised with great caution, but the right to exercise it, like the right to interpret Scripture, is cardinal in Protestantism, and is inherent in every Protestant Church.

In general, therefore, it may justly be maintained that a solid foundation of doctrine, which may be embodied legitimately in authorized symbols, is one among the essential constituents of the Church of God. Even in the earliest stages in the life of that Church, we discover this doctrinal element at the basis of all religious experience; and as the household of faith expands into its later and larger forms, we find this element steadily enlarging in volume and becoming more conspicuous in its influence. It was one of those great characteristics of the apostolic Church, which set it apart altogether from the existing pagan faiths, that it possessed such a system of truth, and aimed to secure adherents only through such education and persuasion as that system of truth demanded. In all later times, the special strength of Christianity in opposition to all false philosophies or teachings, has been largely in the body of doctrine it has held and promulgated; in our time, the power of the Gospel, next to the central fact of a divine

Person who is its Life, lies in what it is as a harmonious, demonstrable, profound, and most effectual scheme of Truth. And is it not an obvious lesson of history that those branches of the Church which have rested less on the priesthood or the sacraments, or on liturgies or polity or other externalities—which have made much rather of doctrine, and have held themselves most strenuously to the task of teaching the world what the Christian doctrine is, have attained the largest growth, the most enduring position, the widest influence?[1]

IV. SACRAMENT DEFINED: NUMBER OF THE SACRAMENTS.—The second impersonal constituent of the Church is seen in the sacraments. Here the first inquiry relates to the nature of a sacrament, and to the number of the sacraments as enjoined in Scripture. According to the familiar Scholastic definition, which lies at the basis of the Romish view, a sacrament is *sacrum signum vel significatio sacrae rei invisibilis*. According to the Catechism of Westminster, which follows substantially the earlier Protestant creeds, a sacrament is a holy ordinance instituted by Christ, wherein by sensible signs Christ and the benefits of the new covenant are represented, sealed and applied to believers. The scholastic definition is expanded, in the Catechism of the Council of Trent, so as to make a sacrament an outward sign—*rem esse sensibus subjectam*—by which, in virtue of a divine institution or appointment, holiness and righteousness are both signified, and effectually implanted.[2] Both the Roman and the Protestant definitions agree on the following points: that a sacrament is an institution, of divine appointment and authority, given not to individual believers separately, but to the Church; that in every sacrament there is primarily an external sign or symbol, simple, definite, unchangeable; that there is also a gracious truth, or series of truths, symbolized in the external rite, and suitably expressed by it; and finally that there exists a divinely ordained connection between the *signum* and the *res sacra* represented, which it is incumbent upon the Church at all times to maintain, and in due form to commemorate. So far forth all branches of nominal Christendom are agreed in their conception of a sacrament; all unite in recognizing the cardinal fact, that sacraments are ordinances or institutions directly imposed upon the Church by God, and have their interpretation and warrant directly from His revealed Word. It is also a matter of general conviction that the sacrament, as thus described, belongs to the Christian rather than the Hebraic or Patriarchal church. In other words, while all discern the germs of these peculiar institutions in cer-

---

[1] On the significance and worth of Church Creeds, see WINER, *Confessions of Christendom*: Preliminary essay. Also SCHAFF, *Creeds of Christendom*, Vol. 1: pp. 3–9. BANNERMAN, *Church of Christ*, Part III: Div. 1: Chap. 2, 3.

[2] MOEHLER, *Symbolism*, p. 197.

tain ordinances enjoined especially upon the Hebrews under Moses, the sacrament proper is admitted to be a distinctive characteristic of the Gospel dispensation.

Protestantism differs from the Church of Rome, first of all, in maintaining that the authority of a sacrament must be derived, not merely from general biblical allusion or recognition, but from the immediate command of Christ Himself. The Eucharist, for example, rests on such a definite, imperative command: Do this in remembrance of Me. Baptism in like manner rests on a direct recognition by our Lord, and on His final commission: Baptizing them in the name of the Father, and of the Son, and of the Holy Ghost. These two ordinances, as we maintain, thus repose on a direct divine warrrant, which makes them obligatory in all ages upon the Church. To set them aside as human ceremonies, or to refuse the observance of them on any natural ground, becomes impossible. Romanism admits the peculiar claim of these two ordinances by placing them above all others as the *sacramenta majora*, and enjoining them especially on its adherents. Following rigidly this test, Protestantism rejects the five ordinances regarded by the Romish Church as a minor species of sacrament,—confirmation, penance, ordination, matrimony, and extreme unction. Churchly penance as a substitute for evangelical repentance is not only without biblical warrant, but is directly contrary to the teaching of our Lord. Extreme unction is a practice of very doubtful authority, and is often made an instrument of spiritual mischief. Matrimony is properly viewed as a religious no less than a civil contract, but clearly has no place among the sacraments, as instituted by Christ. Confirmation and ordination are merely modes of full reception into the Church, or of official investiture within it; and while proper, are in no sense sacramental. The symbolical element, and the direct appointment, are wanting in them all. To regard them as sacraments, therefore, both lowers the proper conception of a sacrament, and assigns to these subordinate ordinances or usages a spiritual value which the New Testament nowhere justifies.[1]

Protestantism also adheres rigidly to the doctrine that the value of the sacraments lies in their representative quality—not in any mystical efficacy embodied in the observance, and transmitted through it to the recipient. It refuses to dissociate the outward sign from the specific truth symbolized, or to admit that the administration of the sign can be of any spiritual avail excepting in conjunction with and through the truth it represents. The declaration of the Westminster Catechism that the sacraments became effectual, not from any virtue in them, or

---

[1] On the number and variety of the usages so regarded by the Papal Church at various periods in its history, see HODGE, *Theol.* III: 492-497.

in him that doth administer them, but only by the blessing of Christ, and the working of His Spirit in those who by faith receive these sacraments—only in virtue, in other words, of the gracious verities they represent, and of the faith by which these verities, as seen in the outward rite, are appropriated by the soul—is the universal doctrine of Protestantism: see Heidelberg Cat., Answer 66. Lutheranism indeed has claimed on the authority of Matt. 26: 26, that Christ is in some way embodied in, with and under the elements in these sacraments; yet the Lutheran Church regards the benefit to be derived from participation in them, not as a mystical transfusion of Christ Himself into the soul, but as an act of spiritual trust in Him and His salvation. For the Romish supposition that the sacrament is an *opus operatum*,—a process by which, through the priestly administration under churchly authority, grace flows immediately from the Church as a reservoir into the recipient, no true warrant can be found in the Word of God. The mischiefs consequent upon the admission of this error, are to be seen on every page in the later history of the Papal Church.[1]

V. BAPTISM DEFINED: ITS GENERAL SCRIPTURAL WARRANT.—Without entering upon any further enumeration of the grounds on which the Protestant doctrine of the sacraments rests, we may pass to the consideration of those two great sacraments which even the Papal Church recognizes as standing far above all other churchly rites: Baptism, and the Lord's Supper. Of these Baptism is to be viewed as the external or introducing sacrament, to be observed but once, and in connection with admission to the Church, while the Supper is the internal and nutritive sacrament, to be received at intervals, throughout the life of the believer, in remembrance or commemoration of Him who appointed it. Setting forth symbolically different elements or aspects of the Gospel, and ministering to different classes of need in the believer, these two sacraments are essentially one in the authority on which they repose, in the high spiritual blessing they incorporate, and in their harmonious expression of what is most central and precious in the Christian scheme.

Baptism is sufficiently defined as the application of water to the person, under the name of the Trinity, in confession of spiritual pollution, and of the need of regenerative grace, and in affirmation of an engrafting into Christ, and of holy covenant with Him and His people. In this general definition, and in the general validity of the ordinance as thus defined, all sections of Christendom are substantially agreed. The attempt to maintain, on biblical testimonies, such as are seen in Matt. 3: 11, 1 Peter 3: 21, Heb. 9: 10, and a few other passages, that the only baptism justified under the Gospel is spiritual baptism, is

---

[1] HALLEY: *The Sacraments*, Part I: Sect. I.

clearly vain.[1] The baptism of the Spirit unto repentance, and the making of the conscience clear in the spiritual sense, are real results, and results of inestimable moment. But the manner in which such references are introduced shows that they are not exclusive; it rather implies the presence and authoritativeness of the formal, symbolic baptism, which is so often directly described elsewhere. Equally invalid is the Socinian position (Racov. Cat. : 345) that symbolic baptism was not designed to be perpetual, but was employed by the apostles only in the case of persons passing over in that age from the world into the Christian faith, as a temporary sign of allegiance. If it be true that our Lord did not Himself at any time baptize (John 4: 2), still His recognition of the ordinance was distinct, and His final command to baptize must be viewed as obligatory, not merely upon the apostles in that era, but upon the Church to the end of time. Hence, while much diversity of judgment exists among believers on points of mode and the like, the Greek, the Roman, and the Protestant (with the minor exceptions just noted) are agreed in regarding this as an ordinance abundantly enjoined in Scripture on all believers, and therefore of perpetual obligation within the household of faith.

The germs of this sacrament are unquestionably to be found in the religious use of water even in patriarchal times, and especially in the washings and purifications of the Mosaic economy; such as appear, for example, in Ex. 30: 17-21, Lev. 8: 6, 16: 24-26, referring to the priesthood; in Ex. 19: 10-14, Numbers 31: 19-24, referring to the people; and in various passages in Leviticus referring to the cleansing of utensils used in religious ceremonies. For the significance of such lustrations, in connection with the idea of spiritual purification, see Isaiah 1: 16, Zech. 14: 1, Ezek. 34: 25, and many other allusions. If the strong, though not conclusive evidence in proof of the baptism of proselytes into the Hebraic communion prior to the time of Christ be admitted here, we are justified in regarding the further idea of spiritual relation or privilege as also incorporated in the Old Test. doctrine. It is at least a suggestive fact that John baptized his converts in this double sense,—the ordinance both typifying their inward cleansing by the Spirit, and exhibiting their outward state as his avowed followers. Inasmuch as neither the people nor the Pharisees seemed to regard the rite as a novelty, and since all classes interpreted it as, in the case of the disciples of Christ also, a mode or sign of proselytism, it is not unreasonable to infer that proselytic baptism was already known in Jewish circles as a mark of religious status as well as of spiritual experience. The question whether the baptism of John was identical with Christian baptism may be determined by its intermediate position

---

[1] GURNEY: *Lectures on the Evidences of Christianity*, pp. 162-166.

between the two economies, and by the spiritual teaching it conveyed; Luke 3: 3-18. Though the new economy had not been formally announced, or the Holy Spirit formally conferred, or the doctrine of the Trinity formally stated, yet the repentance which John awakened was repentance in view of moral impurity confessed, and the new life to which he summoned his followers was in substance, though not in form, the new life in Christ. The submission of our Lord to this baptism (Matt. 3: 13-17) is well-nigh conclusive here. Preparatory and introductory though the observance was in the hands of John, it was still a true budding forth or unfolding of that gracious flower which was to be twined for evermore around the brow of the Church of Christ.

The warrant for Christian baptism starts from the direct institution by our Lord; Matt. 28: 19. Prior to this formal act, the apostles had baptized those who believed on Him; John 3: 22, 26; but from this time baptism was to be a holy institution, associated indissolubly with His Church, and typical both of the indwelling grace that regenerates, and of the elective grace that sets the disciple among the truly redeemed, within the consecrated family and kingdom of God. That from this significant hour, the apostles continued to require obedience to this rite, and themselves to baptize both privately and in the family, and within the churches wherever they went, is abundantly manifest. Note the following instances of individual baptism: the Eunuch by Philip, Saul by Ananias, Crispus and Gaius, and also the twelve disciples of John by Paul:—instances of baptism in the household; Cornelius and his company by Peter, Lydia and her family, the jailer and all his, the household of Stephanas, by Paul:—instances of baptism, more extensively, within the Church; the multitude on the Day of Pentecost, and a like multitude in Samaria. To these historic accounts may be added the abundant references to baptism in the apostolic letters of Paul and Peter,—references which leave no room for doubt as to the full enthronement of this significant ordinance as one of the sacred and perpetual institutions of the Christian Church.

VI. BAPTISM: ITS NATURE AND DESIGN.—Recognizing this general warrant for baptism, we may turn to consider more specifically its nature and design. Here it is essential to exclude at the outset the theory of sacramental grace, whether in the papal or in the prelatic form. The place which the sacraments hold in the economy of redemption indeed justifies the expectation that in the faithful use of them divine grace will be bestowed, even in special measure; and Christian experience testifies abundantly to the spiritual blessings that accompany such observance. In this sense the sacraments are appointed channels of spiritual vitality; the blessing of Christ attending them, and the working of the Spirit being enjoyed in conjunction with them by every true believer. But no biblical warrant can be found for the declaration either that grace lies in the ordinance *per se*, or in the elements used, or that grace necessarily accompanies or directly follows the formal observance. To assert that the sacraments directly or of themselves convey a divine power or grace, which is independent of any spiritual effort or condition on the part of man, and which in the name of Christ is immediately conferred through them as means, under the forms of administration directly provided by the Church as the authorized medium of impartation, is to make them, as sources of spiritual blessing, well-nigh coördinate with the Spirit and with our Lord Himself.[1] Nor does it relieve the error to say with Moehler that the religious energies of the soul are set in new motion by the sacrament, since he adds: Its divine matter impregnates the soul of man, vivifies her anew, establishes her in most intimate connection with God, and continues so to work in all who do not show themselves incapable of its graces. In like manner, the kindred error of baptismal regeneration, or the actual renewing of the spiritual nature of the infant at the time when the external rite is administered, must be rejected as devoid of biblical warrant. As applied to such infants, the sacrament indeed signifies their need of the atoning lustration of the Cross, and of the washing of regeneration through the Holy Ghost; Titus 3: 5.[2] It also justifies the hope of their participation, through the parental covenant, in the spiritual birthright awarded through grace to all believers. Yet the sacrament does not of itself necessarily convey blessings of either class; since it may be administered as a formal rite merely, without any appreciation of its spiritual meaning or relations. The regeneration of a child at the moment of baptism can not on scriptural grounds be either affirmed or denied, inasmuch as such regeneration is a process of the Spirit, who worketh when and where and how He listeth. His efficiency here as elsewhere is sovereign; and the claim of the Church to be the authorized distributor of His grace, or to determine where and how it shall be imparted, is contrary to the teaching of Scripture, and is fraught as a dogma with vast spiritual mischiefs: See Heidelberg Cat., Answers 69–73.

It has already been stated that baptism includes two distinct, and yet closely associated elements: spiritual pollution and purification on the one side, and religious status or privilege within the Church on the

---

[1] MOEHLER, *Symbolism*, p. 193. Catechism Trident.
[2] See also Mark 16: 16, John 3: 5, Eph. 5: 26, which are sometimes quoted in support of the opinion that baptism is regenerative. But the incorrectness of such application is clearly obvious from, 1 Peter 3: 21, 1 Cor. 1: 14–17, and other passages named in the following paragraphs.

other. In the former sense, it represents what is the grand peculiarity of the Gospel as a religious system founded on the second birth. While it does not convey regeneration, the ordinance fitly symbolizes it. It shadows forth the change of heart, John 3: 5; points to spiritual union with Christ through faith, Gal. 3: 27; illustrates repentance as the essential condition of such union, Acts 2: 38; and sets forth the spiritual resurrection which His grace confers, Rom. 6: 4–5. The external element in the sacrament is manifest in the case of every adult recipient; since baptism is associated always with personal confession of Christ, and actual union with His visible Church: Acts 2: 41, 47, and other passages. The inward regeneration is here presupposed, as the proper justification of the outward confession. Baptism, irrespective of a renewed character in such recipient, can signify nothing in the way of spiritual right or privilege; it confers no title, *de jure*, to membership in the church invisible. In the case of an infant, the ordinance must carry the same general meaning, though the membership attained must from the nature of the case be constructive and provisional only,—a membership which becomes complete only when the baptismal covenant is voluntarily owned, and the personal renewing through Christ is sincerely confessed. Some advocates of baptismal regeneration use the phrase in this external sense only, to signify not the second birth, but simply this church relationship pledged and typified in the formal rite.

Comprehensively, the sacrament of baptism thus stands at the threshold of the Christian Church, certifying before the world its belief in the spiritual depravation of all, even of the infants of believers, and in the need and the certainty of complete restoration from this depravity through the grace of Christ, and the agency of His Spirit; certifying also to the forfeited estate and spiritual orphanage of all, even children of disciples, and to the divine assurance of spiritual adoption and kinship conferred on every one who by faith receives Him whom this holy rite so impressively portrays, in His vast redemptive work. It is thus justified, as an institute of the Church, not only by the direct command which enjoins it, Matt. 28: 19; but also by the fundamental truths it represents, and by its vital relations to all profound spiritual experience. See West. Conf. Ch. xxviii: i.

VII. BAPTISM: MODES OF ADMINISTRATION.—Two serious questions here confront us, which require distinct, though it be brief consideration; the question of mode,[1] and the question of subject or recipient.

---

[1] The following works may be consulted on the question of *Mode:* DALE, Classic, Judaic, Johannic, Christic and Patristic Baptism, 4 Vols: STUART, M., Mode of Christian Baptism; BEECHER, E., Baptism, Its Import and Modes; CARSON, A. (Baptist), Baptism in its Modes and Subjects; WALL, W. (Baptist), Infant Baptism, etc.

Three distinct methods of administering baptism are recognizable in Christendom: sprinkling, affusion and immersion. It is difficult to account either for the gradual rise of such variety in method within the Church, or for the gradual disappearance of affusion, if it be supposed that one strict, inexorable, universal mode was clearly enjoined by our Lord or His apostles. These facts lead rather to the conclusion —quite in harmony with the nature of Christianity as a spiritual faith—that while Christ carefully instituted the sacrament as an enduring element in His Church, He intentionally left this subordinate question of method largely to the judgment of the Church in the diversified conditions in which it was, as He foresaw, to be placed in the earth. It is at least presumable that, so long as the essential truths embodied in the sacrament are spiritually held, the matter of ritualistic expression must be incidental in His sight,—freedom and variety in the latter direction being entirely in harmony with loyalty to the doctrine taught, and in some respects even helpful in the fuller elucidation and enforcement of that doctrine. It is obvious, further, that tenacious adhesion to any specified mode, unless it is directly enjoined in the New Testament, must be regarded by Him with disapproval rather than favor, especially if it be accompanied by the condemnation of other modes as departures from the requisitions of essential Christianity, or by the disfranchising of other communions as insufficient and unworthy of fellowship at His table. On the hypothesis, assumed for the moment, that no such direct injunction putting the question forever at rest, is found in the Bible, it is clear that uniformity in administration, in all countries and in all ages, can not be insisted upon, even though uniformity prevailed in apostolic times,—especially if the mode insisted upon be one which can not be suitably, safely, and without liability to perversion, employed at all times and under all circumstances.[1] Such general considerations certainly go far both toward explaining the existence of the variety in administration actually current in the Church, and toward justifying the position here maintained, that no adequate warrant for the use of either of the current modes, to the absolute exclusion of the other as contrary to the Word of God, can be derived from that Word. To these suggestions may be added the broad historical fact that, whatever may have been the usage of the apostolic era, the Church of the first three centuries did not always or even habitually observe one mode; that from this period down to the Reformation the mode which is regarded by some as alone

---

[1] "Whether the person who is baptized, be wholly immersed, and whether thrice or once, or whether water be only poured or sprinkled upon him, is of *no importance;* Churches ought to be left at liberty in this respect, to act *according to the difference of countries.*"—CALVIN, *Inst.*, Book IV: Ch. 15: 19.

possessing divine warrant, almost entirely disappeared; and that since the Reformation, this mode, notwithstanding the most strenuous efforts of its advocates, has never been able to win the suffrages of evangelical Protestantism, but remains at this day the opinion of a relatively small minority in the household of faith. But it is freely admitted here that no general or historical considerations, however cogent, can be conclusive upon an issue which turns directly on the voice, not of the Church, but of the Scripture itself.

It is admitted by all that the biblical question rests primarily on the verbs, βάπτω and βαπτίζω, and their derivatives. Passages in which these words are used tropically, (such as baptizing with the Holy Ghost, Mark 1:8; with spiritual fire, Matt. 3:11; with physical suffering, or personal trial, Mark 10:38; or finally with eternal torments, Luke 3:16–17,) shed but indirect and inadequate light on the specific issues here to be considered. We also discover many instances of direct reference, (such as the general allusions to the baptism of John in Luke 7:29–30, John 3:26, Acts 19:3–5,) where no clear suggestion in regard to mode can be discovered. Careful examination of all the passages, in which these words occur with any reference to the manner of the sacrament, brings to light a considerable latitude of meaning, ranging broadly from cleansing or washing, to dipping or submersion. That there are texts which suggest immersion rather than other modes, may be freely admitted; instances may be seen in Matt. 3:6, 16, Mark 1:9, John 3:22–23, Acts 8:38–39, Rom. 6:3–4, Col. 2:12, Heb. 10:22; also Mark 14:20, John 13:26. Upon these passages, it should be remarked that in the last three, if not in others, the idea of washing or dipping rather than full immersion clearly predominates; that the attempt to run too close an analogy between baptism and burial, based on the references in the Pauline letters, brings in far greater perplexities than it removes; and that in all of the historic instances given, simple affusion applied to one standing in a running stream—as our Lord has often been pictured—answers as well as immersion to the statements made. A second class of texts is found, in which other modes are the more probable; as Mark 7:4, 8, and Luke 11:38–40, applied to the cleansing of the person, and the purifying of the sacred vessels; as also Heb. 9:10, Acts 2:41, 4:4, 10:47–48, 1 Cor. 10:2. In these historic instances, the probability against immersion must be regarded as very strong; and in the last, the reference is clearly to sprinkling or affusion rather than submersion, in either cloud or sea. A third class may be named in which immersion seems altogether improbable; such as Acts 9:18, 16:15, 32–33, 18:8, and others. The apparently insuperable difficulty in the instances where thousands were received into the Church by baptism in a single day, which Robinson (Lex. *art.* βαπτίζω) urges so cogently, is greatly enhanced in at least some other of these instances. The baptism of Paul at Damascus, of Crispus and others at Corinth, and of the households of Cornelius by Peter, and of Lydia and especially of the jailer by Paul at night and within the prison walls, by immersion in every case, is in the highest degree doubtful, if indeed it be not quite impossible. Passages referring directly to sprinkling as a religious rite, based on certain Mosaic observances (Heb. 9: 13-14, 10: 19-22, 1 Peter 1: 2), may properly be quoted here in confirmation of this direct evidence as to other modes than submersion.

What the New Testament yields to thorough and candid inquiry is certainly not uniformity of allusion or usage in favor of immersion, but rather a clear suggestion of that variety, produced by the varying circumstances under which the sacrament was administered, which seems to have grown afterwards into a law or habit in the primitive Church. The most ardent advocate of immersion can establish no higher claim than this, and such a claim those who on general grounds prefer other modes of administration as equally biblical and more convenient, freely admit: see West. Conf., Ch. XXVIII: iii; also, West. Direct. for Worship, Ch. VII: v, where affusion as well as sprinkling is recognized as valid. So far as we can ascertain from Scripture, the cardinal fact thus is, that our Lord and His apostles never determined conclusively the question of mode, but rather granted to the Church that freedom of judgment, that liberty of adjustment to its varying circumstances and conditions, which the vast majority of the churches, ancient and modern, have in fact allowed. The exclusive enforcing of sprinkling by the Papal communion, and the equally exclusive enforcing of immersion by the Baptist communion, are alike unwarranted by the Bible itself and by the history of primitive Christianity, and alike are at variance with that spiritual freedom which is the fundamental law in the Christian Church.

Further questions in regard to the mode of baptism may be considered more briefly. The question whether any administration is valid in which the doctrine of the Trinity is not expressed or implied, must be answered in the negative, as no organization can be a true Church of Christ which refuses to recognize His divinity, and the divine personality of the Holy Spirit, as cardinal elements in Christianity. Baptism by open errorists who cast aside the fundamental doctrines of our faith, is no less invalid than the same ordinance would be, if administered in sport, or in order to excite ridicule or contempt; yet Protestantism agrees with Romanism in holding that the ordinance is not necessarily rendered invalid by the discovered unworthiness of the person administering. The validity of Romish baptism will be determined by the answer given to the question whether the papal communion is, notwithstanding its heresies, a part of the one Church of that Christ whom it professes to receive as the true Savior of men. On this point the French Confession (Conf. Fidei Gall, 1559), says: Nevertheless, as some trace of the Church is left in the Papacy, and the virtue and substance of baptism remain, and as the efficacy of baptism does not depend upon the person who administers it, we confess that those baptized in it (the papal Church) do not need a second baptism. Baptism with milk or oil, or any other material than water, can hardly be counted true baptism; and on the other hand, no previous consecration of the water, or any like preparatory cleansing or disrobing or anointing of the person, can be viewed as essential. Triple baptism in the name of each of the three Persons in the Godhead and repeated baptism, as in cases where the person baptized has fallen into further sin, are alike without biblical warrant. Neither has the ordinance any scriptural connection with the naming or christening of the recipient. Neither is the question of place or agent vital, though baptism as a sacrament of the Church should ordinarily be administered within the sanctuary, and by an ordained administrant. All ceremonies superadded to the observance, such as giving honey or salt to the baptized person, touching his mouth or ears with spittle, breathing upon him by the administrant, or making the sign of the cross upon him, the kiss of peace, the lighted taper, and the like, are superstitious departures from the proper meaning and purpose of the ordinance. Exorcisms and adjurations, such as are practiced in the Greek and Roman communions, have no proper connection with the sacrament. The baptism of bells, altars, sanctuaries, and other objects for the purpose of purification, is a practice wholly diverse from the teaching of Scripture; all such perversions corrupt our estimate of the ordinance, and are obviously at variance with the spirit of Christianity.

VIII. BAPTISM: PROPER SUBJECTS OR RECIPIENTS.—The other important question to be considered relates to the proper subjects or recipients of this sacrament.[1] So far as adult recipients are concerned, this question will be variously answered according to the view taken of the Church, and of church connection. It is maintained here that the Church is not a visible society merely, to whose rights and privileges baptism gives the subject a formal title, but rather that every true Church must be composed of persons who make at least credible profession of piety; and therefore that baptism becomes properly a sign and seal of grace already enjoyed—not a promise of grace to come

---

[1] In addition to the authorities already cited see WARDLAW, Script. Authority of Infant Baptism; WOODS, L., Infant Baptism; HALL, Law of Baptism; RICE, N. L., Baptism, Mode and Subjects; HALLEY, on the Sacraments, Vol. II.

through the observance, or a sign of ecclesiastical place or privilege secured through the formal rite. Waiving the special question as to the qualities of this credible profession, and to the proper judges of such profession when made, it must be held that baptism is not an appointed method of transfusing or of procuring grace, but is simply an emblem of corruption confessed and of spiritual cleansing gained, and that on this ground, and on no other, can the baptized person become entitled to a place within the visible Church. This is the general position of evangelical Protestantism, in contrast with the sacramentarian theory on the one hand, and the papal perversion on the other. We can not accept, without limitation, the striking declaration of Cyprian: He who has not the Church for his Mother, has not God for his Father. In our view, adults are not to come to Christ through the Church, or through outward ordinances, but are rather to come to the Church, and into the enjoyment of the sacraments, through antecedent union with Christ. Protestantism therefore does not baptize all adults who seek its chrism, but only those who seek first, and first find, salvation in and through a personal Redeemer.

But the main question here relates to the propriety of baptizing those who are as yet incapable of exercising such personal faith. The Church of Rome, regarding baptism as necessary to the removal of original sin, and therefore to salvation, administers the rite to all children whom it can reach, without regard to the relation of the parents to the Gospel. The general Protestant position is, that, while it is a sin to contemn the ordinance, yet grace and salvation are not inseparably annexed to it (West. Conf., Ch. XXIX: v), and that therefore even adults, and, *a fortiori*, infants may be regenerated and saved without it. The Scotch Confession denounces as cruel and of Antichrist, the doctrine that unbaptized infants are lost. Yet Protestants vary as to the degree of freedom with which the ordinance is applied,—some granting the privilege to all who seek it, and some to the children of baptized persons only, while others limit the application strictly to the children of believers. This variation in practice seems to be determined chiefly by the view cherished by these parties respecting the amount or measure of grace, to be regarded as flowing into the soul with or through the observance. Over against both the Church of Rome, and the vast majority of Protestant bodies, stands the doctrine strongly maintained by immersionists, that all infant baptism is unauthorized by the Word of God,—personal faith and personal confession being deemed indispensable conditions and concomitants of the external rite. Here the burden of proof rests clearly on those who claim, not that all children, but that the children of believing parents may receive the sacrament, and may gain through it a place and name within the Church of Christ.

The general grounds on which the latter belief is based, may be stated briefly under the following heads. First: it has already been made clear that the Church of God in all dispensations is but one Church. While forms of organization have been changed, while ceremonies and usages have varied in different ages, the unity of the Church as a spiritual organism has never been lost. It is only on the basis of this fundamental truth, that such a question as the present can be successfully considered. Secondly: within this one and indivisible Church, the family as a unit, has always held a recognized place.[1] It is true that God deals in grace primarily with men as individuals,—that the experiences of religion are primarily personal, and that the promises and privileges of the Gospel are given, for the most part, to independent persons. And yet, almost from the earliest manifestations of the Church among men, we find the household sharing with the individual in the blessings of redemption. For many centuries the Church dwelt almost exclusively within the family; and after passing into the tribal, and then into the national form, it still embraced children with their parents within its hallowing circle. Under the Christian economy, whether the baptism of such children be legitimate or otherwise, their place within that circle, and their title to the blessings flowing from such a relationship, can not well be questioned. Thirdly: that God condescended to specialize this connection by entering into formal covenant, if not with Noah or his predecessors, then with Abraham, and with the patriarchs after him, in behalf of their households, and through them with the heads of families throughout the Hebraic dispensation, is also a significant and an unquestioned fact. The primal covenant with Abraham (Gen. 17), can be regarded as nothing else than a holy compact in which, in answer to his parental faith and consecration, the posterity of the patriarch was even through many ages to be blessed spiritually as well as in temporal estate. In its religious quality and aim, in the domestic duties it imposed and in the spiritual benefits it conferred, this covenant was not limited to Abraham alone, but rather was set up as an illustrious example of a like compact into which succeeding patriarchs and indeed

---

[1] "The grand peculiarity of humanity is that, while each individual is a free, responsible moral agent, yet we constitute a race, reproduced under the law of generation; and each new-born agent is educated, and his character formed under social conditions. Hence results the representative character of progenitors, and the inherited character and destiny of all races, nations and families. . . This principle runs through the dealing of God with the human race under the economy of redemption. The family . . is the unit embraced in all covenants and dispensations."—HODGE, A. A., *Outlines of Theol.*, p. 616.

all devout parents under the Mosaic economy might through grace enter. Nor was this privilege limited to parents living under that preparatory dispensation. The same covenant may be entered into under the Gospel, and with even higher warrant, by all believing parents. God still as of old is willing to pledge His grace and favor to the immediate offspring, and even to the remote posterity, of those who, themselves entering into holy relations with Him, desire also to train up their households for His service and glory. As the family regarded as a unit holds a real place within the Church, so the children of faithful Abraham, and the offspring of all who exercise Abrahamic trust, are properly embraced within this covenant of grace.

Fourthly: it is also obvious that the basis of this compact is parental faith. As it was not faith personally exercised at the outset by each member of the Abrahamic family, but simply the holy trust and consecration shown by the patriarch himself, which was the foundation of the original covenant, so God condescends still to accept like parental trust and consecration,—not indeed as a full substitute for personal piety in the child, but as the ground of spiritual privilege conferred upon the child, and the basis of a pledge that through His grace the child shall at length be brought willingly into a personal experience of the same spiritual life. Fifthly: as God has in all dispensations instituted certain visible marks and institutions by which the spiritual relations existing between Him and believers are made known, and as in the case of Abraham He instituted such a visible seal of this gracious family covenant, so it is reasonable to anticipate that such a seal, in some form, would be instituted under the Gospel. In this higher economy, Christ has at least set up the Supper in place of the Passover, and Baptism as the distinctive sign of admission to His fold in the case of adults; and we may therefore well presume that some kindred mark or institution will be given by Him to signalize this gracious relationship of the household within the one great family of grace.—From such general propositions as these, it must be difficult for any thoughtful mind in the light of Scripture to withhold assent. There are doubtless many among those refusing to regard infant baptism as the proper conclusion from these propositions, who still cordially recognize the grand and precious facts which such propositions are framed to describe. Were there no ordinance to mark the household covenant— were there even no formal covenant to represent the underlying verity that the family is treated largely as a unit in the economy of grace, that underlying fact must still be one of untold value in the sight of believing parents under all dispensations.

IX. SCRIPTURE WITNESS TO INFANT BAPTISM: HISTORIC TESTIMONIES.—It is certainly a strong confirmation of such presumption, that Christ and His apostles do so distinctly recognize the claim of infancy to the blessings which He came to confer. When our Lord laid His hands on little children, and prayed for them, and declared their title to a place in the kingdom of heaven, which is none other than His own Church on earth (Matt. 19: 13–15), He laid down afresh, in more spiritual form, what had been the immemorial doctrine of the Hebrews as to the nature both of the Church and of the parental covenant, as already defined. And again, when He commanded Peter to feed the lambs as well as the sheep in that vast fold into which His chosen were to be gathered throughout the world (John 21: 15–17), He laid down a rule of duty which all ministers, all churches, all believing parents to the end of time, are bound to recognize in the training of the young for His service. Nor can we contemplate His significant setting of a little child before His apostles, in order through the vision of its innocent simplicity and trust to rebuke their ambitious strivings, without regarding the act as suggestive of His estimate of the corresponding duty to train up such little ones within His fold, and for His service. And with what our Lord thus suggests, we may fitly associate the declaration of Peter concerning the scope of the Old Test. promise of grace, as including the posterity of believers, Acts 2: 39; the view of the apostles is seen in their counsels to children and parents respectively (Eph. 6: 1–4, Col. 3: 20–21), and the Pauline declaration (1 Cor. 7: 14) that the children even of one believing parent in any given household are to be viewed by the Church as holy, or sanctified, in virtue of such parental faith. In this striking passage, it can not be claimed that the children thus viewed are in all instances capable of exercising personal faith, and are to be regarded as holy on that account; the belief of the parent, and this only, is the specified ground for the position which the apostle counseled the Church at Corinth to take. Even the unbelieving husband or wife is said to be set in better spiritual relations, as a consequence of such belief; and how much more the offspring of a saint standing within the domestic relation!

Several instances of household baptism, more or less fully mentioned, serve to confirm these inferential evidences. Of these the most obvious are the cases of Lydia and her household at Thyatira, of the Philippian jailer and his family (Acts 16: 15, 33), and of the family of Stephanas at Corinth, 1 Cor. 1: 16. Paul puts on record his baptism of Crispus also, of whom it is said (Acts 18: 8) that he believed on the Lord, with all his house. The additional case of Cornelius, who with other inmates of his house was baptized by Peter at Cæsarea (Acts 10: 48), is on probable grounds to be classed with those already cited, as an instance of family baptism, including old and young within the domestic circle. In all of these instances, both the promptness of the baptismal observance, at the very time and place where the associated conversions occurred, and the direct including in each instance of the family of the believing parent, are to be carefully noted. To assert that in each and all of these cases none but adults capable of exercising personal faith were present, and that the sacred rite was applied in every instance to such persons only, is to go very much farther than the laws of sound interpretation permit. There can hardly be reasonable ground for refusing to believe that in at least some one or two of these examples the family was contemplated in its divine unity, and the children of believing parents were, on inspired authority, counted in the holy covenant then and there made by such parents with Christ. It should be added that the strong presumption derived from such recorded instances, as well as from the general suggestions previously considered, is confirmed at many points by the apostolic, and especially the Pauline conception of the Church, viewed as an aggregated household or family of grace. That none but adult believers were in any way counted as members of that divine fold,—that the domestic unit was altogether disregarded, and the children of saints were viewed as having neither place or claim within that sacred fellowship, can hardly be believed by one who studies in its essence and purpose the New Testament Church.

While it is freely to be admitted that these are probable considerations only, and that no direct warrant exists for applying the ordinance of baptism to infants, such as that which enforces the Eucharist upon all believers, still the observance may safely be rested, like the observance of the first day of the week as a Sabbath, on the historic approval and usage of the apostolic Church as here described. The two cases are closely parallel: and in both, the biblical inferences are strongly sustained by the convictions and the practice of believers, after the apostolic age with its peculiar characteristics had passed away. It is a clearly established fact, that if the Church of the second and third and fourth centuries did not enjoin infant baptism, it extensively admitted the ceremony, giving to it the place and significance which circumcision had held in the Hebraic dispensation.[1] That the usage came by degrees to be regarded with greater favor, and was at length clothed with full ecclesiastical authority as one form of the general sacrament, is abundantly evident. Of its position during the long period between

---

[1] See HAGENBACH: *Hist. Doct.*, §§ 72, 137, for the various (and conflicting) judgment of the Fathers from Tertullian in the second to Augustine in the fifth century. "Ecclesia ab Apostolis traditionem accepit etiam parvulis baptismum dare;" ORIGEN.—KURTZ, *Church. Hist.*, I; §§ 32, 58; and other church historians. For modified view, see NEANDER; *Christian Dogmas*, I; 228.

Augustine and the Reformation there is no serious question,—a rite indeed formalized and overloaded with priestly accretions, and therefore void of much spiritual value, yet representing in substance those great doctrines of grace which it was originally appointed to symbolize. The general verdict of Protestantism in its favor is shown by its almost universal observance, outside of the circle of those who hold to immersion as the only admissible mode of administration. Protestants do not agree with the Church of Rome in regarding baptism as essential to the salvation of infants, and therefore make no such extraordinary provision as that Church for the very early administration of the rite, or for lay baptism in special emergency as by midwives or other unordained persons. Yet they agree in emphasizing the importance of the ordinance, as constituting a special form of covenant in which the parents and the church on the one side, and Christ as the Head of the household of faith on the other, bind themselves by mutual vows to train up the baptized infant for the divine service. As to the value of the parental side of this covenant, in the way of stimulating to faithful endeavor and to believing prayer in behalf of the baptized child, there can be no question; the experience of multitudes of pious parents is adequate evidence here. And where churches have been faithful to their part in this sacred transaction, and have become spiritual homes to such children, in the biblical sense, the actual results in the increase of visible membership from this class have been such as to justify the strongest affirmations respecting the salvatory value of the sacrament when thus interpreted. Christ Himself in instances beyond number has set His seal upon the ordinance,—has accepted and approved the covenant instituted through it, by drawing such children into His arms as He did of old, and declaring through the regenerative ministries of His Spirit that of such is the kingdom of heaven.—The precise relation of such baptized children to the visible Church, will be considered at a later stage. It is only to be remembered here that baptism does not create that relation, but simply embodies or expresses it; the covenant then entered into in form, must have existed in substance from the moment when the parental relation to the child was established,

X. THE LORD'S SUPPER: WARRANT AND NATURE.—Associated with Baptism as a fundamental constituent in the conception of the Christian Church, stands the Lord's Supper. The direct and formal institution of this sacrament by the Messiah, is carefully recorded by three of the evangelists: Matt. 26: 20–29, Mark 14: 22–25, Luke 22: 17–20. The purport and spirit of the observance are as carefully registered by John also in the final discourse and prayer of Christ, before He led his disciples out to the Mount of Olives and to Calvary. Paul also was inspired to put on record an account of the institution, in order that the Church through all time might the more fully appreciate its significance; 1 Cor. 11 : 23-25. The direct connection of the sacrament with the Hebrew Passover, as is indicated by the evangelists in their story of the original appointment, brings that historical event (Ex. 12 : 3-20) before us as its type and proper explanation. The great deliverance which the Passover commemorated was, at every stage in the history of the chosen people (2 Chron. 30 and 35: *passim*), the recognized emblem of the far greater deliverance which our Lord through His redemptive sacrifice was to bring, not to the Hebrew only, but to humanity. Hence Christ suggestively connected the new ceremony with the old at the outset, and at the same time took pains to set the two forever apart, as the shadow is forever separate from the reflected reality. So clear is this relationship, and so definite and impressive was the first institution in accordance with it, that all who bear the Christian name in all ages, with few exceptions, have confessed the obligation to observe the sacrament perpetually in remembrance of an atoning Savior,—just as the Hebrews felt themselves perpetually bound to observe the Passover. The disposition to regard the ordinance as a temporary feast merely, arranged by our Lord for His first disciples only, and the disposition to view it as a purely spiritual act of communion in which the formal observance may be entirely dispensed with, are alike at variance with the direct, conclusive, permanent mandate of the Messiah: Do this in remembrance of Me.[1]

Over against the tendency to view this sacred obervance as temporary or as informal, stands the tendency, so manifest in the Church of Rome, and in oriental Christianity also, to materialize or formalize the ordinance by overloading it with ceremonial accretions wholly at variance with its divine intent. This may be seen in the opinion that the sacrament is an actual oblation, in which Christ is really offered up afresh as a sacrifice for the sins of His people. From this view, which has no recognizable basis in the Scripture, has largely sprung the disposition current among Romanists to decorate the Supper with a multitude of unwarranted formalities. In like manner, the kindred theory that the sacrament, like baptism, carries grace in itself, and is to be administered as an *opus operatum*, is altogether without scriptural warrant, and inevitably leads on to just such corruptions as are aggregated together in the Romish Mass. Resting on a false and gross interpretation of the phrase, This is my Body, and maintaining an actual presence of Christ corporeally in the elements employed—they

---

[1] GURNEY: *Evidences of Christianity*, pp. 167-169. The Society of Friends regard the Supper as well as Baptism, as a spiritual observance merely, notwithstanding the explicit command of the Master, and the example of the Apostles.

being actually transmuted into His flesh and His blood,—that theory may easily be used to justify each and all of the grotesque absurdities, which everywhere deface the eucharistic service in the papal communion. Difficulties of a like nature, though less serious, must always beset the observance, on the Lutheran theory that our Lord is ubiquitously present in, with and under the elements, though these are not actually changed into His body and His blood. While we are to guard against the bald notion which Lutheranism justly opposes, that the sacrament is commemorative or historical only—while we are bound to recognize the other gracious relations which it sustains to religious experience, we are still to reject even in its mildest forms the opinion that grace is somehow incorporated in the elements, and is therefore to be received orally by the believer. To say nothing here of the speculative questions involved, such as the corporeal ubiquity of Christ on earth and His presence corporeally wherever His people are assembled to commemorate His death, we are bound to maintain that the benefits of the sacrament are spiritual only, and that such spiritual benefits can in no way be transmitted through any physical process, such as the assimilation of the consecrated elements corporeally.[1]

The essential features in the sacrament are, the use of bread and wine as the elements, the act of consecration and distribution according to the original observance, and the participation in both elements by the Church, in compliance with the precept and example of Christ. To substitute another element for either of those first employed, or to depart radically from the original manner of administration, or to add ceremonial features to it, must be regarded as an unlawful deviation from the divine command. The denial of the cup to the laity, on whatever ground of convenience, is a still more serious departure. The Council of Trent pronounces this a matter of discipline or method, rather than of doctrine; and the usage is justified by Catholic writers, on the ground that the distribution of the cup is liable to special forms of desecration, against which the Church deems it wise to guard. Yet the mandate of our Lord, Drink ye all of it, was addressed not to the priesthood, but to the Church; and the assumed right to do this representatively, in the place of the body of believers, can be regarded as nothing else than a priestly usurpation. The indifference of the papal communion to a point so vital as this is in marked contrast with its strenuous requisitions as to the kind of bread used, the manner of the

---

[1] "They differed from the Reformed only in this, that while the latter were content with the Word and the Symbols as pledges of prevenient grace in the Sacrament, they added to these the real presence and oral communication of the body and blood of Christ, as a most gracious pledge of the forgiveness of sins."—SPRECHER, *Evang. Lutheran Theol.*, p. 457-460. The author does not regard this view as fundamental, or indispensable, in the Lutheran system.

participation, and other minor points in the observance. These minor matters, such as the degree of frequency with which the sacrament shall be observed, or the exact number partaking, or the precise place or posture of the recipient, or the explicit form of prayer or of address, or the singing of a hymn at the close, are left largely to the judgment or to the convenience of each congregation of disciples. The elements may be received at the altar or communion table, or distributed through the sanctuary; the distribution may be made by the person administering, or with the aid of proper assistants; the participants may sit or stand or kneel in the act of receiving the emblems; the bread may be leavened or unleavened, and the wine may be that in common use or the unfermented juice of the grape, and may or may not be mingled with water. So long as there is appropriate adherence to the three essential features already named, these subordinate questions may safely be committed to the spiritual discernment and devout feeling of the household of faith. The spirit of charity finds nowhere a finer field for beneficent exercise; and the autonomy of the individual conscience properly subordinates itself at the table of our Lord to the aggregated judgment of the Christian body. As a practical rule, the usage of any particular denomination is a sufficient guide to personal duty, on all questions not involving the proper substance of the sacrament, as Christ himself has instituted it.

XI. THE LORD'S SUPPER: ITS DESIGN AND PARTICIPANTS.—Resting in the general position that the Eucharist is not a mystical mode of transmitting grace through the Church or priesthood to each participant, but is rather a sublime act of faith and devotion in commemoration of the dying Redeemer who instituted it, we may proceed to consider its object or design more specifically. Five distinct ends are obviously gained through it. Of these the first is discerned in its historic or commemorative quality. For the Supper is an enduring witness by the Church to the transcendent fact, which is central in the Christian scheme—the death of the Redeemer on Calvary. It is a continuous creed or confession proclaimed by His people, respecting their belief that He did actually die according to the evangelical narrative, and that His dying was all that He declared it to be as an atoning and redemptive act. While it would be an error to assert that this commemorative testimony was the only end sought by our Lord in the institution, there can be little room for doubt that this was a primary object. In His purpose this ordinance was to be a perpetual sign that the Passover, and with it the entire economy of which it was representative, had passed away; and that a new economy, resting on a divine sacrifice and conveying spiritual life through a higher form of faith, had come in.* It was to call the Church, and even the world, back from time to time to the remembrance of a fact, which otherwise the world, and even the Church, might soon forget;—a fact which constitutes the grand peculiarity of the Christian dispensation, as a scheme of atonement through sacrifice, and of justification through faith.— But while the ordinance was thus historical in its aim, it was also in the second place specifically confessional and sacramental. It implied from the first a declaration of personal trust in the crucified Savior,— an acknowledgment of Him as the true Lord and Redeemer. It implied also a personal covenant or pledge of discipleship, as the term, sacrament, in a military connection suggests. It was in essence an avowal of willing separation from the sinful world, and of honest devotion to the cause of Christ; 1 Cor. 10: 21. To remember and commemorate Him duly, was impossible to one who still retained his connections with the worldly life; to accept Him, in this sacred act, was equivalent to a solemn purpose to renounce all else for Him.

It is also obvious, thirdly, that this sacrament was designed to bring together in closer, warmer fellowship all who shared in it:—not merely binding them into unity by the consciousness of common convictions and purposes, but also setting before them all the vision of a common home and family of grace. Its form as a feast was itself suggestive of this associating and uniting function; and its place within the Church clearly indicated its design, as a bond of union in the household of faith. As all partake of the bread together, each professes his faith anew to all the rest; and as they drink together the wine, each assures the rest of fraternal affection, and all agree in exalting together that law of love which is the cardinal principle within the Church. And while the communion thus becomes to the individual Christian a holy compact and pledge to be loyal to Him whose dying it so tenderly represents, it also is in these ways a powerful stimulant to Christian union: it binds believer to believer and church to church: it draws into blessed fellowship at the point most vital, all throughout the world who hold to Christ as their Divine Head.—The fourth function of the sacrament lies in what may be termed its anticipatory or prophetic quality. While it points backward to the past, it points forward steadily to a heavenly future: while it brings to view historically the old Jerusalem, it also brings into view the new and free Jerusalem which is above, the Mother of us all. Calvary is its point of departure: Mount Zion is its point of culminating splendor. As a feast, it is typical of the perpetual feast of the redeemed in glory: its bread and wine are emblems of the bread of heaven, and of that new wine which Our Lord pledges himself to drink with His chosen in the kingdom of His Father. Like so many other elements in our holy faith, it has but partial realization here, and is brightly prophetic of much higher festivity, of much nobler fellowship, in that future toward which the Church on earth is ever hastening.

The law of participation in the Supper is sufficiently indicated by these glimpses of its general nature, and of the specific objects sought in its institution. Like Baptism, it belongs as an institution to the Church, and participation in it is a voluntary declaration, not merely of union with Christ, but also of connection with His visible people. And as Baptism presupposes personal faith, at least in the adult recipient, so is the presence of faith the only proper requisite and qualification here. To baptize without regard to character all who are willing to receive such chrism, and then to admit such persons, though unsanctified, to the table of the Lord in the hope that they may somehow receive a mystical grace through a merely formal observance, is a fearful mistake. All the qualifications which are requisite to full membership in any visible Church, are indispensable to this act of commemoration. A gracious state secured beforehand is the invariable condition, 1 Cor. 11: 27–30: all other participants can only eat and drink to themselves damnation. On the other hand, all who consciously belong to Christ, and are by profession within His visible Church, and upon whom no ecclesiastical censures rest, may receive this sacrament worthily. Instances may indeed arise in which the privilege may be granted to persons connected with no organized Church, but in whom the grace of the Gospel obviously appears. But the observance, like Baptism, is churchly in its nature: and it may be presumed that those who openly reject the fellowship of the Church in other respects, are hardly prepared spiritually for this signal act of communion with the people of God. It is to open believers, and to all open believers, that such privilege is to be granted: this is the comprehensive law. It must therefore be regarded as a clear violation of the spirit of the ordinance to shut out from it any true disciple, on account of differences respecting the three orders in the ministry, or the mode of baptism, or the use of other than inspired psalmody in worship, or any like peculiarity not essential to salvation. That communion of saints, which is declared to be cardinal in the first Christian creed,—a phrase which, as Calvin says, excellently expresses the true character of the Church, is at once the legitimate and the only legitimate basis for fellowship at the table of the Lord.[1]

XII. THE LORD'S SUPPER: ITS INFLUENCE AND WORTH: OTHER KINDRED OBSERVANCES.—What has been said respecting the beneficent influence of Baptism as the introductory sacrament, applies with even larger force to the Eucharist. The fact that, while Baptism is to be applied but once, at the outset, this is to be repeated at intervals

---

[1] ROBERT HALL, *Terms of Communion.* *West. Directory,* VIII: iv.

throughout the earthly life of the believer, and may be administered even to the dying saint, shows how great value is placed upon it by the Head of the Church. As a unique and impressive mode of setting forth the cardinal truths of grace, from the rise and fall of man onward to his completed restoration in glory, it is full of precious significance. Hardly any essential doctrine fails to be symbolized in it; it is a picturesque sermon, in which the whole Gospel is incorporated. Those who share in it intelligently, in effect recite again the old Christian creeds, and make again their profession of belief in all the substantial elements of the system of grace. It is also a silent and most effectual monitor as to personal duty; it summons the recipient to careful and honest examination of himself, not merely as to belief, but equally as to his loyalty, his zeal, his devotion. That great law of self-examination which is in so many forms laid upon every disciple, comes to its culmination here; Let a man examine himself, is the divine command, and so let him eat of that bread and drink of that cup; 1 Cor. 11: 27–30, 1 Cor. 5: 7–8, 2 Cor. 13: 5, Gal. 6: 3–4. He who comes to this consecrated table, and goes away from it, without deepened conceptions of himself as a sinner, and of himself as a disciple also, has failed to derive from it some of the most precious benefits it was divinely intended to impart.

Viewed in its relations to the Church, this sacrament possesses values equally great. As a feast, it becomes the basis of a holy and happy fellowship, such as the company of the faithful could in no other form secure. It is the great Christian festival which supersedes the Passover, and all other Hebraic feasts, because it embodies higher truths, and symbolizes a more glorious union. It tends to break down all lines of separation, to silence discords and heal divisions, to develop the sense of mutual dependence and mutual benefit, to harmonize purpose and combine in effort and sacrifice. It thus makes each Church in a more vital sense a holy brotherhood, in virtue of the communion of the membership, each and all, with the one divine and gracious Lord.—In like manner this sacrament becomes a most effective testimony, on the part of the Church, before the world. It certifies in a graphic way to what the Church believes, and is a tender and telling invitation to all who witness it, to accept the dying Savior whose love it commemorates. It presents religion itself, not in a forbidding, but in a winning aspect; the yoke of discipleship which it holds up to view, is an easy yoke; the Gospel which it preaches, sanctified by such divine sorrow, and brought home to the soul by a process deeper than any formal demonstration, has peculiar power. At no hour in its history is the Church more truly or more effectively proclaiming Christ to a sinful world, than when in the true spirit of the Gospel, it gathers thus around the eucharistic table.—Contemplated finally as an expression by the Church of its love and gratitude and loyalty toward Christ Himself, this festival reveals its supreme value. It is indeed an Eucharist—a hymn of gratitude to Him who instituted it, and whom it continually magnifies in His redemptive work. It is also a sacred covenant, forever binding the Church afresh in the bonds of loyalty, and becoming forever a fresh stimulus to duty and sacrifice in His cause. How much the Church owes to these holy stimulations, and how much the kingdom of God among men is dependent for its advances upon the often recurring impulse to activity which this sacrament brings, the experience of the Church in all ages bears ample witness.[1]

With such a holy festival as this, standing in the center, and supplying to it such various benefits, the Church needs no other associated ordinances. The minor sacraments of Rome, however desirable in certain relations, become insignificant in the contrast. This is true also of the washing of feet (John 13: 1-15), of the kiss of charity, or the holy kiss (Rom. 16: 16, 1 Pet. 5: 14), and of the Agape, or feast of brotherly love, which made its appearance in conjunction with the Supper at an early date in the history of the Apostolic Church, (Acts 2: 46) and which seemed at one period likely even to rival the Supper in its place in Christian esteem. Chrysostom describes the Agape in glowing terms as a custom most beautiful and most beneficial, for it was a supporter of law, a solace of poverty, a moderator of wealth, and a discipline of humility. Other Fathers speak of the Agape in similar strains. But we have distinct evidence that even in the days of Paul, this usage was becoming a source of spiritual mischiefs within the Church: 1 Cor. 11: 20-22. Jude also calls attention to those who were foul spots in these feasts of charity, feasting themselves without fear, while wholly opposed at heart to the spirit and aim of the true faith. Peter also, according to some authorities, makes a like criticism: 2 Pet. 2: 13. While the sacred Supper was by degrees perverted in the following centuries into a gorgeous ceremonial, void of quickening power, this revealed rapidly a tendency to degenerate into a worldly feast, quite at variance with the fraternal oneness that expressed itself so strikingly through the community of goods and in breaking of bread from house to house, just after the Pentecost. Designed at first to show forth the equality of believers, and the unity of the Christian household, it became by degrees a luxurious entertainment for the rich in some cases, and in others a species of charity to the poor. Losing its original quality, it came to be in several ways

---

[1] CALVIN, *Inst.*, Book IV: Ch. 17, on the Lord's Supper, and its Advantages; DWIGHT, *Sermon* 160; HODGE, *Syst. Theol.* III: 647-650. Also, VAN OOSTERZEE, DORNER, *in loc;* NEVIN, *Mystical Presence;* STANLEY, *Christian Institutions.*

a source of diversity and disorder within the Church, and at length fell deservedly into disuse, as an institution unwarranted by the Scriptures, and unfriendly to religion.[1]

XIII. ORDINANCES DEFINED: POSITIVE INSTITUTIONS.—The third impersonal constituent of the Church, closely associated with the Sacraments, yet in several particulars distinguishable from them, may be seen in the Christian Ordinances. These may be defined as religious institutions or appointments, imposed by divine authority, and designed to aid both the believer and the Church in the cultivation of piety, and in the discharge of various Christian duties. The cognate phrase, means of grace, is sometimes employed so broadly as to include the sacraments, or the Scriptures, or prayer, as well as these subordinate institutes of the Gospel :—it is sometimes used to describe merely such of these institutes as are combined together in social worship, as preaching, or the singing of hymns. The word, ordinance, is also occasionally used as the equivalent of sacrament. But what is intended here by the term is that series of positive appointments prescribed in the Scriptures, which are associated with the sacraments as elements in Christian culture and service, such as the Sabbath or the Sanctuary. These tributary institutions are not so directly enforced as are the sacraments, by the formal command of Christ himself: neither are they so vitally related to religious experience, or so clearly indicative of the relation of believers to the Church. Yet these statutory regulations are important in many ways as adjuncts to the maintenance of Christianity in the world. They supply an invaluable array of conditions and helps in Christian living: they furnish time, and place, and form for religion: they give meaning and volume to personal and social devotion. Though they are not so immediately associated with the Church, they are still of inestimable value to it: without their aid, the Church could not adequately sustain its interior life, or fulfill its peculiar mission in the economy of redemption. Even in the Hebraic dispensation, we see such tributary institutes standing on every side as aids in religious culture: the altar, the tabernacle, the holy times, the modes of worship, the prescribed ritual, each and all positively enjoined, in order that through them the devout Hebrew might be brought into a deeper, richer experience. Under the Gospel, while what was merely typical is laid aside, and while the formal elements were reduced in numbers and prominence, yet the most essential among these institutes were carefully preserved for the benefit of the

---

[1] "The growth of the churches, and the rise of manifold abuses led to the gradual disuse, and in the fourth century even to the formal prohibition, of the Agape, which belonged in fact only to the childhood and first love of the Church." SCHAFF. *Hist. Christ. Church*, I: 395.

Church and of the believer. It is a serious error to suppose that such positive ordinances are wholly set aside in this later dispensation. Christianity like Hebraism both possesses and cherishes them as being, if not essential to salvation, still indispensable to the healthiest growth, the finest culture and development of the people of God. These positive institutions are four in number: The Sabbath, a sacred time: the Sanctuary, a sacred place: the Means of Grace, a sacred cultus: the Ministry, a sacred form of service. A brief glance at each of these must suffice:

XIV. THE SABBATH—A SACRED TIME, divinely appointed, is seen at once to sustain most vital relations to the life and growth of the Church. The following particulars concerning it may be briefly noted:

1. It was instituted primarily at the Creation, when God at the close of the sixth day, or the sixth geologic period, rested or ceased from His creative labor; Gen. 2: 2–3. This passage can not be regarded as anticipatory merely, by those who accept the general record as in any true sense historic. Traces of the Sabbath as a sacred institute, probably in conjunction with the primal institution of sacrifice, appear during the antediluvian era; Gen. 4: 3, in the end of the days. References to periods of seven days occur repeatedly, as in Gen. 7: 10, 8: 10, 29: 27–28. The Week, finding its origin and model in the example of God, was even at that period a recognized unit in time, sustained by universal consent, on the basis of such divine warrant.[1] It is hardly possible to account for the observance of this period among ancient nations, as originating wholly in natural causes, such as the lunar changes. It is obvious, especially, that the Israelites regarded the seventh day as sacred, before its formal appointment a second time at Sinai; Ex. 16: 22–26. The fact of such antecedent observance both explains the form of the Sinaitic command, Remember, and sheds light on the specific methods in which such remembrance was to be shown. At Sinai the law of the Sabbath became obligatory in a special sense (Ex. 20: 8–11, 31: 13–17), as commemorating also the specific deliverance of the chosen people. They were never to forget the natal day in their national existence, but were to regard it as the fundamental institution on which their civil organization, and also their entire sacrificial system rested; Deut. 5: 12–15, Neh. 9: 14, Ezek. 20: 10–12. The second enactment, specific and national in form, by no means disproves or supplants the original appointment in Paradise. It is a frequent process in the scheme of grace to select existing things, such as the rainbow, and to set them apart for sacred uses; and also to utilize for a further and more specific purpose, what at first existed in a general and anticipatory form. To the devout Hebrew the Sab-

---

[1] *Eight Studies on the Lord's Day:* Study III: *The Week.*

bath was none the less commemorative of the stupendous work of creation, because it was the day on which he was also solemnly and gratefully to call to mind his marvelous deliverance from the Egyptian bondage. We see the same process illustrated in the third enactment of the Sabbath under the Gospel, to commemorate the completion of the redemptive work of Christ, and the still more wonderful deliverance of the soul from guilt and sin through His grace. As creation suggested and involved redemption, so the rescue of the Israelites was designed to stand as a grand historic type of the salvation which our Lord lived and died and rose again to introduce. In its commemorative relations to that salvation, the day receives its final endorsement and coronation.

2. This threefold instituting of the Sabbath, occurring historically at such signal epochs, sufficiently indicates the divine design in its appointment. It was the day, first of all, in which man should call to mind the Creator, the Preserver, the Father and Sovereign, from whom his being and his blessings flowed, and to whom his service and homage were ever to be rendered. It was therefore to be, in a holy sense, the day of rest from earthly avocations and engrossments,—a day in which even the physical man might gain needful repose, and in which his social and moral nature might attain appropriate development. To the Israelite, it was also to be a day fraught with grateful memories of the Providence that had so favored the Jewish people, and of that entire series of divine revelations which had in such signal manner attended the nation, through its supernatural history. It was to the Hebrews a perpetual sermon, full of doctrine and no less full of religious training and stimulation. To the Christian, while it carried along with it most of its preceding significance, it became still more instructive and stimulating, as the day when the Messiah rose from the grave in confirmation of the Gospel He had introduced among men,—when salvation through atoning grace was fully introduced, and the way of life was published to the world. The centuries that have passed since the morning of the resurrection, have only widened the purpose and enlarged the benefits of this holy time. Especially, in the more complex life and movement of the period since the Reformation, the necessity for such a positive provision as this, and the values flowing from it, have become more and more apparent. The design of the Sabbath has broadened steadily, as the ability to use it rightly has increased. To the Church of this age it is seen to be indispensable in a degree never before so distinctly realized. The worship, the work, the religious growth and spiritual influence of the Church, are turning more and more upon the Sabbath; and we may anticipate, that as the Church grows more and more into its true place in the Christian sys-

tem, the Sabbath will become more and more precious in its uses and in its blessings, even until the end of time.

3. That the Sabbath is to be an enduring institution under the Gospel, is apparent not only from these glimpses of its value, but from what we may learn respecting the divine institution in its appointment. Those who hold that as a direct injunction or law, the Sabbath was Jewish only, and that in this aspect it passed away with the other ceremonial functions of that dispensation, lose sight both of its original enactment at the creation, and also of the permanent values it possesses as a time for reverential commemoration of the Creator, who is also the providential Preserver and Ruler of all men. They also lose sight of the solemn significance of the Sabbath as the day that celebrates that redemptive work which, as a revelation of Deity, far transcends creation itself. It is certainly erroneous to regard the day as obligatory with reference only to the minor, intermediate event celebrated at Sinai, while these two far greater events are sustained in remembrance by no statutory provision. The sparse passages sometimes quoted by the earliest Reformers, and also by later advocates of this lower view (Coll. 2: 16, Rom. 14: 5-6, Gal. 4: 10: and others), fall very far short of sustaining their opinion.[1] They are abundantly offset by many passages showing clearly that the obligation to observe the day was intended to be, and is in fact, perpetual : Isa. 56: 6-8, 66: 23: in conjunction with Mark 2: 27, John 5: 16-17, and others. The place of the fourth commandment in the Decalogue is well-nigh conclusive here. That the Decalogue in general was designed to be a moral code for humanity—a species of divine basis for all right and just legislation, the world over, through all time, is clear from the nature of the specific precepts announced, from the manner and form in which they were given, from the teaching of our Lord and the Apostles respecting them, and from their vital relations to the Gospel as a scheme of grace for those who had violated them. No just exception can be made as to the Sabbath : like the prohibition of idolatry, or the law against theft, it was intended to be a law for humanity. It is true that the manner of observing the day has changed; and our Lord himself regards such change as admissible, on the broad principle that the day was made for man: Matt. 12: 1-13. This passage confirms rather than controverts the general view here given. Our Lord himself observed the Sabbath, and sanctified it by such observance: when He allowed works of mercy to be wrought, He by implication forbade all other labor. To interpret His teaching or that of Paul (Col. 2: 16, 22) as involving an abrogation of the fourth com-

---

[1] For a full presentation of this view, see HESSEY, *Bampton Lectures*, 1860.

mandment, is a serious departure from his own declaration that He came not to destroy, but to fulfill.

4. The change of the Sabbath from the seventh to the first day of the week, though resting on no explicit command, is justified by the grand, consummating event of the resurrection of our Lord, which it thus commemorates. As the institution pointed primarily to the divine act of creation, and secondarily to that divine act of preservation which stands out so signally in history as a type of providence overruling all created things in the interest of grace, so it now points to that divine act of salvation, of which the dying and the rising again of Jesus Christ were the most signal incidents. It is significant that our Lord himself introduces the change by His repeated manifestations of Himself on the first day of the week, during the forty days prior to His ascension. The Mosaic Sabbath, as has been said, was not extensible: it could not well be carried beyond the Jewish boundaries, neither could it well express the universal scope, the world-wide relations, of the Gospel economy. The great fact of a new kingdom of grace, comprehending believers in all lands and ages, and made forever glorious by the perpetual presence of a divine King, could not be adequately set forth through it. It pointed too much to the past, and to a past which the Hebrew alone could appreciate, while the day of the resurrection pointed forward to a millennial future in which humanity might share together. Hence our Lord himself, by his gracious appearings again and again on the first rather than the seventh day, not only suggested the observance of the new, but authorized the quiet supplanting and withdrawal of the old,—following here precisely the same method as in the introduction of the Christian, as a substitute for the Hebraic Church. In harmony with this divine purpose, we find the disciples, even before the ascension (John 20: 19, 26) and regularly afterward (Acts 2: 1, 20: 7, 1 Cor. 16: 2, Rev. 1: 10), assembled together as by a divine warrant, to celebrate the day on which the Savior arose. The peculiar title applied to it, the Lord's Day, is indicative of their estimate, and of the justifying ground on which they made the change. On this general warrant, which the Church in all subsequent ages has pronounced sufficient, the Christian Sabbath now stands,—justified by considerations hardly less clear or strong than those on which the Church itself is established as a permanent institution in the Gospel scheme.

5. Respecting the manner of observance, common usage is adequate to determine the external question whether that observance shall begin with the evening of the seventh, or the morning of the first day. Other external questions, such as the proportion of worship, public or private, the administration of the family life, the measure of social

fellowship, the amount of personal enjoyment or of travel admissible, are also to be determined by the individual conscience, or by the judgment of the household of faith at any given time. Works of necessity, and works of mercy also, are warranted by the example of Christ himself; Luke 13: 14–16, Luke 6: 7–9. But all labor for purposes of gain, and all employment inconsistent with the supreme design of the day, as well as all forms of personal or social pleasure which tend to prevent the soul from gaining the spiritual benefits which the day was designed to secure, are by clear implication forbidden. The question respecting the validity or the extent of legislation, whether by the church or by the state, in support of the Sabbath—whether by specifying acts forbidden, or by enjoining special duties, is one in which only a general warrant of Scripture can be invoked. The main rule here is, that this holy time is not to be observed in a ritualistic or pharisaic spirit, in a rigid or technical temper, but in a mood entirely in harmony with the great facts of grace, to whose reality it so beautifully certifies. If the Sabbath is for man, the Sabbath is still more obviously for the Christian and the Church, and its observance is but one aspect or condition of that holy devotion, that joyous and unwearied service, which the Church is ever offering to her ascended Lord.[1] It may be added here, that the Sabbath is the only sacred time directly warranted by Scripture. The various feasts and fasts of Romanism, and the kindred observances instituted by some sections of Protestantism, may have sprung from a right desire to increase the religious, in contrast with the secular elements in human life. But their tendency, like that of the Agape, has been downward habitually, and what at first was holy time, has too often become at last a holiday. Christmas itself, with its holy associations, has come to be, even in Protestant circles, more a gay carnival than a holy feast.

XV. THREE ASSOCIATED ORDINANCES DESCRIBED.—The other divine institutions which stand in a relation to the Church not unlike that of the Sabbath, are the Sanctuary as a sacred place, the Means of Grace as a sacred cultus, and the Ministry as a sacred form of service. These may be considered still more briefly:

1. THE SANCTUARY, as a place sacred to the worship of God, existed in some form from the earliest ages. We indeed see religion first revealed in the individual life; the closet, or its equivalent, was the first temple. Enoch walking with God, Abraham alone in his tent, Isaac meditating at eventide, Jacob at Bethel, are historic illustrations of this primary fact. Yet community in faith led early to community in worship; and around the rude altars which were the first places of holy convocation, the pious met and shared in the appointed forms of de-

---

[1] GILFILLAN, J., *The Sabbath;* a good practical treatise.

votion; Gen. 8: 20, Noah; Gen. 12: 8, Abraham. Suggestions of such social worship in places provided for the purpose are found in the history of the Israelites prior to the Exodus. In conjunction with that event, God made direct provision for the Tabernacle, as such a place for religious assembling; Ex. 25: 8–9: and the elaborateness of this provision shows His estimate of the importance of such a tributary institution. The history of this Tabernacle, during the Sinaitic wanderings, and afterward at Gilgal and Shiloh and Gibeah, until its final transfer by David to Mount Zion (2 Sam. 6), constitutes a most interesting chapter in the history of the Hebraic Church. During this long period, the conception of such a place in which God should especially dwell and be adored, was wrought permanently into the Jewish mind; the tabernacle became an indispensable accessory to the Jewish worship. In process of time this conception was further realized in the Temple, which took the place of the Tabernacle as the recognized center of the national devotions—the material embodiment, in its amazing splendor and beauty, of the religious life of the people; 1 Kings, 6 and 8. The second temple erected in the days of Ezra, though less magnificent, sustained the same relations. So also, even from the age of Samuel, synagogues arose in Hebrew cities and villages, as accessories on a smaller scale, subservient to the same spiritual end. In the time of Christ, we find the national faith, though corrupted and formalized, still erecting appropriate sanctuaries in which it might abide as in a home, and where the ancient worship it still loved might receive appropriate expression; Luke 7: 5.

Under the Gospel, the sanctuary sustains a still more intimate relation to the social life and activity of the Church. That deep religious instinct which we thus trace in the history of the people of Israel, and which in its cruder forms leads men even under the impulses of natural religion to erect altars, to consecrate groves, to rear splendid temples, in honor of the deities they worship, rises to its culmination in Christianity. The disciples indeed worshiped privately at first, and afterward for a time in whatever suitable places might be procured; but at length the sanctuary begun to be reared everywhere as an enduring representative, from Jerusalem and Antioch to Corinth and Rome, of the faith whose adherents it sheltered. Such places are as essential adjuncts to church life as is the Sabbath. They bring believers together as in a common home: they stand forth in society as a perpetual invitation to the unbelieving world to come in and hear the truth; they constitute a silent, but most effectual witness to the reality of the religion which they represent. And the obligation of each Church of Christ to provide itself with such a habitation—one which in its structure shall be conformed to the spirit of Christianity, and which shall worthily commend the Gospel to the interest of all who observe it—is one of the most urgent among the duties which any such organization owes to itself, or to the holy cause it maintains.

2. THE MEANS OF GRACE, as the phrase is frequently employed, are certain forms or methods of worship, imposed by divine authority, and together constituting a species of sacred cultus in devotion. These are sometimes called distinctively The Ordinances; Presb. Form of Gov.: Chap. VII. At the first they consisted simply of sacrifice and prayer; after the Exodus, the offering of praise and the reading of the law were added; at a later date the exposition of the law was introduced; and as the Sacred Books increased in number, history and prophecy were also read and expounded in connection with the law. Vocal praise especially grew into prominence in the age of David, in conjunction with the costlier and more elaborate sacrifices then offered. The simple ritual of the tabernacle was, by successive modifications, transmuted into the gorgeous ceremonial of the temple; and this ceremonial was observed, so far as practicable, through the succeeding centuries down to the era of our Lord. Not merely on special occasions, but in the ordinary Sabbath worship, whether in the temple or in the humble synagogue, these elements of devotion were essentially the same. Numerous illustrations of these statements may be gathered from the historical portions of the Old Testament.

While the early Christians ceased from sacrifices, the one great Sacrifice having been offered, they retained substantially the other elements in the Hebraic religious cultus, suffusing them throughout with the nobler truth and the higher temper of the Gospel. To the reading of the law and the prophets, they added the testimony concerning Christ, and concerning salvation through Him. As the evangelical narratives and the apostolical letters were prepared, the reading and exposition of these became an important feature in their social devotions. While prayer and praise were retained in accordance with Jewish usage, the basis and scope of prayer, the substance and the tone of praise, were vastly enhanced. The functions of the priest and the scribe gave way by degrees to those of the Christian preacher. So throughout, while the worship of the Church sprang as the Church itself had done from Hebraism, yet like the Church it assumed from the first a broadened form, a higher quality, in harmony with the larger faith to which it was subservient.[1] In the Papal communion we see these sacred institutes of devotion, like the sacraments, overlaid with showy formalisms wholly at variance with the New Test. conception of worship. We find a vast, pompous, splendid but unscriptural liturgy coming into existence, incorporating indeed these simpler ele-

---
[1] SCHAFF: *Ancient Christianity*, I; 118. MOSHEIM: *First Three Centuries*, I; 185.

ments, but destroying in large degree their spiritual meaning and effect,—a liturgy in great measure Judaistic in form, and capable as a spectacular observance of making deep impressions on the beholder, but with relatively small power to spiritualize or to edify. Protestantism agrees rather in regarding worship as consisting of prayer, praise, and the reading and exposition of the Word, in addition to the sacraments. The offering of gifts for church uses or for charity, and occasional fasting or thanksgiving, and the administration of discipline, are sometimes added to the list, as secondary forms of devotion. The proportion of these elements varies in different communions, and at different periods; and the matter of proportion, like the matter of written or unwritten forms, is to be determined in each instance by the judgment of the particular body. Such matters as standing or kneeling or bowing in prayer, the use of Christian hymns, or of versions of the Psalms only, and the like, may safely be referred to the same court for decision. What is vital, as Protestants affirm, is to maintain the right of each and all of these elements as authorized and obligatory forms in worship, and to set them all in their proper adjunctive relation to the spiritual culture of the Household of Faith.

3. THE MINISTRY, regarded simply as a sacred form of service, may be classed among these impersonal constituents of the Church. The conception of a series of divinely appointed modes of offering to God social worship, carries with it the conception of an ordained leadership, through which the Church may be aided in such joint devotions. The historic foundations for such ministerial service are laid—if we go back no further—in the appointment of Aaron and his sons, and also of the Levitical order, as helps to the Hebrew Church in this holy task of worship. The priestly office especially was an indispensable assistant in such a cultus as that provided in the Mosaic economy. During the theocratic and particularly the royal era, we see this ministerial adjunct growing into greater prominence, and being more and more widely utilized. The subsequent rise of the prophetic body, as accessory in the task of educating, training, rearing the Church, is another fact of the same class. Without such a ministry as this, viewed simply as a divine ordinance, not only would the Hebrew worship have fallen to the ground; the Sanctuary and the Sabbath would have lost their practical value; the national faith itself would have ceased to be the controlling power we find it to have been throughout the national history.

Without anticipating the consideration of the minister of Christ in his personal qualities and relations to the Church, we may here observe that the Christian ministry, as a service, stands properly among those ordinances which in the divine economy are made tributary to the proper organization, and even the healthful existence of the household of faith. This ministry is in the new dispensation all that the priesthood was in the old. The mode of election to it varies;—the service is no longer hereditary. The call to that service is more distinctly spiritual; it involves a deeper experience of religion, higher natural endowments, clearer providential indications, and profounder spiritual movings toward the service. No anointing with oil by the hand of some antecedent priest is essential; it is the Church itself which bestows the requisite endorsement. So the functions united together in this concrete ministry are higher. None but spiritual sacrifices are now to be offered; prayer and praise are to be presented, not for the people, but with the people; the law is to be enforced from a different plane of authority, and the Gospel is a message to be announced in a spirit and method in harmony with its own nature. But such a ministry is no less essential to the Christian than the priesthood was to the Hebraic Church, but rather infinitely more. The sanctuary is of less moment; the Sabbath is hardly more vital. Even the sacraments, contemplated in their peculiarly close relations to the church life, are dependent on the existing of such an office as this. A church without such a form of service within it, can be in only a very inadequate sense a Church of Christ.

With these glimpses of the Ministry and the Means of Grace, of the Sanctuary and the Sabbath, viewed as so many adjunctive institutes or ordinances, our review of the impersonal constituents of the Church may be terminated. No other kindred ordinances or institutions can be added to the list. The tendency to question the authoritativeness or sacredness of these, and the disposition to add to their number any human contrivances in the interest of religion, are alike to be condemned. The Church needs no other sacred time or place—no other sacred worship or service. Equipped with such tributary institutes, and blessed as we have seen with its two great sacraments, and with a compact and adequate array of inspired doctrines, the Church is beyond doubt abundantly qualified of God for that sacred mission to which it is appointed—a mission of grace, wide as the world in scope, and extending in time down to the millennial age.

CHAPTER III.

THE PERSONAL CONSTITUENTS OF THE CHURCH:

ITS MEMBERS, ITS OFFICERS.

The impersonal constituents of the Church, considered in the previous chapter, exist only for the sake of, and in tributary connection with, its personal constituents. Doctrines, Sacraments, Ordinances, find their value solely in the relations they sustain to the persons who compose the Church. Whatever in that divine organization is external and formal, must be viewed always as accessory merely to what is interior and vital. The Personal Element is of necessity supreme and controlling. This element may properly be divided into the two classes, the Members and the Officers, associated together in the Church.

I. THE PERSONAL ELEMENT SUPREME.—The natural tendency to exalt the Church as a great external organism, at the expense of the persons associated in it—to set the institution above the individual, and to subordinate his convictions, his interests, and even his rights to its domination, is one frequently appearing in ecclesiastical history. Church doctrines, for illustration, especially when moulded into confessional form, are often imposed upon believers to an extent for which there is no warrant whatever, either in the Scriptures, or in the nature of the organization that imposes them. Church sacraments and ordinances have in like manner been often robed with assumed authoritativeness, and pressed as obligatory, in ways equally unwarranted, and equally hurtful to the souls of men. The Church is regarded by virtue of a certain divine right as prescribing faith, ceremony, service; and obedience and submission, constant and absolute, are declared to be the supreme duty of all who dwell within its communion. In the Church of Rome we find this tendency embodying itself in a dominating priesthood, to whose rule all private members are supposed to be made subject by divine arrangement, and whose great function it is supposed to be to enforce the prerogatives and prescripts of the Church as absolute, on every one who owns allegiance to it. In some branches of Protestantism we see this tendency manifesting itself in milder, but equally unwarranted forms: we see the organization exalted into an undue place in the Christian scheme, invested with an undue measure of authoritativeness, and thus transformed sometimes into an instrument of tyrannical usurpation. The institution is set far above the person, and even above the whole body of persons who are united in it; the organism is made superior to the life that vitalizes it; and the result is too often a species of Vaticanism hardly less unworthy than that of Rome itself.

A slight consideration of the question will be sufficient to make clear the dangerous errors underlying all such ecclesiasticism, whether Roman or Protestant. The relative estimate which our Lord himself placed upon what is impersonal and what is personal in Christianity, is an adequate guide at this point. His declarations concerning the value of the soul, His sedulous ministries to the souls of men, His plan of salvation for souls through personal union with Himself, all conspire to show that in His view the exterior elements of the Gospel derived whatever worth they possessed from their perceived relations to this, the supreme aim and end of His redemptive scheme. The Soul was always held by Him far above the Church, viewed as an institution merely. And as the Sabbath was made for man, so in His estimate all other ordinances, each of the sacraments, and every doctrine He proclaimed, were made for man, and found their supreme use in the influence they exerted upon his spiritual life. There can be little question that the Apostles held the same view, and acted on the same high principle, in their organizing of the Church, and in their enforcement of the several institutes and observances incorporated with it. While they taught on the one hand a due subordination of the individual believer to his brethren in the Lord, and while they maintained absolutely the right of the Church to administer the Christian sacraments, and to enforce obedience to right law, even to the exclusion of the unworthy, they never exalted the Church unduly: they never enforced its claims or prerogatives in a dominating spirit. In their view, the disciple was higher than the institution,—the personal element rose above, and properly subordinated to itself, all that was impersonal merely. And in the teaching and course of Christ, and of those who, under His guidance, gave shape to the primitive Church, we may easily learn the universal and the perpetual law. That Church is not a mechanism or a crystallization, but rather a vital organism instinct with personal life. Within its sacred enclosure, and under its gracious influence, the human soul is to hear and accept divine truth, to be anointed and sealed through the sacraments, to be cultured and stimulated through the means of grace into vigorous spiritual life. In a word, it is the Personal Element which renders all impersonal elements worthy, and which above all else should make the Church itself glorious in our eyes.

II. Church Membership: Preliminary View.—What has been said already respecting the true conception of the Church, will serve to show that membership in it must be obtained by methods in harmony with the nature of the organization. Individuals are not to be born into it precisely as they are born into the family, or made members in it precisely as they come into connection with the state within whose territory they have their birth. The connection in this instance is not natural but spiritual,—piety is its essential basis and justification. And as faith is an active principle in the soul, the connection which faith establishes, must be voluntary,—the outgrowth, not of nature, but of gracious choice. The Church is built essentially on this foundation. The chosen generation, the royal priesthood, the holy nation, the peculiar people, to whom Peter refers in such glowing terms, are persons who have been called out of the darkness of nature into the marvelous light of grace—called out also from the darkness of their natural relations into the light and glory of the household of faith, in order that they might through such attained piety show forth the praises of Him who has granted them this spiritual calling. The same conclusion is reached, if we contemplate the end or design of the Church, whether toward God as in worship, or toward man as in testimony. These imply a voluntary and active connection, based on moral predispositions, as their proper condition. True worship is indeed spontaneous, but not in the sense in which the singing of birds is: it is rather the spontaneous outflow of a will thoroughly absorbed in God, and inwardly devoted to His glory. And the only testimony to which the world listens receptively, is the testimony which breaks forth from hearts that are freely surrendered to Christ, and that find supreme delight in witnessing to Him.

Hence all notions of church membership which ignore the active, voluntary, holy personality that must pervade it—which find analogies rather in those merely natural relations into which without choice or purpose of our own we are born, must be set aside as inadequate. It is impossible that the administration of baptism, whether to an infant or to an adult, or the mere manducation of the sacred emblems in the Eucharist, can entitle the recipient to a place in this divine household. Nor can any enactment of the state, or any payment of tithes imposed by law, or any ecclesiastical declarations, however comprehensive, institute such a connection. Even in the Hebraic dispensation, the distinction between membership in the nation and membership in the church inevitably worked itself into prominence, and in the latter portion of the period became still more prominent. Under the Gospel, the maintenance of such a distinction, is vital to the entire conception of the Church; to deny it would be to Judaize our Christianity. In holding this view, it is not needful to ignore the peculiar place which the pious household sustains in the plan of grace, or to refuse to the children of believers any manner of connection with the Church. But the general law of membership remains undisturbed; the bond of union must ever be spiritual. What disastrous consequences follow every deviation from this principle, on whatever side, will be apparent from a brief survey of the theories of membership which have been held within the various sections of Christendom.

III. MEMBERSHIP IN THE PRIMITIVE CHURCH.—Reverting first to the Church Apostolic, we see at once that, just as the disciples found the proper norm or form of the new organization in the Jewish synagogue, so they found the spiritual basis of that organization in the piety, or the faith, which had been the recognized foundation of both the Patriarchal and the Hebrew Church. They knew already that all were not the true Israel who were of Israel externally, but only those who by the possession of a kindred experience had become in heart the children of faithful Abraham. The transient organization which John the Baptist had set up on the basis of sincere repentance, and of obedience to righteous law, had doubtless emphasized the lesson which both the teaching of the prophets, and the course of the national history, had enforced. What our Lord had taught them respecting religion as a matter of heart and spirit primarily, respecting the true nature of repentance and conversion, respecting the quickening influence of faith, and its power to transform the whole man into likeness to Himself, had rendered it impossible that they should contemplate church membership as having any other than a spiritual foundation. And when they came to contemplate the great truth, that the Church they were organizing was to include Gentile as well as Hebrew,—all men of all nations who would heartily receive and follow the Messiah—this impossibility became a thousand fold more distinct and more decisive. In such an organism, none other than the religious qualifications of which the faith of Abraham was both forerunner and symbol, could have been introduced.

Hence we find the recognized basis of membership in the Apostolic Church, to be simply an avowed and authenticated belief in, and acceptance of Jesus Christ as the Redeemer of men. The record furnished in the earlier chapters of the Book of Acts is decisive on this point. The message of Peter at the Pentecost was the message of the whole body of disciples: Repent, believe, be baptized for the remission of sins, receive the Holy Ghost, and enter heartily on the new life He imparts. Those who received his word, and they only, were baptized; those who were baptized, continued in the doctrine and fellowship of the new organization; and the Lord added to it day by day those that were being saved. From the rule thus established at the outset, the apostles never swerved. Whatever disposition naturally remained to cling to the old national test, and to give the Hebrew, if not an exclusive right, still a special eminence within the household of faith, seems to have disappeared almost wholly after the experience of Peter at Samaria, and the introduction of the Gentile into full membership. That parties should have arisen, either from the natural assumption of supremacy by the Jewish converts, or from the natural jealousy of converts from other nationalities, is certainly not surprising. But the obvious fact is, that no serious attempt was made in any quarter to reduce the standard and test of membership which the miraculous events of the Pentecost had set up, or to exclude any persons of any class in whom the evidence of true discipleship appeared. That unconverted persons sometimes became members, on their profession of faith and acceptance, is made clear by the instance of Ananias and Sapphira, and of Simon of Samaria; Acts 5: 1–10, 8: 13–24. But we have abundant proof in the letters of both Paul and John, and of Peter and James also, that such instances were viewed as wholly exceptional; and that the young Church was made by such terrible illustrations still more strenuous in insisting upon the spiritual standard already described. It is needless to refer to specific evidences of this fact. The frequent warnings against hypocrisy and delusion, the strong injunctions to the exercise of faith, and to the culture of a genuine Christian life, the assertion of the right of the Church to administer discipline, and the actual expulsion of persons found to fall short of the standard prescribed, show decisively the spiritual principle on which the apostolic churches were planted.

It is a familiar fact in ecclesiastical history, that this standard remained without challenge, until the persecutions of the second and third centuries on one side, and the rapid development of worldliness within the Church on the other, gave occasion for a more exact analysis and exposition of the primitive terms of membership. It was perhaps inevitable that, under these two adverse influences, the simple but searching test of the apostolic age should give way to more external or formal conceptions of church connection. As an offset to this downward tendency, Montanism appeared in the latter part of the second century, not merely insisting upon such thorough application of the biblical rule as would exclude any and all who might be unbelievers, but also setting up an extraordinary standard of holiness, to which but few among genuine disciples could attain. The two noted schisms of Felicissimus at Carthage, and of Novatian at Rome, in the third century, originating in the endeavor to exclude finally from the Church all who had lapsed under persecution, were also movements in the interest of stricter adherence to the apostolic standard. Donatism, rising into prominence in the fourth century as a further protest against the looseness and the imperialism current in the Church, in like manner took high ground not merely against those who had proven unworthy, but also in favor of the most rigid scrutiny of the spiritual state and the personal confession of all who sought church membership. Amid many extravagances, and even serious errors as to the real nature of the Christian life, these parties were striving to maintain, in the presence of prevailing downward tendencies, the doctrine and practice of the early disciples. But these tendencies were too strong to be resisted. Even Augustine took ground against Donatism as a fanatical and impracticable extreme: and became the representative advocate of the more formal, less searching view of discipleship. To him we probably owe the first special emphasizing of the distinction between the visible Church and the Church invisible, with its natural consequent in the more definite exaltation of the outward profession, as distinguished from the spiritual faith professed.[1] Under such advocacy, the Church came to be contemplated more and more as an external society, and connection with it involved little more than a declaration of belief in Christianity. In resisting the teaching of the stricter school, which indeed was often extreme and impractical, and sometimes wildly fanatical, the Church gradually lost its hold of the New Testament doctrine, and fell away into a grosser view—the precursor of that still more serious departure, whose historical outcome was the Church of Rome.

IV. GREEK AND PAPAL VIEW OF CHURCH MEMBERSHIP.—From the fifth to the sixteenth century, this superficial theory of membership, harmonizing so well with other formal tendencies in both the Eastern and the Western Churches, excluded almost entirely the primitive doctrine. As the Church came to be regarded more and more as a visible organism, with a fixed geographic center, whether at Constantinople or Rome, and with an authoritative head, whether patriarch or pope,—as the ministry came to be viewed as a priesthood through whose touch all grace must flow, and the sacraments were esteemed as mystical instrumentalities for the conferring of that grace which the Church was supposed to contain, much as a goblet contains wine, it was inevitable that saving faith in Christ, as exercised prior to all external profession, should sink gradually out of sight. Men came to

---

[1] "There are many reprobates mingled with the good, and both are gathered together by the Gospel as in a drag-net: and in this world, as in a sea, both swim enclosed without distinction in the net, until it is brought ashore, when the wicked must be separated from the good, that in the good, as in His temple, God may be all in all." *Civitas Dei*: Book 18: 49. For the history of these struggles, see Mosheim, Neander, Gieseler, Hase, *in loc.*

the Church, without religious experience of any sort, to receive a blessing which the Church alone could confer. Children came into the fold through baptism, and the membership thus instituted was never dissolved, except in cases of grievous heresy or of extraordinary crime. The outward confession was the only requisite needful: the inward basis and justification of such confession, as defined in the New Testament, was no longer required; and the Church was consequently filled with those who merely received its formal chrism, and were content with proclaiming before men their formal allegiance, not to Christ, but to Christianity.

As the Greek and the Romish teachings differ but slightly, we may find sufficient illustration of the error common to both, in the authorized declarations of the latter communion. The Roman Catechism of 1566, (I: 10, 7–8) recognizes the distinction between the good and the unworthy, by describing the former class as bound and joined together within the Church, not only by the profession of faith and communion in the sacraments, but also by the spirit of grace, and the tie of charity. But it also declares that both classes are properly included within the Church, and are to be allowed there, as the chaff is permitted to grow among the wheat. Bellarmine, *Eccles. Milit.*, Chap. II, defines the church as a company of men, who profess the Christian faith, and are bound together by participation in the sacraments, under the government of authorized pastors, the Roman Pontiff as vicar of Christ on earth being supreme. The first of these three qualifications in his view excludes all infidels, all Jews, Turks and Pagans, and all heretics and apostates; the second excludes all catechumens who have not received the eucharist, and all excommunicated persons; and the third shuts out all schismatics who may possess the true faith and the sacraments, but still are not under the divinely ordained government of the priesthood. He emphasizes these qualifications as external and visible—setting them over against the Protestant demand, as he defines it, that internal virtues are requisite to constitute church membership; and finally declares that the Church is a body of men as visible and palpable as the assembly of the Roman people, or the kingdom of France, or the republic of Venice.

That this is a wide and disastrous departure from the doctrine of the Apostolic age, will be obvious at a glance. The sources of the error are easily seen in the deceptive notion of organic visibility, in the false conception of the priesthood, in the kindred error concerning the sacraments as elements of grace, and in the crude and low views of Christian character, accepted everywhere in the Papal Church. Its harmful consequences are seen as easily in the merely external professions allowed, and in the wholly unspiritual relationship sustained by multitudes within that communion. And no argument more conclusive or crushing against this theory can be needful than that which is furnished directly in the history of Romanism since the Reformation, and in the present spiritual condition of the Papal Church. Oriental Christianity, misled in the same way, opening its doors to all who will acknowledge its ecclesiastical authority and submit themselves to its sacramental discipline, shows still more painfully in its multiplied formalisms and in its utter deadness spiritually, how disastrous, how fatal this error as to the law of church membership is. Certainly, it is impossible to build up a true Church of Christ on such foundations; if the external tests of admission have no profound spiritual basis, no vital experience of saving grace to rest upon, they became of necessity a mischievous formality, a deadly snare.

V. PROTESTANT DOCTRINE OF MEMBERSHIP AFTER THE REFORMATION.—Passing over from the view current in the Greek and Roman communions, to the general teaching of Protestantism, especially during the century following the Reformation, we fail to find in that teaching any really adequate recognition of the primitive doctrine. The comprehensive declaration of Hugo, that the true Church is the Multitudo Fidelium, and of Savonarola, that the true Church is composed of all those who are united in the bonds of love and of truth by the grace of the Spirit, were indeed accepted, and incorporated substantially into the newly formed Protestant Creeds. The French Confession of 1559, for example, defines the Church (Art. XXVII) as the company of the faithful who agree to follow the Word of God, and the pure religion which it teaches: who grow in grace all their lives, believing and becoming more and more confirmed in the fear of God. This Confession admits that there may be hypocrites and reprobates among the faithful, but declares that their wickedness can not destroy the title of the Church,—a title which rests on the spiritual reception of the Word and of the holy Sacraments. The Confession of Augsburg in like manner describes the Church (Art. VII) as the congregation or assembly of the saints, or of believers; in which the Gospel is rightly preached, and the sacraments are rightly administered.[1] Most of the Symbols of the period make similar declarations, yet there was evident shrinking, in many cases, from the full application of the spiritual and searching principle avowed. Various influences conspired to prevent such application. Many persons doubtless united with the several Protestant bodies, merely as a form of declaration against the Church of Rome, or as an expression of their adherence to the general principles, such as the right of religious freedom and of the private inter-

[1] In the edition of 1540: Congregatio membrorum Christi, hoc est, Sanctorum, qui vere credunt et obediunt Christo. Schaff. Vol. III: 13. See also Conf. Basle, Art. 5.

pretation of Scripture, on which Protestantism rested. Again, in many minds an intellectual acceptance of the doctrine of justification by faith, in contrast with the Romish theory of justification through works imposed by the priesthood, was regarded as a sort of substitute for hearty faith in Christ Himself as a personal Redeemer. Moreover, the dialectic disputations among the Reformers on questions largely speculative, and the multiplication of creeds to express slight differences, turned the thoughts of many away from the more vital matter of belief and trust in the Savior. To these causes may be added the entangling alliance everywhere existing between the Church and the State,—an alliance which divided widely the provinces of Central Europe into Catholic and Protestant, and which tended everywhere to obliterate the distinction between political citizenship and church membership.

In addition to these general hindrances to a full return to the New Testament doctrine, we may note the special influence of the views then current with respect to infant baptism, to the place and rights of children within the Church, and to the spiritual efficacy of the sacraments. The Romish usage of confirmation was substantially retained by both the Lutheran and the Reformed bodies: the recitation of the Commandments, and of the Creeds and Catechisms, was widely accepted as a sufficient qualification for communion. Though Christ Himself was regarded as the source and giver of salvation, yet connection with the Church and participation in the sacraments were too often contemplated as steps toward rather than signs of salvation; and if such connection was accompanied by general propriety in conduct, or the absence of heinous sin, it was too often held to be sufficient. Among the Lutheran bodies little more than this was insisted upon: and even the Reformed, notwithstanding their general inclination toward greater stringency in such directions, were disposed to condemn those advocates of a more stringent view, whom the Augsburg Confession stigmatizes as Donatists and such like. Calvin himself regards all as entitled to membership who, by confession of faith, regularity in conduct, and participation in the sacraments, acknowledge God and Jesus Christ. He indeed pronounces it a disgrace, if persons of immoral life occupy a place among the people of God, and declares that if churches are well regulated, they will not suffer persons of abandoned character among them, or admit the worthy and unworthy promiscuously to the table of the Lord. Yet he lays large stress on what he styles the judgment of charity in regard to all such persons, and laments the imperfection of the times, as shown in the inability of the churches to exercise discipline, even in the case of gross offenders.[1]

---
[1] CALVIN, *Inst.* Book IV: Chap. I: 15.

VI. CURRENT OPINION AMONG PROTESTANTS: THE FORMAL VIEW.—Without dwelling upon the multiplied illustrations of the Protestant doctrine of church membership during the sixteenth and seventeenth centuries, or on the defective usages which sprang up in consequence within the various Protestant communions, we may turn at once to consider existing opinions among those who together wear the Protestant name. These opinions may with sufficient exactness be thrown into two main classes: those which lay stress chiefly on the external or formal relationship, and those which emphasize especially a change of heart through grace, and a conscious Christian experience and life, as the essential condition of membership. Of these the formal or external view may first be considered:

The Church is contemplated, according to this view, as a visible society simply, having a prescribed system of administration and ordinances, and an ecclesiastical right of discipline,—existing in virtue of a formal covenant, and capable as an organization of conferring certain external privileges, apart wholly from the spiritual state or desert of the recipient. This visible society sustains only an external relationship to Christ, and is made up merely of professing adherents, and held together simply by the possession of these outward rights and prerogatives. Into this visible society any one may be introduced who submits to the ordinance of baptism, and who avows his general faith in Christianity. Of its external privileges, such as participation in the Supper, he may by such formal connection become partaker, though he be conscious of no real union of soul with Christ as his personal Redeemer. From the visible fellowship thus established, nothing but an authoritative separation, through excommunication on account of demonstrated sin, can expel him. The entire connection is an outward and formal one; the possession of grace in the heart is not presupposed or implied in it. The conditions are, the declaration of what may be termed historical or intellectual belief in Christianity as a religion, and an outward conformity with the prescribed rules of the visible body. The adherent professes to be, not an infidel or scoffer, but in an external sense a believer; and as such seeks for himself and his children the outward advantages, which connection with such an organization confers.[1]

This wholly formal conception of membership is based on a very broad, and indeed unwarrantable distinction between the Church visible and the Church invisible. It is supposed to be justified by what our Lord teaches, in several parables and elsewhere, respecting His Church on earth as a mixed society, containing good fish and bad, tares and wheat, within the one visible organization. It assumes the ex-

---

[1] BANNERMAN, D. D., *Presbyt. Alliance Proceedings*; 1880, p. 525.

istence of a certain outward covenant, and of a series of merely external privileges, of which those who are not true believers may properly avail themselves. It sets forth the sacraments, not as the signs and seals of regenerative grace enjoyed, but rather as the appointed marks of an external union, and consequently as advantages or benefits which those who are not Christians may share. It reduces the standard of admission to a simple application, and makes membership a mere form; surrendering the question of qualification wholly to the applicant, unless he be a notoriously profligate person. And wherever the connection between Church and State exists, this union is constituted even without formal action by either party—the inhabitant of a given territory becoming, *de facto*, a member of the legal Church. So, wherever baptism is regarded as conferring not a constructive, but an actual and complete membership, the baptized child, submitting at a given age to the ceremony of confirmation, becomes, or is, without further inquiry, an authorized member in the visible society that baptized it. Thus Blunt,[1] representing the high Anglican view, defines the visible Church as the whole body of those who have been baptized, and who have not been authoritatively separated from the Church by excommunication. That this is a departure from the doctrine of the Thirty-nine Articles is obvious, but it is a departure to which the theory of one comprehensive state church, and the theory of baptismal regeneration, inevitably compel their advocates. The state churches of Northern Europe, and extensive sections of European Lutheranism, are based on substantially the same misconception.

A modified or intermediate theory, retaining many of the characteristics of the preceding, appears in the view held in certain sections of British Presbyterianism. This opinion recognizes on the one side the insufficiency of the Romish test, and demands something more than a surrender of the understanding to the dictates of the Church in matters of faith, and a formal submission to its ordinances. But on the other side, it maintains that an intelligent profession of belief in the Gospel, coupled with conduct and life in harmony with such profession, is all that the Church may properly require. It denies that a saving belief in Christ is the only title of admission to the Christian society, and questions the right of that society to require from the applicant credible proof that he has any such title. In the language of one of its advocates, this theory holds that the Church stands revealed before the eyes of men, embodied as an outward system of administration and ordinances and discipline: and that men are called upon to enter within this Church, and are promised that, if they do so, they shall enjoy certain advantages even outwardly, and distinct

---

[1] *Dictionary of Doct. and Hist. Theology: Art.* Church.

from any saving benefits in this church state. This position is justified on the ground that the biblical conception of the Church as visible demands it, and on the further ground that any closer test than this cannot be applied without assuming for the Church an unwarrantable degree both of authority and of spiritual insight.[1]

The serious error in all such teachings lies primarily in the ignoring of the cardinal principle, that the only legitimate membership possible is that which rests upon repentance and faith and a holy life; and secondarily, in the assumption that the visible church is something other, more external and formal, and altogether less comprehensive and spiritual in its demands, than the true Church of Christ on earth. The distinction between the visible and the invisible household of faith is indeed justifiable, and is in certain directions important. But clearly no warrant exists in Scripture, or in the perceived nature of Christianity, for such an application of that distinction; and the consequences following such application are themselves abundant proof of its unlawfulness. To those who are familiar with the history of the conflict in New England during the last century over the Half-Way Covenant, as it was termed, no further evidence of such unlawfulness is needful. The practical result everywhere, as in that historic illustration, can only be to fill the Church with an unregenerate membership, to the irreparable injury alike of its true spiritual quality, of its standing before the world, and of its power to discharge adequately its great commission to disciple the nations.

VII. Current Opinion among Protestants: The Spiritual View.—This view may be defined in general as a closer return to the doctrine and usages of the Apostolic Church. It may be well described by a brief reference to the historic illustration just named. Prior to the middle of the eighteenth century, the churches of New England, in their attempt to establish a theocracy both ecclesiastical and civil, had received multitudes of persons who indeed accepted Christianity as a system, and believed in such sound standards of doctrine as the Westminster Confession, and who were also for the most part moral in life, and practically beyond the reach of church discipline, but who still were not Christians at heart, and therefore were only an enfeebling and demoralizing element within the church. That such a condition of things could not exist permanently, is apparent from the nature of the case: an element like this must either be excluded from the spiritual body, or press that body down to its own unspiritual level. With the purifying process that finally wrought out that exclusion, the name of Jonathan Edwards is indissolubly associated. His earnest and powerful presentation of the proper qualifications for church fellow-

---

[1] Bannerman, James. *Church of Christ:* Vol. I, p. 75, *seq.*

ship and communion, based as it was on his high and strong scheme of Christian doctrine, prepared the way for the introduction of better, more evangelical tests of membership. In his memorable treatise, Edwards shows with convincing power what saving faith truly is as a profound, vital, regenerating experience,—what it really is to receive Christ in His person and His offices as a personal Redeemer, and to attain and possess the spiritual life, of which such a reception of Christ is both the beginning and the permanent source. He also examines the profession of such faith; showing what it involves as a personal covenant with the Savior, and to what vast changes of thought, feeling, conduct, it commits the soul that intelligently makes it. He emphasizes also the public and visible element in such profession, as something done before the Church, and before the world,—the organized church being not merely a witness, like the world, but also a party to the compact thus made by the professing disciple primarily with Christ Himself. Against all connection with the Church through baptism, or by virtue of civil position, or any similar external process—against all mere profession of adherence to Christianity as a system, or mere submission to sacramental grace, or mere pledges of external morality, he enters strong, effectual protest. In a word, he brings out afresh, with great vividness, the simple and searching tests applied by the apostles, and demands for these full recognition, cordial acquiescence.[1]

The views of Edwards, made conspicuous as they were by the sad conflict through which he was compelled to pass in maintaining them, and made still more conspicuous by the revivals that were showered upon New England largely in consequence of their promulgation, have been extensively accepted in America, and within evangelical circles in Protestant Europe, as expressing the substantial doctrine of Scripture on this vital subject. Postponing here the subsidiary question as to the relative responsibility of the individual making a visible profession, and of the Church that receives him to membership on that profession, we may safely hold with Edwards that nothing less than such a spiritual state as has been described, can constitute any person a worthy candidate for admission to the organized household of faith. It is true that the visible Church is set forth in the Bible as a net enclosing good fish and bad, as a field containing wheat and tares growing together unto the harvest, as a companionship in which men like Ananias, and Simon the sorcerer of Samaria, are found. It is true that even in the apostolic circle Judas had a place; and that no insight of man is able always to detect hypocrisy, and no power vested in the

---

[1] EDWARDS, *Qualifications for Full Communion.* Also, *Thoughts on the Revival of Religion in New England.* Consult also his treatise on the *Religious Affections:* and BELLAMY, *True Religion Delineated.*

Church is adequate to the task of its own entire purification. There is some force also in the conception of the visible Church as an external society, having certain rights and prerogatives vested in it, while in that position. But all this furnishes no justification for the inference, that the Church as visible is to lower its standard from a saving belief in Christ credibly evidenced to the body, to a general declaration of adherence to Christianity, and an outward submission to the sacraments, even though these be accompanied by a commendable morality in the person seeking admission. At this point the modified view advocated by Bannerman is hardly less defective theoretically, while in practice it is far more dangerous, than the purely formal theory allowed largely in the Anglican, and practically followed in many of the Continental communions. A glance at the New Test. teaching will convince any one that the apostolic Church never admitted any one to its fellowship in order that he might enjoy certain outward advantages wholly apart from his spiritual estate—without any preëstablished relation to Christ within the Church invisible. Its invariable requisite was nothing less than a saving belief in the Savior Himself, consciously possessed and duly authenticated, not by a moral, but by a distinctively holy life.

VIII. MEMBERSHIP IN THE PARTICULAR CHURCH.—Reducing this conception of saving belief to its several elements, we discover four definite qualifications for church membership—each and all of which are indispensable. These qualifications are, first, a spiritual knowledge of God, especially as revealed in the Gospel, as Father and Son and Holy Ghost: second, repentance for sin as committed against God, and trust in the divine mercy, especially as that mercy is manifested in and through Christ as a Redeemer: third, obedience to God, and cordial devotion to His interests and kingdom, culminating under the Christian dispensation in personal conformity with Christ, and loyal consecration to His service: fourth, a public declaration of such faith and devotion, and a holy covenant with God to be His servant, followed and confirmed by voluntary union and communion with His people, and, under the Gospel, with some branch of the Christian Church. It will be obvious that these four elements are essential expressions of true piety under all dispensations, and that they consequently have always been, in greater or less degree, the indispensable prerequisites to true church membership, even in the Hebraic or the Patriarchal era. It will also be obvious that, while all are essential to membership in the Church invisible, they are all, and especially the last, essential to a just connection with any visible household of faith. From the nature of the case the latter connection must presuppose their existence, and assume it throughout, or the connection established must be throughout formal, meaningless, dangerous to all spiritual interests, whether of the Church or of the individual soul.

Hence, in the particular church, it is indispensable that great care should be taken at this most vital point. The following conditions are requisite here. First: there must be an open profession or confession, not merely of general adherence to Christianity or general belief in the Gospel, but of personal piety,—individual faith and trust in Christ Himself for salvation. Secondly: this profession or confession must be credibly evidenced, not merely by a moral life, but by the possession and manifestation of those spiritual experiences and graces, which are the direct outgrowth of a living piety within the breast. Thirdly: this evidence must be received and considered by the particular church, through some suitable and appointed method—the profession must be believed by that church to be genuine, and to represent a regenerate state in the applicant. As the household of faith must share with him in the issue of his act, so it is bound to form some just estimate of the spiritual condition which the act symbolizes. Fourthly: there must also be in every such case a voluntary acceptance of the covenant and creed of the organization, and a cordial submission to its legitimate regulations and authority. Loyalty not merely to the Church at large, but to the particular body, is of necessity implied in such a step; otherwise, the connection becomes little more than an abstract declaration, having but slight influence on any of the parties, and of small value as a contribution to the general cause of Christ.

Some who admit the need of the first and second of these specific qualifications, question the propriety of requiring the third, on the ground that the particular church is in fact incapable of forming an accurate judgment respecting the spiritual state of any applicant, and that the assumption of the right, or the acknowledgment of the obligation to do this, is consequently improper and mischievous. It is said that the visible Church is and must always be a mixed society; that the effort to expel all unworthy members, or to keep the Church absolutely pure, has always been a failure; that Christ intended that His Church should, even until the day of harvest contain tares, as well as wheat ready for His garner; and that the responsibility for connection with the Church must not be assumed by the body, but must be thrown entirely upon the person applying for admission. It is broadly affirmed that this responsibility can not properly be in any degree shared by the church or its appointed officers, and that they ought never to be understood as passing judgment upon, or as endorsing the validity of the evidences of a gracious state, furnished by the applicant. No such judgment, it is said, is expressed or implied in receiving any one into the fellowship of the Church: all that is requisite is, that there be no positive grounds for pronouncing him not to be a Christian.[1]

The answer of Edwards to this intermediate position is the just and conclusive answer. He maintains that the particular church must share with the professing disciple in the solemn act in which he is engaging; and that it is sacredly bound to settle for itself, no less than for him, the question whether his profession is credible,—may be accepted as the outward evidence of a truly regenerate nature. He holds that while there is always some liability to error in such judgment, yet the church should reduce such liability to the lowest possible degree, and should be satisfied with nothing less than substantial assurance as to the spiritual state of the applicant. He defines the element of credibility in the case, not simply as what may in a negative way be believed, but rather as a positive judgment founded on outward manifestations that ordinarily render the judgment probable. Can there be any doubt that this is the wise and scriptural position? How can any church refuse to step in with its counsel and oversight, at such a juncture in the spiritual experience of those who seek its fellowship? When we bear in mind how many such persons are young or ignorant, or are in a variety of ways exposed to serious delusions respecting their religious purposes and estate, how can we justify a church in simply opening its doors, and allowing them to enter in, upon their own unchallenged declaration, provided they are not openly unworthy? The credible evidence in such cases must be, not negatively that which may be believed, but positively that which convinces. Those who are appointed by the church as judges, must inquire respecting piety as well as knowledge (*Pres. Directory:* Ch. IX: 3-4), and the duty of inquiry clearly carries with it the duty of guidance and of judgment. They must be convinced, as far as ascertainable indications go, that the applicant is indeed, as he professes to be, already a child of God. This is a reponsibility which no particular church can evade or transfer: it belongs essentially to every organized household of faith. As the

---

[1] MASON, JOHN M., *Church of God,* p. 52-58, *seq;* HODGE, CHARLES, *Theol.,* Vol. III: 544-6: 569-78: HODGE, A. A., *Outlines of Theol.,* 646. The first author goes on to argue that there are positive advantages to be gained by the Church through the admission of unregenerate persons, and through the mixed condition of things resulting. And the second, in arguing for the admission of baptized persons to the communion and to church fellowship, adds the remark that it is to be feared that many such have come short of eternal life who, had they been received into the bosom of the Church, and enjoyed its guardian and fostering care, might have been saved: III, 576. For another statement, see DORNER, *Christ. Theol.* IV: 337-9. While he holds that the Church must not identify its judgment with the judgment of Christ as absolute and final, he maintains that the Church can not grant admission where impenitence is seen to exist,—the Church judging the applicant thus far.

grounds of exclusion from the Church must be the same as the grounds of exclusion from heaven, so the terms of admission must be the same essentially as those of admission to heaven: and for the requiring of these terms, and the decision respecting their existence, every such church must be directly accountable to Christ.

IX. MEMBERSHIP OF CHILDREN OF BELIEVERS.—One further question remains,—the question respecting the relation to the Christian Church of the children of believing parents, and especially of those who through the sacrament of baptism have been visibly associated in covenant with the particular church. It has already been shown that, in the economy of grace, the pious household, as well as the individual believer, has a legitimate place and claim, and that the believing family may properly be contemplated as, in some important senses, a unit within the Church. It has been shown that in the Christian as in the two antecedent periods in the history of that Church, the Abrahamic covenant stands as a great fact in the scheme of grace, full of promise and of blessing. It has been shown that the baptism of the children of pious parents, as a sign of this covenant relation, is warranted by Scripture, and is justified in the experience of the Church of Christ. It follows from these propositions that such children are in a true sense, born within the pale of the visible Church, may properly be baptized, are entitled to its continuous nurture and care, and do even inherit a certain species and measure of membership within its sacred inclosure. To this general view even those who regard infant baptism as an unauthorized mode of expressing this covenant relation, might easily give assent.

At this point we come upon a wide variety of opinion and usage. The Papal Church at one extreme regards this membership as conferred in and through such baptism, and therefore claims as its lambs all baptized children, whatever may have been the spiritual state of the parents. At the other extreme, we find persons who hold that church membership can exist only in and through personal faith, and who therefore regard the children of believers as standing, prior to conversion, in the same place essentially with the children of unbelievers,— wholly outside of the visible Church. The rite of confirmation, according to the papal view, does not establish, but simply confirms or ratifies an antecedent membership. Hence the Romish communion can set up no spiritual standard of admission, and is consequently constrained to suffer the disastrous issues of its error in the strange mixture of good and bad, wheat and tares, in its multitudinous membership. Of the antithetic error of denying to such children any covenanted relation to the visible Church, nothing further need be said; it is sufficient to note its disastrous influence in many ways on church life and growth. The general Protestant position lies between these two extremes; yet neither the doctrine nor the practice of Protestant bodies can be said to be in any sense uniform. As in respect to the membership of adults, so here the formal and the spiritual theories stand in wide contrast.

The formal theory exalts the merely external relation, at the expense of the spiritual experience and life which that relation at least anticipates. It tends decidedly, as in the Churches of the Reformation, and as in current Prelatism and Lutheranism in Europe, toward the Papal view; contemplating the connection as substantially one of form and of outward privilege. Accordingly, access to the table of the Lord is made to turn chiefly on the capacity to recite the Commandments and the Apostolic Creed; fellowship in the Church is assumed as a species of natural right, under these external conditions; and the membership thus gained stands rather as a social mark, than as the sign of a gracious state. The Westminster Symbols expressing the general doctrine of the seventeenth century, emphasize strongly this external aspect of the connection, while they also bring out more distinctly than any antecedent Confession, the more spiritual view implied in their emphatic phrase, knowledge and piety. On the one side they introduce, or at least give currency to, the doubtful distinction between member and communicant, and thus furnish foundation for such defective conceptions of adult membership as were expressed in the Half-way Covenant of New England. On the other they directly impose upon the Church not merely the obligation to care for such infant members spiritually, but also the further duty to discipline them when they become adults, for their failure to come to the table of Christ, or to lead a truly Christian life.

The spiritual theory affirms the fact of a real connection established at birth and ratified in baptism, and accepts in full the obligation of the Church to train up in knowledge and piety those who through parental faith stand in that connection. It regards this as an anticipatory or constructive species of membership; it views the connection as prospective and prophetic. It maintains also the obligation of parents to bring up such children as within the Church rather than without;—to educate them directly and zealously, with reference to their assumption in due season of such duties as devolve upon converted adults within the household of faith. It asserts the duty of the Church to contemplate such pious offspring as its own,—to make ample provision for their training in divine things, to instruct them in all Christian duty, and to guide their young feet into the way of peace. But on the other hand it regards full membership as involving something more than this; it demands a higher qualification than the mere rite of confirmation, or any general profession of adherence to Christianity, or even blamelessness in life; it calls for a true change of heart in the baptized child, no less than in the unbaptized adult who has lived long in sin, wholly without the fold of grace. In a word, it holds to the existence of a genuine and most blessed relation, which has in it large spiritual possibilities, and which may be expected to issue, if all parties are faithful to their covenant, in a complete and perfect union at once with the visible Church, and with the Church invisible. This relation is the historic antecedent to full membership; it is membership in the germ, and might therefore be called by that name. But it is not a connection which properly brings the child under the executive government of the Church, or which exposes it to ecclesiastical discipline for its failure to discharge religious duties. The assumption by the Church of a derived right, for example, to excommunicate such a baptized child, on its coming to mature years, for the neglect of religion, or even for immorality, is unwarranted by the nature of the relation, as thus described.[1]

X. THE CHURCH AN ORGANIZATION: OFFICES AND OFFICERS REQUISITE.—Besides the membership who constitute its personal material, the Church, in order to the proper execution of its functions, requires— as we have already noted—an organization of this material into unity under some definite form of constitution. Without such organization the life of the body can not be adequately sustained, nor can the ends contemplated in its existence be effectively secured. The Bible therefore not only sets forth the qualifications requisite in the members of this divine body, but describes that body as a living organism, in which each member has an appointed place, and in which all the members are fitly joined and compacted together by that which every joint supplieth, Eph. 4: 16. The two metaphors by which the Church is habitually described in the New Testament, will sufficiently illustrate this statement. Viewed on one hand as a family or household of faith, every particular church is a unit, animated by what may be termed a common life, and regulated by distinctive principles which are higher than individual impulse or aim. Viewed on the other as a state or kingdom, the particular church still more obviously requires organization, a constitution and laws, a real and effective government. All that is requisite to the full equipment of the two inferior institutions, the family and the state, for the full performance of their respective functions in human life, must be in like manner requisite to the exist-

---

[1] MASON, J. M., *Church of God*, pp. 166-173. The author affirms the right of the particular Church to inspect conduct, and to exercise authority, but does not claim the right to administer discipline. See on this point, *Presbyt. Digest*, pp. 671-2. HODGE, *Church Polity*, p. 215.

ence and efficiency of the Church. It is especially obvious that such organization is an essential element under the latter conception;—if the Church is to be in any sense a kingdom, it must have organization, laws, offices and officers, such as its nature and its aims demand.

Without anticipating the full consideration of the nature of church government, we may note here the necessity for officers—representatives of such government—as well as members to be governed, within the organized family and kingdom of grace. Various illustrations of this necessity might be derived from the constitution of the Hebraic, and even of the Patriarchal Church. Under the Gospel the evidence is still more distinct and conclusive. The Messiah in constituting His Church, clearly made provision for the official investiture and the administrative functions, first of the apostles, and then of those who should succeed them in the discharge of this spiritual trust. The perfecting of the saints individually, and the perfecting of the organized body for its great mission, required that long before His ascension He should be training special men for such administration, and then that at the ascension He should give to His Church apostles and prophets, evangelists and pastors and teachers, by whom the composite organization should be guided, edified and governed; Eph. 4: 11-13. These official persons were not to be a class separate from the Church, and vested with an inherent right to control it, and with authority to transmit that right to others, independently of the choice of the body to be governed. They were rather members of the Church, divinely chosen and set apart from their brethren for this service; and were to act under full responsibility to the Church as well as to Christ for the manner in which they should discharge their difficult commission. In the full sense, no company of believers can be regarded as a Church which is not thus organized and officered; even where this is denied in form, it is not excluded in fact. An unorganized body of disciples, without a constitution, without rules, without leaders, may enjoy a degree of temporary fellowship, but they can not declare themselves a church according to the New Testament standard. They may wear the name, but certainly they can attain no distinct view or experience of the divine reality.

Contemplating the officers of the Church simply as among its personal constituents, antithetic to its membership as already considered, we may briefly examine the names and functions, the position and authority, of those who are called to sustain this relation:—meanwhile postponing the broader question respecting the nature of the government to be administered through such official instruments. Distinguishing for the moment between the officer and the office, we may observe in general that all of the offices mentioned in the New Testament may be divided into two classes, the temporary and the permanent.

XI. TEMPORARY CHURCH OFFICES.—The first class of offices to be considered in this connection are those which by their nature were limited to particular epochs or exigencies in the history of Christianity, or those which are essential occasionally, but not permanently, in its progressive career. The prophetical and apostolic offices belong to the first division; the office of the evangelist and of the deaconess to the second:

1. The prophetical office appeared prominently in the Christian Church during the first century, as it had existed during a large portion of the preceding period. Its appearance was probably included in the promise in Joel, quoted in conjunction with the miraculous events of the Pentecost, Acts 2: 17. The warnings of our Lord with regard to false prophets, show that such an order was to exist under the Gospel: Matt. 7: 15, Mark 13: 22. Examples of true prophesying may be found in Luke 1: 67, Acts 11: 27-8, 13: 1, 21: 10-11: various references to the prophetic order occur in the epistles, as 1 Cor. 12: 28-9, 14: 1-3, Eph. 4: 11. Like the Jewish seers, these New Test. prophets taught as well as foretold future events, Acts 15: 32, 1 Cor. 14: 29-32. It may be that the power of speaking in unknown tongues, and the kindred power of interpretation and of discerning spirits, dwelt largely in them. Obviously their presence and their work were both a prominent and a peculiar feature in the life of the primitive Church.—Yet their mission clearly ended with the first century. The claim of ability to foresee the future through divine aid was indeed occasionally made, during the second and third centuries, as the same claim has been made in modern times. But facts have never verified the claim. The office evidently belonged, like the other charisms, to that particular period in the career of the Church,—it was supernatural altogether, and as such was just then needed as a confirmatory witness to the divinity of the Gospel. But the necessity for it ceased when the Church had once obtained an assured position, and the function therefore passed away. While we can not on Scriptural grounds affirm, that no exigency will ever arise in which the gift of prophecy will again be conferred, before the final consummation, we are warranted in affirming that no such endowment exists now, or has existed at any period since the decease of John, the last and greatest of the historic prophets: Rev. 10: 11, 22: 6.[1]

2. The apostolic office also ceased with the death of John. The peculiarity of this office clearly lay in the function of witnessing to

---

[1] On the Prophetical Office and Teaching, see ALEXANDER, on Isaiah, *Introduction*. Also STANLEY, *Hist. of the Jewish Church*, Lect. XIX: XX.

the person and mission of Christ,—a function which from the nature of the case could have been imparted to none but those who had actually seen and heard Him, and which in fact could have been exercised by none even among such competent witnesses, but those to whom a divine commission had been directly given. The apostles, in other words, were a body of men selected by our Lord as His disciples in a special sense, to accompany Him during His earthly ministry, in order that they might be qualified, as only such a body could be, to certify before men after His decease to what they had personally seen and heard; Acts 1: 2, 8, 1 John 1: 1–3. The introductory commission given to them (Matt. 10: *passim*), and the full commission described in Luke 24: 44–48, show that, while they were to become also bishops and teachers permanently caring for the Church which was to be organized by their efforts, this peculiar and inalienable function of bearing personal witness, was to be their more immediate duty. Their own declarations as to this apostolic function, especially in connection with the election of Matthias to the apostolate (Acts 1: 21–22), are decisive on this point: Acts 3; 15, 5: 32, 10: 39–41, 13: 31, and many others. If it be maintained on what seem to be reasonable grounds that the election of Matthias was divinely directed, and that his election shows that the function of witnessing might properly be transmitted beyond the original circle of the twelve, it should also be granted that the description of the qualifications requisite in this instance, shows conclusively that such transmission could have been justified only so far as these untransmissible qualifications might be found. As witnesses, in the sense here described, the apostles could have had no successors, at least beyond the small circle of those who, with them, had companied with the Lord Jesus all the time that He went in and out among men, in His mediatorial mission. No command to transmit their function of witnessing beyond this limited range anywhere appears; no affirmation that this would occur, can be found in the New Testament; by the nature of the case such transmission was impracticable.

The attempt to prove that the apostolate, in this sense of the term, was in fact transmitted not only to Matthias and Paul, but also to Barnabas, Apollos and Epaphroditus, and was thus made a permanent office within the Church, rests on very slender foundations. In the case of Paul, we find his claim to the apostolic office based directly on his possession of supernatural qualifications kindred to those possessed by the original group; he had personally seen the Lord, and had been miraculously commisioned to testify to what he had seen: 1 Cor. 15: 8–10, Gal. 1: 12. In respect to the others named, the term, apostle, is clearly used in the same general sense in which we find it applied, probably, by Paul to Andronicus and Junias (Rom. 16: 7), and elsewhere to other persons who were messengers or helpers of the churches. The reference in Rev. 21: 14, to the twelve apostles of the Lamb—a reference dating nearly two generations after the death of our Lord—implies that the original number had never been exceeded. The allusions by Paul and John to persons whom he styled false apostles—who say they are apostles and are not, are also suggestive in this connection: 2 Cor. 11; 13, Rev. 2: 2. That the real apostles filled other functions, and sustained wider relations to these churches, is obvious from the case of Paul himself who, though he styled himself an apostle, 1 Tim. 2: 7, was also called a prophet, Acts 13: 1, a bishop or elder, Eph. 3: 7, 8, and an evangelist or teacher, Acts 13: 2-4. Naturally the apostolic group continued while they lived, to be not merely witnesses to the great facts touching the Messiahship, but also leaders in the entire process of planting and edifying the Church, wherever it was established. This general office of leadership and ministration was of course transmissible, though even here the supernatural charisms which in their case accompanied the office, and the inspiration which sustained and aided them in it, could not be conferred by them on their successors in this task.[1]

3. The evangelistic office makes its appearance rather as an occasional form of ministration, or a temporary function, than as a permanent equipment of the early Church. It finds an illustration in the mission given by our Lord (Luke 10: *passim*) to the seventy who, in addition to the twelve, were to go forth for a season as His messengers to the lost multitudes of Israel. Apostles and others seem at times to have assumed such a special service, as Philip in the desert toward Gaza, Acts 8: 26-40; Peter going down to Caesarea, Acts 10: 23-48; Paul and Barnabas laboring in Cyprus and in Western Asia, Acts 13: 2-14. The more general biblical references (Eph 4: 11, and elsewhere) show that this type of Christian work was extensively assumed under some sort of commission, by numbers in the primitive Church, and was continued throughout the apostolic century. The disciples who went forth preaching the Word, or heralding the good news of the Gospel, even to the uttermost parts of the earth, were filling this evangelistic office. Like John the Baptist, they were forerunners of the more permanent work of organization and edifying that was to follow, under the blessing of the Spirit, wherever they successfully proclaimed

---

[1] NEANDER, *Planting and Training*, etc., p. 150; MOSHEIM, 1: 91: *Note:* "By its very idea as the primitive, authentic body of witnesses the apostolate is unrepeatable, because it rests on the uniqueness of the relation of the first generation to Christ, and on their immediate selection and education by Christ." DORNER, *Christ. Doct.* IV: p. 334.

the great salvation. We find their successors in those who in the centuries following bore the Gospel to the farthest East, and to the tribes of northern Europe; or in the missionaries of modern times, as they traverse the globe on the same errand of mercy to lost humanity. Apparently, they were never intended to become a separate, independent class, existing within the organized Church, by the side of others who sustain the ministerial office, and assuming to themselves some special class of ministerial functions. The application of the title to those who are called to no evangelistic work such as has just been sketched, but who labor occasionally in aid of Christian pastors, as in seasons of revival, is one which the New Testament nowhere suggests.

4. To complete this review of church offices which are temporary or occasional rather than permanent, a glimpse at the office or function of the deaconess may be taken here. The instance of Phœbe, deaconess or servant of the Cenchrean Church, gracefully alluded to by Paul as the succorer of himself and of many, and also his reference to Mary, and to Tryphena and Tryphosa, at Rome, are quoted as indicating the existence of such an order of persons in other households of faith; Rom. 16: 16, 12. His allusion to a certain class of godly women (1 Tim. 5: 10), and to the wives of deacons (1 Tim. 3: 11), and a like allusion in Titus 2: 3, are regarded as confirming this indication. The place which holy women evidently occupied in the circle of grace, even during the life-time of Christ (Luke 8: 2–3, for illustration), and also the peculiar type of social life which was developed at the Pentecost, and in which women shared as freely as men, have seemed still further to confirm the belief that official position was early conferred on woman within the Church. Such a step would certainly be in harmony with the spirit of a religion, which from the outset aimed at the emancipation and exaltation of woman, as one of its immediate results. It is also certain that the office of deaconess, with the special function of caring for the sick and needy, instructing the young, watching over certain church interests, and ministering to martyrs and confessors for the truth, existed early in both the Eastern and the Western Church. In the Apostolical Constitutions, a form for the ordination of women to this service was explicitly prescribed. A substitute for such a class of church servants is provided in the Romish communion, and in some sections of Protestantism, through the appointment of special orders of nuns and sisterhoods, devoted through life to the interests of religion. Yet the office, if any such existed at the beginning, must have been but occasional and partial; it can not be said to have held its place broadly in the conviction and favor of the Church. In some communions it is still in some degree and form retained. The current tendency in the most spiritual sections of Protest-

autism to supply women with appropriate spheres and opportunit'es for useful service in the Church, though it may result in no such official investiture, is a fact in which all true friends of an active, fruitful Christianity may well rejoice.[1]

XII. PERMANENT CHURCH OFFICES.—Contemplating still the office rather than the officer, and inquiring simply respecting those official functions whose existence and exercise are indispensable to the proper organization and effective work of the Church, we may note three distinct spheres of such activity which demand careful consideration.

1. The office of instruction, including both the enlightening and edifying of the Church, and the education of society in the Christian faith, stands first in this series. That such a function is essential to the healthful development of organic Christianity is obvious. It is just at this point that we discover one of the marked contrasts between Christianity and the great natural faiths,—in the appeal which the former constantly makes, not to superstition or to the esthetic taste, but to the reason and the capacity for rational trust. It lays before the mind a system of truth to be apprehended and believed, as the basis of all the further experiences it awakens in the heart or in the life. And in order to the proper presentation of such a system of truth, it needs competent agents and representatives,—persons to whom this task of instruction may properly be entrusted, and by whose effort the body of believers may be edified, and the Gospel effectively commended to men. Even during the apostolic age, and while the Holy Ghost was miraculously poured out on many, and the disciples in general enjoyed peculiar opportunities for knowing the truth for themselves, such teachers were appointed, as we know, to aid the Church in this primary task of edification. The presence of inspired prophets, of holy evangelists, of progressive inspiration, did not obviate the necessity for such a class of qualified instructors. Various titles besides that of teacher were given to those filling this function: pastor or shepherd, Jer. 3: 15, compared with Eph. 4: 11, 1 Peter 5: 2–4: minister or steward, 1 Cor. 4: 1, 12: 28: bishop or overseer, Acts 20: 28: presbyter or elder, 1 Peter 5: 1. Other functions are indeed included in such titles, for the reason that those who were primarily called to be teachers, were also, for the most part, empowered to assist the Church in other official relations—especially in government. Yet any one who studies carefully the Pastoral Letters, will see at a glance how primary and how vital, in the judgment of the apostles and their associates, this work of instruction was. Nor has time rendered this

---

[1] SCHAFF, *Hist. of Apostolic Church*, I: 135; BINGHAM, *Antiquities of the Christian Church*, Book II: Ch. 22. For a valuable Art. in favor of the office of deaconess as permanent, see *Presbyt. Review*, Vol. I: No. II. A. T. MCGILL, D. D.

office less important. As the Christian scheme of doctrine has developed into theologies and creeds, as the antagonisms between this divine system and human heresy and unbelief have become more distinct and complex, as the sum of saving faith has grown into more extended form during the ages since the New Testament was written and compiled, the need of such teaching and such teachers has the rather steadily increased. Not merely or mainly the unfolding of new aspects of divine truth, but rather the more careful explication and defence of that truth against all error, and the general education of believers and their children, and of all who are willing to hear the Word, constitute the chief vocation of those on whom this office rests. Neither do any indications appear that such a vocation will ever be needless. The Church of Christ will have such teachers, at least until millennial times: and those sections of the Church which appreciate this need most fully, and most thoroughly provide for it, are most certain to grow into progressive influence, into millennial maturity.

2. The office of government stands second in this series of permanent church functions. Without entering here on the general consideration of the Church as a kingdom, administering a system of laws under divine guidance, we may simply note the fact already adverted to, that government has in reality existed within the Church in all ages, and that the task of administering such government has always been committed to men chosen and ordained for this purpose. Postponing all questions as to the biblical form of church polity, or to the proper mode of administration, we may still recognize the existence and prominence of this governmental function. Especially are such existence and prominence apparent under the Gospel economy. That the apostolic Church had rulers, is a fact as unquestionable as the kindred fact that it had teachers. Some of the titles already named, such as bishop or pastor or elder, indicate this as an undoubted feature of the primitive Church. Ruling was as essential as instruction in an organism so constituted, and sent forth on such a mission; and provision was therefore divinely made for this necessity, in the selection of persons qualified to rule, and in their official investiture within the Church. We see the apostles and other chosen brethren acting officially in this way, as early as the Council at Jerusalem; Acts 15: 22-23. More general allusions to such a class of rulers appear in Acts 20: 28, Rom. 12: 6-8, 1 Cor. 12: 28, Heb. 13: 7, 17, 24, and other passages. But it is quite apparent that the function of teaching and the function of ruling were not always vested in the same person. While the distinction is not formally drawn out, as it would probably have been, if the two functions were always assigned to different persons, it still is clear that the distinction was sometimes recognized; 1 Tim. 5: 17, 1 Peter 5: 2-3.

That rulers existed as a class under divine warrant in the apostolic Church is thus evident, whatever may be held as to the precise duties devolving upon them, or the extent of the authority wielded by them. And what was necessary in the apostolic Church, may be presumed to be all the more necessary since the gift of inspiration has ceased, and since the miraculous manifestations of a divine presence and control have been withdrawn. In all countries and ages this function has in fact been found to be indispensable to the proper constituting and full efficiency of the visible household of faith. Even where such organization is regarded as wholly spiritual, and where all formal official investiture is condemned as incompatible with the nature of the family of grace, the essential fact in the case remains; the official function still finds recognition.

3. In connection with the two primary offices of instruction and government, we may note a third office which appeared very early in the primitive Church, and which, like the two preceding, seems essential to the full constituting of the Church for its great mission among men, —the office of administration. The sphere for such an office lies outside of both teaching and ruling,—it includes the general care of the organized body, in what may be described as its external work and relations. The germ of the office appears in the provision made for daily ministration to the saints, during the peculiar experiences following the Pentecost; Acts 6: 1–6. The line of distinction between the spiritual and the temporal in church life was there clearly drawn by Peter; and the provision then made, continued to exist long after the special need which he so tersely describes, had passed away. There was seen to be a large sphere of oversight and administration, not merely in the distribution of church charities, but in many other directions, in which the teacher or ruler could not so effectively act,—which required a separate class of official persons. Without referring to general allusions to the diaconate, found in the Pauline epistles (Phil. 1: 1), we may note the careful description of the Christian deacon in 1 Tim. 3: 8–13, as proving beyond question the existence of such a class, and the importance of their functions in the apostolic age. Nor was this an office which existed for a season only. The need which created it at the first still exists,—is in fact as extensive and as enduring as the Church. While the special call which first produced the office has passed away, other and broader aspects of that call have become equally apparent and equally urgent. Rather is it true that with the more complex development of the Church,—with the widening variety of needs, and the multiplication and more elaborate classification of official duties, the necessity in the case has been greatly enhanced. May it not even be affirmed that this office of administration, though

perhaps inferior in sphere, fills a place in the permanent life of the Church, no less vital than that of government or instruction, and must therefore be as legitimate and enduring a constituent in its organization as they?

In the three offices thus sketched, all the great primal needs of the Church of Christ are fully met. Wherever provision is properly made for instruction, for government, and for administration, in the broad sense just defined, any church organization may regard itself as fully equipped alike for inward efficiency and for outward growth. No other official functions are needful; under these three terms all legitimate church functions and services may be classed.

XIII. OFFICERS REQUISITE IN THE CHURCH.—The consideration of these three offices, or classes of official service, suggests at once the further fact, that every such office requires a person in whom its functions are for the time embodied, and by whose active services these church needs are efficiently supplied. Respecting this personal element, some further suggestions may here be introduced:

The conspicuous place of the ministry within the Church will, under this general view, be apparent at a glance. Whether that ministry be regarded as essentially one order, or as divided into three distinct classes—whatever the theory as to the way in which this order becomes possessed of its high functions, or to the measure of accountability to the Church for the use of its official position, there can be no question as to the underlying truth, that a church without a minister is not in the full scriptural sense a church. In forming our conceptions of the minister in this relation, we are indeed carefully to distinguish between the biblical germ in which the office originated, and the ecclesiastical development that has followed with the ages. For, it is quite obvious that the simple servant of the Church, who at first, as bishop or pastor or elder, had general charge of the flock of Christ under apostolic warrant, had his lines of labor and of duty much less closely defined, and was himself much less consciously and distinctively an official person, than his successors are under any existing form of church polity. The three classes of function which have been described, were also far less obviously separate, and flowed together within the grasp of one and the same person much more freely. For the elaborate division of this holy order into a succession of officers, invested with varying grades of service and prerogative, and for all the formalities and dignities with which this order is now decorated, even in the simpler forms of current ecclesiastical organization, one looks in vain to find any definite provision in the constitution of the primitive Church. The minister of Christ, as sketched in the New Testament, was on the one side a simple pastor or teacher of his brethren, and on the other an overseer or ruler, inspired by love, and animated in all his administration with the benignant temper of service, but without special title, or any high official prerogatives. The sketches which Paul has given in his letters to Timothy and Titus show us, as no uninspired description could do, just what the minister was designed to be, and what during the apostolic age he doubtless was: shepherd and bishop, pastor and overseer and ruler, and robed in these functions with a saintly grace peculiarly his own, still in every station the servant, even the slave, of his brethren for the sake of Christ, his Lord: 2 Cor. 4: 5.

The call to this sacred office was peculiar. It was not an inherited vocation like that of the Jewish priest: it was not a special investiture transmitted from apostolic hands, without the action or approbation of the Church. The glimpse of church method given in the election of Matthias, doubtless became an example largely and reverently followed. While we see the apostles, and others under their sanction, officially appointing elders in every city (Titus 1: 5), and thus organizing the Churches as by divine warrant, we have clear, concurrent indications that the call of God habitually verified and approved itself in the estimate of the Christian flock. No one assumed the sacred office for himself: the summons of the Spirit, the acquiescing judgment of His people, were its recognized ground and basis, Heb. 5: 4. The essential elements of this call remain the same at all periods: first, such natural endowments and such a measure of culture as will enable their possessor to fill the office adequately: secondly, personal experience of religion, and a supreme willingness to be exclusively devoted to this service: thirdly, providential indications pointing toward that service as a life vocation: and fourthly and supremely, the movings of the Holy Spirit in the soul, intelligently apprehended, and the concurrent judgment of the visible Church. Undoubtedly such a call should not be a single or a casual experience: it should be heard again and again, and should become the controlling impulse and motive in the life.[1]

The functions of the Christian minister are easily apprehended. While they include primarily all that is implied in the term, instruction, they also include some prominent share in the government, and even in the general administration of the household of faith. Though he is not to assume the exercise of such administration or government to the exclusion of others, or to claim a right to such exercise apart from the judgment or determination of the church, as Romanism affirms, yet there is a certain concentration of offices in his person, such as

---

[1] VINET, *Past. Theol.*: Introduction, sec. 7. Also, BRIDGES, *Christian Ministry:* BURNET, *Pastoral Care:* BAXTER, *Reformed Pastor*, Part I: WAYLAND, *Ministry of the Gospel:* Letter 2.

makes him of necessity a central agent or factor in all departments of the church life. It is his sacred vocation, in the highest sense of that term, to edify those who are divinely committed to his charge; building them up not merely on their most holy faith, but equally in all the diversified aspects of their religious experience and calling. It is no less his high task to represent the Gospel, and to proclaim it by every available method to all persons of whatever class, whom he may be able to reach. Like the Church itself, or the sanctuary within whose walls he chiefly ministers, he is to stand forth in the community as a visible, permanent representative of the divine faith which he proclaims; ever bending his energies to the one business of leading mankind to salvation, and to this end laying aside all other vocations and interests in life. Of the inherent worth, of the peculiar privileges and dignities, of the sublime rewards of such a ministry, when animated by the apostolic spirit, and conducted according to scriptural principles and methods, volumes might be written.

Nor is this sketch peculiar to the Christian minister. At the first, he shared even the primary function of instruction, and eminently the functions of administration and of government, with others whom the church recognized as qualified to discharge these high trusts; and their activities were hardly less essential than his to the healthful condition of the visible body of believers. Doubtless the two latter functions were not always separated by broad lines; as the teacher governed, the ruler also instructed, nor is it unlikely that those holding the diaconate sometimes taught, or even ruled, in churches where abundant materials for filling such official positions were not easily found. The Stephen whose name stands at the head of the list of deacons, was full of faith and power; he wrought miracles and wonders among the people, and so testified to the truth in disputations in the synagogue, that his opponents were not able to resist the wisdom and the spirit with which he spake,—finally attesting his faith and loyalty to the truth in martyrdom. And from the apostolic usage, we may learn the universal law; that as in that age, so in all ages there should be other official persons as well as the minister in the visible Church; that to these persons no less than to him, are the tasks of government and administration and even of instruction assigned; and that upon those who fill such offices, special honor and privilege as well as responsibility do fitly rest. Without adverting here to any particular questions suggested at this point, such as the separation or blending of these functions, or the creation of one or two classes of such adjunctive officers, or the manner in which they shall severally receive their appointment and **authority**, we may rest for the present in the general facts and principles just given. It is specially incumbent upon Protestantism to emphasize these related offices and officers, since the Papal Church has so largely ignored them; and to give to those who administer and to those who rule, the just share of both the dignity and the control which the Papacy confers on the priesthood alone.

XIV. CHURCH OFFICERS: FURTHER QUESTIONS NOTED.—The general doctrine here presented, sheds light on the specific question of official investiture. It is one of the fundamental errors of the Church of Rome, that the priesthood is an office transmitted from generation to generation through the priestly orders, and without the voice or approbation of the Church. It is the priesthood, not the congregation, which selects and constitutes the priest; it is the clerical body in conclave assembled, not the Church, which chooses and officially crowns the pope. Protestantism admits the existence of no such prerogative. It refers all official investiture on the one side directly to Christ, and on the other immediately to the Church. No minister, for example, becomes such without authority of the Master, authenticated by the judgment of His people; no person however qualified can receive or hold office of any class in any other way. The right to transmit official prerogatives independently of the Church was not claimed even by the apostles, neither did the leaders of the primitive Church act in any instance as if such right were vested in them. Christ and His Church alone can create even the humblest among the official servants in that divine household.

It follows also that the authority vested in church officers is not native in the person, but belongs to the office—is not inherent but delegated: and is therefore to be exercised under a due sense of responsibility to those who confer it. This authority is also limited rather than comprehensive: it includes just such functions and duties as the Scriptures and the church assign to the person holding it; it conveys no warrant for official administration beyond the bounds thus described. All attempts to intermeddle with whatever lies outside of such boundaries, all effort to lord it over the heritage of God in directions where the individual conscience or the claim of the body of believers is by divine right supreme, all assertion of dignities or enrobing in the purple and pomp of hierarchy, are both treason to the Church and disloyalty to Christ, its divine Head and Lord.

As official authority is limited in sphere, so it is in many ways limited in time and opportunity. It is indeed a common Protestant view, and one which has some measure of biblical warrant, that all official investiture in the Church is for life. Yet many sections of Protestantism limit the sweep of this principle by affirming a distinction between the office itself and the exercise of its functions, and by regarding the latter as temporary and occasional, though the former be permanent. These practical limitations are often extended so far, on account of mental inadequacy or advancing age or spiritual incompetency, or the failure to command church support, that the official title becomes a fiction,—ceases to be anything beyond a name. And it may well be questioned, whether an office, which for any such cause can never be exercised by the incumbent, might not, for the welfare of all the parties, and in the interest of Christian sincerity, be formally surrendered. It would probably be a decided gain to the common Protestantism, if the length of time during which any church office should be held, were in all cases distinctly bounded, if not by some periodic limitation in time, still by the manifested competency of the person appointed to fill it.

It may finally be suggested here that no peril more subtle, no evil more disastrous, attends the Church of Christ on earth, than those which in various ways accompany this problem of office and official function. More than all external causes, and possibly more than all internal heresies and controversies, has this problem agitated, convulsed, divided Christendom, from the apostolic age down to our own. It lies at the foundation of most of those conflicting conceptions of polity and order, which have so often rent the one Church into a series of separate denominations, not merely at variance in opinion, but antagonistic in spirit and action. In the particular church, it is easily recognized as first among those divisive influences by which the household is torn into sections and embittered by factious conflicts, inimical if not fatal to the spiritual life of all the members. Here personal ambitions, partisan feelings, intestinal strifes, sectarian narrowness and bitterness, find their chief sphere and opportunity. Here the best affections of disciples are arrested in their action, the purest purposes are frustrated, and the noblest elements in Christian manhood are crippled in their action and influence. In a word, the spirit of hierarchy is the ever threatening peril, the chiefest evil, of organic Christianity. And the only possible antidote lies in the broadest, most continuous and urgent enunciation of the holy precept of our Lord, embodied for His Church through all time in the golden sentence, which to every one holding official station within that Church is a supreme commission: I AM AMONG YOU AS ONE THAT SERVETH.

CHAPTER IV.

THE CHURCH AS A DIVINE KINGDOM:

GOVERNMENT, POLITIES, DISCIPLINE.

The impersonal and also the personal constituents of the Church have now been passed in brief review. The next question to be considered relates to the peculiar organization in which these various elements are embodied,—to that Church viewed as a divine structure, vested with the right to govern and discipline itself, and qualified to stand forth in human society as an independent and enduring kingdom of grace. Three topics here present themselves for investigation: Church Government in general, Polities in the Church, and Church Order and Discipline.

I. THE CHURCH AS A STRUCTURE: GENERAL CONCEPTION.—Even in the patriarchal age, the Church is seen to be, not an aggregate of dissimilar elements, but a living organism, bound together in every part by the common principle of piety. In the Hebraic Church, formal and external as the uniting tie appears in conjunction with the Hebrew commonwealth, the same spiritual structure is still apparent; the Church is an organized institution within the State, and as such maintains its vitality and efficiency even while the State is passing into decay. Under the Gospel this self-organizing capacity, and this independent life, are still more manifest. While our Lord lays broad and sure foundations for His Church, and makes adequate provision for its organization under the guidance of His apostles, He commits the task of specific construction to the spiritual body itself. He provides doctrines, sacraments, ordinances; He brings together the company of those who believe, and defines their mutual relations and their common work; He lays down the fundamental principles of Church government. But He leaves them to organize themselves, according to such models as the Jewish Church, and possibly the Hebrew or the Roman state, placed before them. While in His appointment of the twelve, and of the seventy, and in some other specific provisions, He makes place for government and for offices and officers, He chooses to lay the work of organization upon His disciples, under the direction of His Spirit, and of His commissioned representatives. The reasons for such a procedure have been noticed already; the fact is unquestionable, and in many ways is one of deep significance.

Thus the Christian Church, at the Pentecost a simple aggregation of disciples, soon became by virtue of such inherent capabilities, and under such guidance, a spiritual structure, more complete and beautiful than the Patriarchal or the Hebraic Church had ever been. The New Testament was its constitution, and whatever laws it needed from time to time, were framed by it on this divine basis. Apostolic inspiration indeed guided it, but in such manner as left free room for the exercise of a sanctified judgment on all points of detail, whether in enactment or in administration. The offices of the bishop, the pastor, the elder, the ruler, the deacon, sprang into being as they were needful; government grew progressively into shape and power. Before the close of the apostolic century, we see the Church standing forth everywhere, from Jerusalem to Rome, not always in the same form, or always under the same regulative conditions, but in all varieties a living institution,—as firmly built up on constitutional foundations as the Roman State. It was no longer an aggregate or accumulation; it was an organism, a spiritual kingdom.

As such, the power of the keys—as it is termed—was fully vested in the Church. Granted at first to Peter, and to the other apostles as in trust, this power was not to be transmitted by them to a hierarchal body of their own construction, and acting independently of the Church, but was to be transferred to the household of faith and wielded by it. Such hierarchal investiture with the right to govern the Church, from age to age, without the choice or option of the flock, is simply a prelatic fiction, never suggested in Scripture and fraught— as the history of the Papacy has shown—with immeasurable mischief. It is the Church, and the Church alone, which through such agencies or instruments as it selects, wields this sacred dominion in full responsibility to its ascended Lord. Among the forms in which this power of the keys is to be exercised by the Church, the first is the right to determine, under the direction of Scripture, the terms of admission to its circle; the second, is the right to make and to enforce all laws and regulations needful to the completeness of its organization, or to its full efficiency as an organized body; the third is the right to discipline unfaithful members, as by admonition or by withholding from them certain privileges, sacramental or otherwise, entrusted to its keeping; and the fourth is the right to purify itself whenever needful, by the expulsion of errorists or grossly unworthy persons. In general, every church has an inherent right under the guidance of the Word of God, to take whatever steps are necessary to its strengthening, its development, its perfection, as a branch of the Church of Christ among men.

And this right is vested, not in any group of officials appointed by foreign authority to act for the body, but in the body of believers themselves. Within biblical warrant they may indeed commit the exercise of this right to persons chosen for the purpose, but they can not alienate that right, or free themselves from final responsibility for the manner in which it may be wielded by their representatives. In a word, the Church is a self-governing organism; official persons, acting for it, are agents only.[1]

Hence the Church is in a true sense the Kingdom of God on earth. This phrase is variously used, both in Scripture and elsewhere. It refers sometimes to the general providence of God, as exercised in sovereignty over His earthly creation, and sometimes to His moral government as wielded over men or nations. In the sphere of grace, the phrase points sometimes to the holy sway of religion within the individual soul, or to the progressive influence of the Gospel as a sovereign force in human life, or to the ultimate triumph of God over all enemies, in the complete establisment of His gracious dominion. It is thus obvious that the Kingdom of God and the Church of Christ, whether visible or invisible, are not always synonymous in meaning or coterminous in extent. Yet in its essence the Kingdom is gracious rather than providential, and the Church is ever the central sphere within which the Kingdom becomes specially manifest. And as the sway of grace progresses in the earth, it may be anticipated that the bounding lines of the two conceptions will draw together more and more closely, until finally in the fullest sense the Kingdom and the Church will become one, with Christ as the recognized Head in providence and in moral administration, as well as in grace.

II. CHURCH GOVERNMENT DEFINED AND JUSTIFIED.—The term, government, may be defined as the regulation or constraint of individual action, by proper authority administering law in the interest of human society. It implies first of all, the existence of a community of individuals, who are to be brought into subservience to some common control. Such community involves more than casual or occasional association: government never springs into existence through transient contact, but is rather an outgrowth of fixed, enduring fellowship. There must be a society in the true sense, with recognized rights and interests, and with power to regulate individual freedom within such limits as these interests and rights may prescribe.

The existence of law, and of an authority empowered and adequate

---

[1] CUNNINGHAM; *Church Principles*, Chap. XI: Church Power. LUTHER, *Articles of Smalcald.* "The keys belong not to any man, but to the Church. Wherever the Church is, there is the right of administration, under the Gospel."—HODGE, *Church Polity*, p. 142. LYTTON; *Church of Christ*, Book III, Chap. II.

to enforce law, is also implied in the idea of government. Whatever the source from which such law may have been originally derived, or whatever the inherent qualities of the law as announced, the control exercised over the individual will and life must be a control under law. No private person becomes a law unto himself, or is a source of law to others in this connection: it is society which prescribes the principles and rules by which its members are to be controlled for its welfare. It is society also which gives form and efficiency to the authority by which law is administered and enforced. Such authority stands forth in the community as the representative both of law, and of the social force through which law is to be applied to individual life.

This general definition of government is applicable to the Church, and eminently to the Christian Church, at each of these three points. That Church is not a casual fellowship, a transient association, but a settled community, held together by a common life, and having interests and rights which it is bound to protect and to foster. It is a community existing under law,—law derived primarily from the Scripture as an authoritative source, and enjoined through the personal command of Christ as its Head, but defined and applied to each member, in the interest of all, by the community itself. It is a community divinely invested with authority to enforce its own regulations,—possessing the right to require obedience, or within certain limits to visit disobedience with discipline or punishment. Its exercise of such authority is declarative and ministerial only, but is on this account none the less significant or effective. The Church is thus, in its constitution, a government,—a spiritual community controlling its members, through the administration of scriptural law by appropriate authorities, for the furtherance of those great ends in whose interest it was divinely established.

Such church government is plainly justified by many practical considerations. It might be argued from analogy that, since government is essential to the welfare of both communities and individuals in other spheres—since both the family and the state depend largely upon it for their comfort and their usefulness, the Church needs to be organized in this form, in order to accomplish most efficiently its own spiritual ends. These ends indeed differ widely from those sought in the state or the family, and from their own nature must be differently secured. It is also obvious that in the household of faith, the principle of self-government has far wider field for action: the several members may be expected, under the consciousness of immediate responsibility to Christ as well as to His people, to control their private action with closer reference to the common good. Yet Christians do not always govern themselves wisely, or properly shape their conduct so as to secure the best interests of all; and so far as they are defective in such respects, as children in a family, they obviously need the just constraint, the regulative guidance, of the common body. What we observe in this direction in all other deparments of life, is seen to exist at least in some measure within this spiritual sphere.—This argument is strengthened by what we know respecting the social constitution of the Church, as a company of persons varying widely in sex, age, social condition, varieties of temperament, natural types of character; and therefore needing on many sides such organizing and regulating power at the center, as will transform their association into a permanent blessing to each and to all. The peculiar nature of the fellowship into which such diversified individuals and classes are introduced, adds emphasis to the demand for such governmental control. If the multiplied impulses, tastes, desires, plans of such an aggregate are to be turned to good account—if all are to be drawn into unity around the great verities of grace, and animated by the same holy affections and purposes, and fully utilized for the furtherance of the Church itself, viewed as a community, that community must assume the form of a kingdom as well as that of a family, and must robe itself as such with all rules and authorities adequate to secure these vital ends.

Contemplating government in its relations to the purity, and to the spiritual unity of the Church, the argument for its existence is still further strengthened. It is of course admitted that the chief agency in this respect lies in the purifying power of grace in the believing heart—in the hallowing and unifying influence of holy love, throbbing in the breast of each believer, and drawing all spontaneously into oneness, and into loyalty to the truth and to the common organization. Yet experience has shown that some external regulation is needed in addition to these inward forces;—that law and authority are needful to guide these inward sentiments into right and useful expression, and that the sentiments themselves grow into strength and perfectness only when they are thus trained by the experienced hand of the Christian community. The history of church organizations is conclusive here: for those which are best governed, are precisely those in which these results appear in most satisfactory form and measure.—That government is essential also to the growth of the Church, and to its success in the accomplishment of its divine mission, is another practical argument for its existence. Whether we contemplate the Church at large, or any particular church, we see at a glance that the sublime ends for which these are established, can not be effectively attained without organization—without law and authority directing the movements of each member for the general good. And on this, as on the preceding grounds, it may justly be argued that government is indispensable, as an organizing, controlling, inspiring, productive factor in church life.

III. CHURCH GOVERNMENT IN SCRIPTURE.—These general considerations in support of the right of Church government to exist, are abundantly confirmed by what we actually see of this element in the history of the Church, as recorded in the Bible. Recurring to the patriarchal period, when the Church dwelt chiefly in the family, we find Noah, Abraham, Jacob, exercising spiritual as well as natural authority in their families; Gen 18: 19. In the Hebraic Church, we find at first a strictly theocratic rule, determining both the duties of the body and the obligations of the individual, and in all cases requiring loyal obedience as a condition of membership. By degrees this right to govern is transmitted to the priesthood, and still later to the prophetic order, under a double sense of accountability, first to Jehovah, and then to His people. The law by which all were to be guided, was divinely revealed: and the functions of the religious ruler were limited to the promulgation and enforcement of that law. At length we observe the singular phenomenon of church government as thus constituted, surviving and even increasing in vigor, while the civil government first associated with it is broken down, and passes out of sight.

Under the Gospel, the fact of government is distinctly stated by our Lord, though its full realization, as we have seen, belongs to the apostolic age. While Christ more often adverts to His spiritual kingdom as a dominion within the soul (Luke 17: 20-1), or as a holy force working in human society (Matt. 13: 33), He sometimes uses the phrase with evident reference to the relation of believer to believer within the Church, and to the Church itself as a spiritual empire. We may also note here the marked passage, Matt. 18: 15-18, which as to both principle and manner, lies at the basis of all legitimate church discipline. The corresponding passage, Matt. 16: 19, illustrated by the more specific reference in John 20: 23, if we substitute the true, instead of the false or papal interpretation of the words, is a plain investiture, not of Peter as primate, or of the apostles generally, but of the Church itself with the right of government. And while, for reasons already stated, the Messiah did not proceed to organize His Church formally, with complete law, and with adequate authorities appointed by Himself, we still find church government resting essentially and firmly on what He said and did.

The apostolic teaching, based on that of our Lord, is specific and abundant. Thus we see the Christian Church, at the very outset of its career, taking on a governmental as well as a domestic form; we see it meeting in council at Jerusalem, in order to consider and determine doubtful questions; we see it in several ways exercising administrative authority, enacting laws and rules for the guidance of disciples, and assuming executive control over the movements of those who were going forth among men as its representatives. The Book of Acts is a record of spiritual administration on the part of the Church, as well as of personal activity on the part of the apostles and their associates. At a later stage, we find Paul not merely inculcating the principles by which judicial administration should be controlled, but also commanding the church at Corinth to exercise discipline, and himself assisting it in such exercise; 1 Cor. 5 and 6: 2 Cor. 2 *seq*. Both James and Peter, John and Jude, in various passages affirm the right of the Church to protect itself against the unworthy, even by disciplinary processes. Not only were saints to separate themselves from the evil; they were also authoritatively to separate the evil from them—to purify the body of Christ even by the expulsion of vicious or heretical members. Government is also indicated as a right inherent in the Church, by the numerous injunctions in the apostolic writings with regard to church work—injunctions which could not well be carried into effect without such government as a bond of organization, and as an essential condition of efficiency in service.

Two mistakes are to be guarded against, at this point. The first is the error of indifference to government,—an indifference too often exhibited in disastrous forms, especially in Protestant communions. One of these forms appears in the prevalent disregard for church discipline, with its natural consequence in the weakening and corrupting of the household of faith. Another is seen in that spirit of individualism, which is habitually regardless of prescribed modes of activity or service, and which refuses on the slightest grounds to submit to legitimate regulation and restraint. The second error appears in the assumption, so often at least implied, that government is an end in itself, rather than a divine means to the better accomplishment of other and higher ends. Thus in the papal view the Church is often regarded as existing for the sake of government—rather than government as an instrument employed by and for the Church. The natural relations are thus subverted, and what was divinely appointed as a blessing, is changed into an agent of tyrannical usurpation.

IV. VARIETIES IN CHURCH GOVERNMENT: DIVERSE POLITIES.—At this point we are confronted by the fact that, while church government is thus clearly warranted by Scripture, and while the main principles in government and the general rules for construction are so definitely laid down by our Lord, and so corroborated by both the teaching and the example of His Apostles, such government exists in the world in very wide and even antagonistic varieties. We are confronted by the further fact, that each of these varieties has claimed and is still claiming for itself special and even exclusive biblical warrant: and that the struggle between these antagonistic types on this ground, has been and still is one of the most prolific sources of conflict, schism, disaster, to the common Christianity. The question whether such a state of rupture is ever to be brought to an end—whether the divided and contesting organizations of Christendom, are ever to be harmonized and unified around this issue of government, is also one which forces itself, in many ways, upon the attention of those who believe at heart in the one, holy, catholic and apostolical Church of the Nicene Creed.

It would be a shallow and unjust view to attribute these diversities wholly to evil causes, such as the ignorance or weakness or wickedness of men. Every student of ecclesiastical history indeed knows how large a part human ambitions, human jealousies, human selfishness and sin, have played in the development of these diverse polities within the one Church of Christ on earth. Protestants point to the shameful career of the Papacy at various stages, as an illustration of this general fact; and the adherents of the primacy of Peter in turn point for like illustration to the conflicts, the disruptions, the persistent antagonisms, which have so painfully appeared in the history of Protestantism since the Reformation. But no great and permanent type of Church organization can justly be said to be a product of human sinfulness, wholly and alone.—It is also true that human ignorance, showing itself in the entire failure to see, or in the partial or distorted view of, what the Scriptures clearly reveal on this grave question, has had much to do, if not with the formation of these diverse polities, still with their development and application. Passing beyond what the Bible has plainly taught, and theorizing for themselves on what they suppose to be scriptural indications, men have often gone widely, disastrously astray, even where the desire and the purpose were not unworthy. Human weakness, likewise, as well as human ignorance, has had at times much to do with these ecclesiastical growths: it has yielded too often where resistance was needful: it has too often suffered human ambition, or a misguided zeal, to introduce what stronger convictions, firmer religious principle, would have constrained it to resist.

Yet broader and higher causes must be recognized in conjunction with these, in order to the adequate explanation of these remarkable diversities. Some of these causes are natural, social, political. There are men, for illustration, whose mental tendencies incline them strongly toward a monarchal, or toward a democratic form of government, first in the state and then in the church; and whose preferences, readily seizing upon whatever biblical material may be found to justify these natural tendencies, lead them to frame church constitutions and regulations according to such personal predilections. There are also social influences and usages, as seen in the general arrangements of society, which predispose men toward corresponding arrangements, so far as the Scripture permits, within the household and kingdom of grace. Especially is it true that political principles and institutions,—the forms of civil government, the theory and practice of legal administration, the varieties of public office and station—have had much to do with a corresponding construction of the Church. That the Roman State, for example, with its multiplied officials, its elaborate rulings, its legal pomp and domination, affected largely the shaping of the Church long before Leo I. became the imperial Pope of Rome, and still more decisively from the date of his accession down to the Reformation, is a fact too obvious to be questioned. The general rule which ecclesiastical history at many points suggests, is that, wherever monarchy prevails in the state, a monarchal development appears in the Church, and wherever a democracy exists, the Church tends to become democratic. Is it not just to recognize deeper causes of this class as conspiring with human ignorance, weakness, sin, in producing the varieties of government we are contemplating?

Is it not possible also, that some reasons for such variety may be found in the Scripture itself, and in the nature of Christianity, viewed as a free and expansive faith, having the world as its area, and destined to include all classes and degrees of humanity within its governmental control? In one aspect, Christianity is obviously a monarchal system—a purely royal religion; in another it is essentially democratic—a spiritual republic. But the kingship of Christ, and the brotherhood of believers, are to some extent antithetic principles; and their practical application, as regulative guides in ecclesiastical construction, may result in either a monarchy or a republic, or in a blending of both in varying proportions. Moreover, the Hebraic Church, though it was the natural model of the Christian, and though it gave definite form to the earlier Jewish churches at the outset, could not well have been carried in its original type, and with its marked Jewish features, into Gentile countries, and made the authoritative norm of the numerous churches springing up in Western Asia and Eastern Europe, in states of society wholly unlike that in which it originated. It is at least certain that such a process could not have been carried on, without either a direct and positive command from our Lord Himself, or the inspired and authoritative word of His apostles. But no such command or word, clear, imperative, sovereign, appears in the New Testament. As has been intimated already, our Lord seems to have left the matter of organization very much in abeyance. Neither have the apostles so fully defined their conception, as to make imperative one unvarying and fully authoritative mode of construction for all lands and times. Are we not therefore justified in the general conclusion, that as in the mode of baptism, and in some other particulars, some variety of usage existed under the apostolic warrant, and is therefore still admissible under the authority of the common Gospel? And would it not be a vast advance toward the peaceful settlement of many controverted questions in church polity, if such a measure of freedom were recognized as vested in each and every church, under the supreme action of those general principles of organization which are plainly stated in the revealed Word?

Without discussing the questions thus raised, or attempting any full solution of this difficult problem of diversity, we may pass on to a very brief consideration of the particular varieties of polity exhibited in the history of the Christian Church. These may be thrown broadly into two general classes: government by the priestly orders, government by the church. Government by the priestly orders exists in two leading varieties, the hierarchal and the prelatic. Government by the church also exists in two leading varieties, the democratic and the representative. Four distinct conceptions of church government thus make their appearance historically in Christendom, though rarely without some degree of admixture with antithetic elements. A brief glance at each of these, as they present themselves historically, may now be taken.

V. THE PAPAL POLITY: ITS POSITION AND CLAIM.—This hierarchal variety of government by the priestly orders, as distinguished from the body of believers, may be briefly described.[1] It maintains in general that the Church of Christ on earth was intended to be one and indivisible,—a visible organization having a recognized center, a central power, one code of laws, one belief, and one mode of worship. It maintains that this one Catholic Church was authoritatively established by Christ and His apostles, has survived and flourished from the apostolic age down to our own time, and is destined thus to live and prosper till all oppositions are overthrown, and the Christian world is brought into tributary allegiance. It maintains that Rome is the divinely chosen center and seat of this Church; that the Pope of Rome is its proper head and sovereign, acting as vicegerent of Christ on earth; that it is given to him to determine its doctrine, worship, and laws, and that obedience is to be paid to him by the faithful throughout the world. It maintains that beneath the Pope, in whose hands

---

[1] The following Catholic authorities may be consulted: MOEHLER, on *Symbolism*; KENRICK, on *The Primacy*; DOLLINGER, *The Church and the Churches*. Also NEWMAN and MANNING.

the scepter of spiritual sovereignty is thus placed, there are inferior orders and classes of clergy, existing by scriptural warrant, to whom spiritual grace is entrusted, and by whom, under accountability to the supreme pontiff, the Church is to be instructed and governed. It maintains that the government of the Church has from the beginning been vested in these priestly orders, and is legitimately wielded by them; and that this is the polity directly and exclusively prescribed in the Word of God. No other mode of government has any scriptural basis or justification, and all churches organized on any other basis are not churches in the biblical sense, but are schismatical, revolutionary, and worthy of condemnation. Wide diversities of opinion exist within this general definition, as with reference to the degree of authority vested in popes and councils respectively, and the rights and prerogatives of inferior and superior clergy. But all agree in the fundamental position, that government as to spiritual things belongs, not to the private Christian, or to the particular congregation, but to the hierarchy, and in the last resort to the reigning pontiff sitting as supreme ruler over the entire household and kingdom of grace.

The arguments advanced in support of this theory of church government are of three classes: scriptural, historical and philosophical.— The scriptural argument starts with the promise of the primacy, said to be found in John 1: 42, as explained in Matt. 16: 17–19, and further illustrated in Luke 22: 31–32. In these passages, we find, it is alleged, a marked prominence given to Peter at the time of his selection to be an apostle: we find in his name and in his personal declaration of faith, evidence that in his own person as a believer he was to be the rock on which the Church should afterward be built: we find in the investiture with the keys of church authority, an indication that such authority was to be entrusted to him and to his successors to the end of time: we find in the further commission to strengthen his brethren, direct proof that he was to be set above them as their teacher and guide, and in like manner was to be ultimately the teacher and guide of the whole Church. The promise thus given was verified, after the resurrection of the Lord, in the formal appointment of Peter, John 21: 15–17, with a supreme commission to feed, protect and keep the flock of Christ. Corroborating evidence is supposed to be found in the general place held by Peter, sometimes with James and John as associates, at the head of the apostolic circle. The actual exercise of this primacy began at once, after the ascension, as is evident in the first, and the succeeding chapters in the Acts of the Apostles: Acts 1: 15, 2: 14, 3: 1, 15: 7, and other illustrations. Further evidence as to the primacy appears in Gal. 1: 18, 1 Peter 5: 1: and in verse 13, where Peter speaks as bishop of the Church at Rome, the mystical

Babylon. It is further alleged that these evidences that Peter was set at the head of the apostolic group, and was made the central personage and head of the Church, with full authority to wield the power of the keys, and to transmit that power at his decease to others, are conclusive as to the intention of the great Head of the Church. And further, that this primacy was never questioned either by the other apostles or by the primitive Church, but remained as an unchallenged institute at the very origin of Christianity, and became a law of construction by which the Church is to be forever bound. In further illustration, it is said that the Catholic Church follows exactly the model furnished by the Jewish Church;—that the pope is in the latter substantially what the high priest was in the former: that the inferior clergy correspond with the Mosaic orders of priest and Levite: and that the authority vested in the clergy under the Gospel, is essentially the same authority which was exercised by the Old Testament priesthood. On these scriptural grounds it is maintained that the Roman Catholic is the only truly biblical Church.

The historical and philosophical arguments adduced in support of this conclusion may be briefly summarized. It is alleged, that the early Fathers interpreted these passages concerning the promise and institution of the primacy as the Church of Rome now interprets them, and that Peter was always, in fact, held in special reverence by the primitive Church as chief among the Apostles:—that reliable tradition, as well as the reference in 1 Peter 5: 13, shows the apostle to have been the first bishop of Rome:—that the Roman see was regarded on this account, even from the first century, as having special authority on all questions of faith and order:—that, as the field of Christendom extended, this supremacy was more and more freely accorded, until we find at length the papal authority fully and freely exercised wherever the Church was planted: and that, with the exception of the Eastern and of the Protestant schism, this sway has actually been wielded, by universal consent, from the earliest centuries down to our own time. Such are the main lines of historical evidence adduced.—The philosophical argument rests chiefly on certain considerations relating to the historic continuity, to the compact and elaborate adjustments, to the peculiar solidarity, and to the efficiency and majestic sway of the Papal Church,—especially as noted in contrast with the opposite weaknesses alleged to exist in the multiplied and antagonistic forms of Protestantism. That Church, it is affirmed, approaches much more nearly than these Protestant organizations to the ideal set forth in the Bible, and corresponds more exactly to our highest dreams as to the Church of the future. While Protestantism reveals only a fragmentary and desultory life, the Church of Rome, which is none other than the

Church Catholic or Universal, reveals a degree of unity, of strength, of capability, which on philosophical grounds justifies the conclusion that it is the Church, the only Church, of Christ among men. Its claim to universal allegiance is therefore unquestionable, imperative, supreme: all refusal to yield such allegiance is schismatical and sinful, and must bring the soul into condemnation.

VI. THE PAPAL POLITY CONSIDERED.—The answer of evangelical Protestantism to these claims is clear and strong. Reverting to the scriptural argument, we may note, first, the incorrect interpretation of the crucial passages named, with reference to the promise of the primacy. Thus, when Peter was styled the rock, in connection with his notable confession, our Lord clearly referred to the confession itself, and to the spirit of trust which led to it, and commended these, rather than the personality of Peter, as the basis on which His Church was to be established. He praised the firmness, the endurance, the sublime confidence shown by the Apostle, and declared that all acceptable belief in Him must exhibit these qualities. This is illustrated in the place given to such loyal confession in the apostolic letters: Rom. 10: 9-10, Eph. 2: 20, 1 Cor. 3: 10: also Acts 4: 10-12, 8: 37, as examples. Again, so far as the power of the keys, or of ecclesiastical authority, is concerned, we find that what was entrusted to Peter in Matt. 16: 19, was in like terms entrusted to all the apostles in John 20: 23, and to the Church as a body, Matt. 18: 18. It is also obvious that the other apostles were shepherds of the flock as truly as Peter, through authority derived not from him, but directly from Christ himself: Peter recognizes this in his exhortation to all elders of the Church, whether apostles or otherwise, 1 Peter 5: 1. Again, his commission to strengthen his brethren, after he had passed through the painful experiences connected with his denial of Christ, is nothing more than an injunction to fraternal fidelity, such as frequently appear in more general form in the Epistles. Nor can anything more be made of the prominence assumed by Peter, either while Christ lived, or afterward, as described in the earlier portions of the Book of Acts, than an exhibition of those qualities of temperament and age which made him a leader in the apostolic group even while our Lord lived,— a leadership which, however conspicuous, nowhere presents itself in the aspect of an official primacy.

Very much may be quoted from the New Testament in direct antagonism to the papal claim. Thus, our Lord, on various occasions, plainly discountenanced the idea of gradation among the apostles (Mark 9: 33-37), and rebuked the desire for eminence which He discovered among them: Matt. 20: 20-27. His rebukes to Peter, for his inconsiderate forwardness, are especially frequent: as in immediate conjunction with the alleged promise of the primacy, Matt. 16: 23, and again in connection with the washing of the feet of the disciples, John 13: 6–10, and again with the rash affirmation of fidelity, just before the denial, Luke 22: 31–34. The denial itself, as faithfully recorded by the other three evangelists, and referred to by John, stands out in very strange contrast with the papal assumption; and the relations of this event to the subsequent history, and especially to the noted interview at the Sea of Galilee, lead us to a very different conclusion from that which Romanism has drawn from the inspired narratives. We search in vain through the records of the Acts for any clear sign of an official primacy, either claimed by Peter, or assigned to him by either the apostles or the Church. His place in the events of the period is habitually that of an equal among equals: while he leads in the proclamation of the Gospel outside of the circle of Judaism, he shares this work almost from the first with Paul, who finally becomes the chief apostle to the Gentiles: among the Jewish churches, he in like manner shares the control with James, and indeed with the apostles generally; Acts 15: 22, Gal. 1: 18–19. We should also note here the conflict in judgment and authority between Paul and Peter, recorded in Gal. 2: 11–14: and in which Peter was to be blamed, for the manifestation of the same moral weakness which had appeared so painfully in the denial itself. Setting all these glimpses of the career of the apostle over against those quoted in proof of his primacy, we can be led to no other conclusion than that this alleged primacy, and the vast fabric of priestly usurpation which has been built upon it, are without adequate warrant in the Word of God.

Protestantism rejects as inadequate both the biblical and the traditional evidence with regard to the asserted bishopric of Peter at Rome. Whether the obscure passage, 1 Peter 5: 13, refers to the literal Babylon in Chaldea, or to Jerusalem as the spiritual Babylon, or to some smaller place bearing this name, or to Rome itself viewed as the mystical Babylon, it affords no distinct evidence that Peter had given up his apostolic function, and assumed that of a Christian bishop, at Rome or elsewhere. The tradition that he was martyred there rests on foundations equally slight. Nor is the testimony of the Fathers as to this point, or as to the primacy in general, or to the apostolic eminence of Peter, either harmonious in itself, or in the aggregate in any high sense conclusive. It is freely admitted that, after a long period of progressive departure from the simplicity of the primitive era, and after protracted struggle among rival bishops claiming supremacy in Christendom, Rome won the victory, and became and remained in the West, the visible center and seat of supreme ecclesiastical power. But this development, as Protestantism maintains, was unscriptural, abnormal, and injurious to the best interests of Christianity, and is on these grounds to be rejected as illicit. The claim of Romanists to an unbroken oneness is far from being warranted by facts; both the violent separation from the Eastern Church, the revolutionary schisms within the Papacy, and the later revolt of Protestantism, disprove the claim. We set the Reformed doctrine of a spiritual unity, at least partially verified among the Protestant communions, over against this conception of an outward organic oneness, and claim that the highest illustrations of true biblical unity, are found in such communions even in their present disparted condition, rather than within the fold of Rome. What is claimed for the completeness in organization, the efficiency, the power and majesty of the Catholic Church, however true, by no means proves that the polity of that Church is either scriptural or on philosophic grounds desirable. Deeper insight leads to quite the opposite conclusion; and the present attitude of the Papacy toward personal rights, toward civil liberty, toward progress in thought and in spiritual experience, is painful evidence against both the polity and the priestly despotism planted upon it. On these grounds, evangelical Protestantism, in all its varieties, rejects the hierarchy as, if not an unbiblical excrescence upon Christianity, still a type of government in which human elements, subtle and corrupting, have too largely perverted an institution of God into an instrumentality of man. While its polity is not the worst feature in the Papal communion, that polity, taking away from the people their prescriptive rights, and setting up instead a government of the priesthood, and for the priesthood, must ever be condemned at the tribunal of a free and spiritual Christianity.[1]

---

[1] The question whether the papal polity is unscriptural, should never be confounded with the broader and more complicated question, whether the Roman Catholic Church is to be regarded as a branch of the Church of Christ. For it is conceivable that a true Church may be organized upon a false ecclesiastical basis, and that such a Church may retain its essential faith, its spiritual quality, even though it be iniquitously governed. It is conceivable also that a true Church may exist, even where its essential faith has been overlaid with many human accretions, and where formalizing tendencies, corrupting usages, and the like, have seriously burdened or impaired its spiritual life. On the ground of such distinctions, Protestant writers have largely abandoned the older position, that the Church of Rome is a synagogue of Satan—in head and members an embodied Antichrist, and have simply condemned the papal polity, and the embodied papacy, as being a conspicuous form of that Antichrist to which Paul in his letters to the Thessalonians so vividly refers. When it is remembered how much of saving truth is retained in the Romish communion, and what measure of religious influence that communion wields in the world, and what multitudes of sincere believers are embraced within it, utter condemnation of the body, *capite et membris*, seems a serious departure from the crowning law of Christian charity. See Hodge, Ch., *Theol.* III; 822. *Church Polity*, 205-210. Smith, II. B., *Life*; appendix A.

VII. THE PRELATIC POLITY: ITS CLAIM OUTLINED.—Viewing Prelatism in general, without reference to specific varieties or shadings, we may observe that, while it rejects the Romish conception of the papacy as unwarranted by Scripture, and injurious to the Church, it still retains in substance the papal view as to the inherent right of the clergy to govern the household of faith. It harmonizes, in other words, with the hierarchal rather than with the democratic or representative theory of government of the Church, by and for the Church. It holds, with the papist, that the apostolate was designed to be a permanent office, and was in fact perpetuated from the apostolic age, under the title of bishop, and with the apostolic functions and prerogatives essentially embodied in it. It claims that this transmitted oversight and control of the churches, in particular districts or dioceses, was a characteristic feature in church management from the beginning, and that it stands forth, under direct apostolic sanction, as the only authorized mode of ecclesiastical administration, for all succeeding times. It also joins substantially with the papist in affirming the existence, by scriptural warrant, of two subordinate orders of clergy, priests and deacons, to whom certain powers and duties are assigned, and who possess, under the episcopal jurisdiction, the right to share in church government. With the papacy, it maintains further that these three orders, existing by divine right as revealed in the Bible, are essential to the proper constitution of the Christian Church, and consequently that no religious organization can be regarded as a church in the full sense, unless it is thus constituted. In some of its varieties, Prelatism admits that certain prerogatives, such as the choice of those who may hold position in the particular church, are properly vested in the laity: but as a rule, it reserves the function of government essentially to the clergy, as of divine right, independently of the people. In some varieties, it also admits the right of the laity to a voice in respect to church doctrine and canon, and to general administration, but still strenuously exalts the clergy into special prominence as an independent order, with a threefold classification, with prescriptive rights and a special investiture of dignities, not accorded to them by the people, but conferred on them in the New Testament, and by apostolic decision and precedent. In some varieties of prelatic polity these claims as to those holding the office of bishop are greatly modified, and that office is viewed as little more than a judicious mode of oversight and administration,—the authority reverting chiefly to the two remaining orders, or to the body of believers.

Prelatism, as thus outlined, claims for itself a distinct biblical and historical warrant. This warrant is derived partly from the analogy of the Mosaic priesthood, with its three distinctive classes, severally invested by divine appointment with certain inherent rights and prerogatives. It is held that this arrangement was intended to typify and introduce the form of government, which God designed to establish in the Christian Church. It is held also that, when Christ organized that Church during His own life, the three orders were preserved by Him, He being Himself the great High Priest, while the apostles and the seventy corresponded to the priests and the Levites respectively. It is further held that, when our Lord ascended, He made provision for a continued triplicity by the advancement of the second and third classes to fill the vacancies made by His departure, and by the appointment of the diaconate as a third body of subordinate clergy. And as the apostles thus became primates in the Church, vested with peculiar jurisdiction and oversight in the place of the Master Himself, they were authorized to fill vacancies in their own number, or to increase that number, as occasion should arise. As Paul was supernaturally commissioned, and as Matthias was supernaturally selected under apostolic direction, to serve in this bishopric, so Timothy and Titus and others were chosen and set apart by the apostles themselves for like service; and thus abundant provision was made for the preservation of this apostolic office in the Church to the end of time. It is maintained that such preservation has in fact occurred, and that bishops as a class, separated by certain vested peculiarities from all other ministers, and empowered supremely to rule within and over the Church, are an essential requisite to a scriptural organization of the body of Christ. It is held also that this interpretation of Scripture was generally accepted and endorsed by the early Fathers: and that, as the primitive Church took on maturer form, the episcopate, if not at first universally established, came to be the universal feature of organized Christianity. Both the Eastern and the Western Church, it is alleged, were thus prelatic in structure, long before the struggle among leading bishops—the metropolitans and archbishops and patriarchs, each jealous for his own dignities—eventuated in the supremacy of the papacy at Rome. It is maintained that the institution of the papacy, being a departure from the scriptural model, did not annul the antecedent episcopacy, and that the latter, being faithfully transmitted from century to century, remained, and continues to be, the authorized mode of polity for the Church throughout the world. By some advocates, it is admitted that the distinction between bishops and presbyters, or the ordinary clergy, did not exist at first, and was not universal during the apostolic age, but gradually came into existence as an authoritative development from the biblical germ. It is admitted by others that no such distinction exists now, in the nature of the office; and that the administration of government by bishops is in large degree a provisional arrangement for the better guidance and control of the Church, and is therefore prelatic in form, but representative and democratic in substance.¹ On the latter basis, this polity is strongly defended on philosophic grounds, as furnishing a wise and just and effective form of government,—one which protects the Church against the agitations and disruptions to which bodies not thus organized are subject,—one which harmonizes well with the best existing varieties of civil rule, and which naturally attracts to itself the finest elements in society, and is in close affinity with the highest types of Christian civilization.

VIII. PRELATISM EXAMINED.—With the modified forms of the prelatic polity just described, no broad scriptural or historical issue is requisite. It is the Prelatism which allies itself with the Papacy and with oriental Christianity, in holding that goverment is a function of

---

¹ The fiction of a direct apostolical succession, verified by historic records, with no gap at any point, is now abandoned by most Anglican authorities, though long maintained as the only ground on which the prelatic polity can stand. More moderate advocates hold that such a demonstrated transmission is not essential: that the episcopal office justifies itself rather on general grounds as an ancient and biblical institution: that it has been widely and happily recognized during the progress of Christianity: and that, although the polity based upon it may not be the only one authorized in Scripture, it is still the polity best adapted to secure the interests and advancement of the Church. It is admitted by most authorities of this class that there was originally no distinction in office indicated by the terms, bishop and presbyter, and that the distinction which appeared later was rather an outgrowth of experience, than the carrying out of a strict biblical injunction : LIGHTFOOT, *Commentary on Philippians:* Essay on the Christian Ministry. STANLEY, *Christian Institutions:* Chap. x. Essentially the same general view is advocated by JACOB, *Eccl. Polity of the New Test:* and HATCH, *Organization of the Early Christian Churches.* This is a significant departure from the Romish and the Oriental dogma, which maintains, not only the original distinction in office, but also the historic transmission, the transfusion of apostolic grace, and the original and supreme jurisdiction, as essential features of the episcopate. The Church is in the Bishop, is the apothegm of Cyprian, and substantially this is the doctrine of the hierarchal school generally. On this basis the ordination of ministers otherwise than through the bishop, is invalid, and persons so ordained have no proper claim to the ministerial office in any grade, neither can any church constituted in any other way be a true Church of Christ : PALMER, *Church of Christ,* Part VI: The Episcopate. LYTTON, *Church of Christ:* Origin of the Ministerial Function. BLUNT, *Dict. of Doct. and Hist. Theol:* art. Apostolical Succession, and others. In the Methodist Episcopal communions, the office is regarded as neither hierarchal nor in a strict sense diocesan, but rather as a ministerial function or mode of service, justified by the uses it subserves, and not contrary to Scripture : POPE, *Christian Theology:* Vol. III: p. 358. Such is essentially the position of several other Protestant communions, organized more or less fully on the prelatic basis. The Reformed Episcopal Church, for illustration, adheres to the episcopate, not as an institution of divine right, but as a very ancient and desirable form of Church polity: see *Declaration of Principles.*

the clergy rather than a prerogative of the people,—which claims that the episcopate is the only form of polity revealed in the Bible, and is the only legitimate basis of Church organization,—which regards all ordination other than episcopal as invalid, and pronounces schismatical and sectarian all other varieties of administration, against which on many grounds, biblical and otherwise, earnest protest must be made by the adherents of free, popular, effective Christianity.

While it is admitted that the Jewish Church stood forth everywhere within the bounds of Judaism as the natural norm of the new Church to be organized in Christ, we find no suggestion in Scripture of any such close imitation of the offices and methods of the former, as is implied in the parallel on which Prelacy so largely rests its claim. Christ was to be, not merely during His earthly life, but perpetually, the Head of His Church; nor have we any evidence in His own words that He intended at His decease to set up a body of representative men, who should be authorized to act henceforth as His vicars on earth, above and over His Church. If there were any such evidence, it would be an inevitable conclusion from it, that He who had chosen the twelve to this distinction, had also chosen one among the twelve to be their ruler—the high priest and vicegerent of the whole Church in His stead. Neither is there any proof of a transfusion of apostolic grace, or of a supernatural investiture of priestly dignities, which were in turn, by a process quite outside of the Church as an organism, to be transmitted to certain chosen successors, and by them to others, who were to be high priests and apostles at once to the Church for all coming time. The biblical proof that such transmission actually occurred, as in the case of Timothy and Titus, and others who are called apostles or bishops or overseers, is wholly inadequate. The apostolate of Paul, and that of Matthias—if he actually filled the apostolic office—supply no proper parallel. It is doubtful whether Timothy ever resided permanently at Ephesus, where he is presumed to have been bishop: he appears far more often in other places and relations: Acts 17: 15, 18: 5, 19: 22, 20: 4, in connection with 1 Tim. 1: 3, 2 Tim. 4: 9, 13. In respect to Titus, asserted to be first bishop of Crete, a similar uncertainty exists: Titus 3: 12. As to Barnabas, styled an apostle, in Acts 14: 14: to Epaphroditus referred to in Phil. 2: 25: to Silvanus, associated with Paul and Timothy as an apostle, in 1 Thess. 2: 6: and to Andronicus and Junia, or Junias, called apostles in Rom. 16: 7: or to the angels, or apostles, of the seven Asiatic churches, we really find nothing that warrants in any high degree the conclusion that any one of these persons was ever ordained to a special apostolic service, or was ever recognized by the Church as a legitimate successor of the original Twelve. The special function of the original group, as witnesses to the great facts of the Messiahship was, as we have already seen, an untransmissible function: by the nature of the case these later converts could not have discharged it. And so far as the general oversight of the Church was concerned, we have on the one side no clear evidence that the apostles were one and all bishops, and on the other side abundant proof that not merely the persons named, but others also, shared with the twelve in the great task of organizing and governing the nascent Church. In this work the bishop and the presbyter were one and the same; and as bishops or presbyters, the apostles stood on entire equality with their official brethren, except so far as the possession of supernatural charisms, and especially the gift of inspiration, gave them peculiar, though temporary eminence. In the New Testament, as candid and competent scholarship now admits, no distinction such as is claimed for prelacy, appears at any point. It is needful only to add that the inspired record of the institution of the diaconate conclusively shows this to have been in no sense a priestly, but rather an administrative office, such as a layman might fill: and on this side also, the dogma of a threefold ministry fails to justify itself at the bar of Scripture. The analogy sometimes drawn from the appointment of the seventy (Luke 10: 1) in no degree justifies the counter claim.[1]

It is freely admitted that as we pass beyond the apostolic period, traces of defined episcopacy begin to make their appearance: that during the second and third centuries these traces still increase in number and prominence, and that this increase continues in both the East and the West, until in the fifth century the long evolutionary process culminates in the patriarchate at Constantinople, and in the papacy at Rome. But we may justly ask whether this was a legitimate and healthful outgrowth from the germs planted, the principles prescribed, the spirit inculcated by our Lord and registered in the inspired Word? The argument for the prelacy, like that for the primacy, fails disastrously at this point. The process described has in it too many human elements, is too much a growth of pride and ambition rather than of grace, and is too obviously a movement away from the cardinal law of Christian equality, and from the doctrine of church right and church power laid down in the Epistles, to be contemplated with favor. What we really see in it is a humanizing tendency—a disposition to bring the Church into closer affiliation with the imperial Roman state: a tendency and disposition repressed at first by the teaching of Christ and the apostles,—repressed also by the prevalent spirit of the early Christians, by the outward condition of the Church, and

---

[1] For a full, and effective, argument on these biblical questions, see COLEMAN, *Manual on Prelacy and Ritualism:* Ch. VI, especially. Also, BARNES, *Apostolic Church.*

by the persecutions often raging; but at length breaking forth, especially in the great municipal centers, and affecting more and more the general feeling, until it reached its acme at last, not in diocesan prelacy, but in a hierarchal papacy, wholly at variance with both the letter and the spirit of the New Testament.

Nor is the historical argument for prelacy improved, but rather weakened, by every further trace of its development, down through medieval into modern life. Even where the prevalent tendencies inspired by the Reformation, and native to the mind of Northern Europe, have kept it largely in check, the prelatic spirit has not justified itself in the deepest convictions of that multitude of the faithful who, in the phrase of Savanarola, constitute the true Church. Though sustained by state authorities, and affiliating by a natural impulse with the monarchal rather than the democratic principle, it can not be said to have held its own, when tried at the bar of Christian intelligence and experience. The admissions made by many of its most eminent advocates as to its lack of distinct biblical warrant, are suggestive at this point; and their general plea for it on the ground of its beneficent working and influence as an ancient and efficient scheme of church organization, is one which requires large modification. Yet these objections are not to be urged too strongly, in view of all that a modified and liberal episcopacy, sympathizing spiritually with the people, has wrought—especially in English history. And where such episcopacy is regarded, not as an order with hierarchal powers, but as a mode of ecclesiastical organization, having the good of the people as its aim; and where the propriety of other modes of organization are admitted, and other Christian communions are acknowledged to be true Churches of Jesus Christ, opposition to this system may well yield its strenuousness, and may even be changed into cordial esteem.

IX. INDEPENDENCY: ITS GENERAL POSITION.—We pass at this point from the hierarchal to the popular type,—from government by the clergy in their own right, to government of the people, by and for the people. And as in the former type two varieties appeared, the papal and the prelatic, so in the latter we find two distinct varieties, the democratic and the representative. It is not to be assumed that these two varieties exist always in pure or unmixed form; they are often interblended practically, for the obvious reason that as to their underlying and regulative principles, they belong to one and the same class. Of these two varieties, we may consider first the purely democratic, under the title of Independency.[1]

---

[1] Authorities to be consulted here: ROBINSON, J., *Works*; MATHER, C., *Ratio Disciplinæ* and *Magnalia*; PUNCHARD, *View of Congregationalism*; DEXTER, H. M., *Congregationalism*; HYDE, J. T., *New Catechism*, 42.

In this form of polity, the autonomy of the particular church or congregation is affirmed as the fundamental principle in church government. It maintains that only true believers, with their families, have any right to a place in the household of faith: and that this divine household is fully empowered to judge of the qualifications of all persons seeking fellowship with it. It holds that every company of believers, in such number as can conveniently assemble together, and are by mutual consent organized for this purpose, is an independent Church, vested with absolute right and held under inalienable obligation to govern itself, under a supreme responsibility to Christ alone. It affirms that the principles to be regarded in such government are fully laid down in the Scriptures; that the interpretation and application of these principles belong to the particular organization; and that in the act of governing itself on this basis, every such organization is to be controlled by no human authority outside of itself, whether ecclesiastical or political. It further affirms that but two classes of officers are described in the New Testament, the minister and the deacon; it regards the diaconate as essentially an administrative office, concerned with the charities and external interests of the church chiefly; it repudiates the doctrine of more than a single order or class of ministers, and refuses to the clergy any influence or control in government beyond what may belong to them as members in the particular church. In general, it defines a church as a voluntary association of persons professing godliness, and bound together in holy covenant, to which full ecclesiastical power is directly committed, exclusive of all foreign jurisdiction—an organization wholly free and independent in itself.

Such was the original doctrine of the Brownist or strictly Independent party in England with whom this type of polity, in its modern form, may be said to have originated. Two important modifications have appeared in more recent times: the first recognizing the propriety of committing the government of the church, in part at least, to representative persons chosen from the body for this purpose: the second, affirming the duty of fellowship among the churches, in conjunction with this autonomy of the particular church. The worth of the former modification will be considered in another connection. To the latter, the system of Congregationalism, as distinguished from strict Independency, owes its origin. The fundamental position is well defined in the Cambridge Platform: Although churches be distinct, and may not be confounded one with another; and equal, and therefore have not dominion one over another; yet all churches ought to preserve church communion, one with another, because they are all united unto Christ, not only as a mystical, but as a political Head, whence is derived a communion suitable thereto. The modes in which this correlative duty of fellowship finds expression, are ecclesiastical councils for the solution of specific questions, local or provincial conferences meeting statedly for the consideration of common interests, and general or ecumenical assemblages, convened for the contemplation of issues, doctrinal and ecclesiastical, in which all the churches organized on this basis are alike concerned. The action of such associated bodies is held to be strictly advisory or declarative, and therefore may not directly control the administration of any particular church: still the important principle is here admitted, that all particular churches are in fact one Church, because they are spiritually united together in Christ, as their mystical and their political Head.

This variety of polity claims for itself a definite, if not an exclusive, biblical warrant. The Cambridge Platform, following the Brownist leading, and the spirit of the age, declared that the parts of church government are all of them exactly described in the Word of God, and that it is not the province of man to add or diminish or alter anything in the least measure therein. The Scriptural argument as generally presented, may be condensed in the following propositions: that the matter, or material, of a church is saints only, Rom. 1: 7, 1 Cor. 1: 2, Phil. 1: 1–7: that the form is one organized body politic, 1 Cor. 12: 12, 20, 27, Eph. 2: 20–22: that the quantity to be included is as many as can meet in any one place, Acts 2: 1, 5: 12, 14: 27, 1 Cor. 14: 28: that the power of government is vested wholly in the church itself, Matt. 18: 17–19, 1 Cor. 5: 4–7, Rev. 2 and 3: that the only officers authorized are ministers and deacons, Acts 6: 1–6, 15: 23, Phil. 1: 1, Eph. 4: 11–12: and that the choice of officers rests exclusively with the church itself, Acts 1: 15–26, 6: 2–7, 14: 23, and other passages. It is held that this was the constitution of the apostolic churches; that the term, church, is nowhere used except with reference to the single congregation; and that the plural, churches, is invariably employed to describe the congregations of a given region. It is held that the only fellowship recognized among these churches in the apostolic age, was by advisory councils such as that convened at Jerusalem; and that these councils were never empowered to exercise formal jurisdiction in any way over the particular household of faith. It is also held that, in the earlier history of Christianity, after the apostolic century, this was the authorized and exclusive mode of church organization: and that the later modes, as the episcopal and papal, were unwarrantable departures from the scriptural model, in the interest of human pride and ambition. Independency thus claims historic as well as biblical warrant, and on this ground asserts its right to be regarded as the only proper mode of church organization. Many of its advocates lay great stress on its intrinsic equity, on its harmony with human rights and with free and just government, on its influence as an element in spiritual culture, and on its efficiency in producing an intelligent, active, earnest, useful church life. With a large proportion of its adherents in our time, considerations of this class have greater weight than the biblical argument itself,—especially where the legitimacy of other modes is admitted, by the recognition of churches so organized as being true parts or divisions of the one Church of Christ.

X. THE CLAIMS OF INDEPENDENCY REVIEWED.—Many of the general positions here taken, may be accepted in substance by those who are opposed to what has been denominated the hierarchal type of church government. All who are neither papist nor prelatist, agree in rejecting the fiction of the three orders, and in maintaining the absolute parity of the Christian ministry. They agree in ascribing to the Church, and even to each congregation, the right to govern itself, so far as this is set over against the assumed right of the clergy to govern, in virtue of a divine appointment and independently of responsibility to the household of faith. They also agree in affirming the duty of every member in that household to share either personally or representatively in its administration, and to associate himself responsibly with the church life and work. In a word, all who are neither papist nor prelatist, agree substantially in regarding the Church of God on earth, not as an empire or an oligarchy, but rather as a spiritual democracy,—a holy brotherhood of saints, in which the principle of equality is the fundamental law, and in which those who rule, in whatever station, are still the servants of all, in the name of Christ.

Yet most who hold these general positions, fail to find, either in history or in Scripture, sufficient basis for the claim of Independency in the exclusive form urged by many of its adherents. It is admitted that, if we go back beyond the period when the papacy rose into supremacy, or the earlier period when episcopacy was the prevalent polity, we find simpler modes of church organization in existence, conforming at some points to this purely democratic conception. It may also be admitted that, especially among the Gentile congregations, exact uniformity did not prevail, and that in some of them clear approaches to strict democracy are apparent. Some of the allusions in the Book of Acts, and also in the Epistles, certainly justify this admission. But beyond this it is clearly impossible to go. The presumption that a pure democracy was at once established, in every instance where a church was organized, whether on Gentile or on Jewish soil—that one uniform mode was inflexibly followed, in whatever form of civil society, and without regard to the antecedent experience or culture of those uniting in the organization; and especially that a type of government which had literally no representative, or even suggestion among the civil governments then existing, and which neither the Jewish believer trained in the synagogue system, nor the Gentile believer disciplined under the imperial sway of Rome, could possibly have comprehended at the outset, was invariably instituted wherever Christianity was carried, is certainly one which it is difficult for any mind that appreciates these conditions even to entertain. To assume that such a pure democracy was thus everywhere introduced, and enforced as the fundamental law of church construction, is a step which nothing but the clearest, most positive and unquestionable affirmations of the New Testament could warrant.

More specifically, the following objections to the claim of Independency may justly be urged: First, if we set aside so much of the biblical teaching as is held by the adherents of the representative, in common with the adherents of this democratic theory, the remainder is found to be too casual and too slight to sustain the extensive fabric of inferences based upon it. The assertion of the Cambridge Platform as to the fullness and exactness of the inspired testimonies, is far from being verified by facts. That the particular churches in Jerusalem, in Antioch, in Ephesus, in Rome, and wherever else the Gospel was embraced, were in each and every case organized on this purely independent basis, with ministers and deacons set in their respective places, and assigned to a specific work of teaching and administration, while in each and every case the church literally governed itself, without exterior counsel or control of any sort, except the apostolic, is a supposition for which, be it true or otherwise, no distinct evidence can be found in the New Testament. The claim is at the best inferential, and the inference is at the best doubtful.—Secondly, there is conveyed in this theory an inadequate conception of the true province and worth of government, as a central feature in all church organization. That the apostles refer (1 Cor. 12: 28, 2 Peter 2: 10) to governments as among the charisms and prerogatives bestowed on the primitive Church,—that the function of ruling was under such divine guidance entrusted by the particular congregation (Rom. 12: 8, Heb. 13: 7) to certain persons among its members,—that these were not always ministers or deacons, but in some cases at least (1 Tim. 5: 17, Heb. 13: 17), were a distinct class or order of church servants, and that this representative administration occasionally, if not frequently, took the place of that exercised democratically by the whole body of believers (Acts 20: 17, 22), may be affirmed, if not positively, still at least with considerable basis of probability. What is said also, especially in the Corinthian Epistles, respecting the administration of discipline, strongly suggests the presence of an executive force, composed of representative persons, and adequate to carry into effect the decisions of the Christian household.

Thirdly, strict Independency clearly fails to give just prominence to the scriptural doctrine of the fellowship of the churches, and the sacred unity of all in the one great Church of God on earth. It is a strained interpretation of the use of the singular term, church, which leads to the affirmation that the disciples at Jerusalem, at Antioch, and other points where they were quite certainly counted by hundreds or thousands, were in every case compressed within one and the same church organization. A much more natural inference is that, however many the congregations were, they were united together, by some species of confederation, as the one Church of Christ, in the several cities named. What current Congregationalism recognizes in councils and conferences, if not some more compact and effective form of fellowship, doubtless existed in the apostolic age, both within and without the bounds of Palestine. The doctrine of the essential unity of all churches in the One Church, with all its vast practical suggestions and consequences, was also familiar to every one who had ever listened to the Pauline letters to the Ephesian and Colossian disciples: Eph. 1: 22, 5: 23, Col. 1: 18. The epistles of Peter and John inculcated the same vital lesson: they taught believers, Jew and Gentile, their essential oneness in Christ, and on that foundation urged habitually the duty of Christian fellowship, saint with saint, and church with church. Hardly credible is it that, in the presence of such teaching, a strict independency or even a form of association merely casual or occasional, should have come to be the accepted and the uniform mode of organization for the Household of Faith.

XI. THE REPRESENTATIVE POLITY STATED AND JUSTIFIED.[1]—The remaining species of polity of the popular or democratic type, bearing the general name of Presbyterianism, but existing wherever Protestantism has extended, under wide varieties in both title and construction, agrees in principle with much that is found in the other polities considered. Historically it had its modern genesis, like the two preceding Protestant varieties, in the investigations and the struggles of the Reformation. While all the reformers were agreed in rejecting the papal theory and practice, they still were unable to harmonize upon one adequate substitute. Some among them went back to the Fathers of the second and third centuries, and there found and

---

[1] Authorities to be consulted: Presbyterian Forms of Government, British and American: GILLESPIE, *Aaron's Rod Blossoming*; RUTHERFORD, *Peaceable Plea for Paul's Presbytery*; CUNNINGHAM, *Hist. Theol.* Chaps. II: XXVI; BANNERMAN, J., *Church of Christ*: Part IV; MILLER, S., *Presbyterianism, etc.*; SMYTH, T., *Treatises on Presbyterianism*.

adopted the scheme of diocesan Episcopacy, while others, going back still further to the apostolic age, found and embraced the scheme of absolute Independency,—both classes claiming scriptural as well as ecclesiastical warrant for their respective positions. Prior to both in the order of time, and claiming like biblical justification, arose the Presbyterian scheme of government, both in the particular church and among the churches, through a system of representative or delegated authorities, set apart specially for this purpose. This form of polity agrees with Independency in maintaining the parity of the ministry, and in denying their right to rule over the church without its consent; and also in regarding the diaconate as an administrative and charitable, rather than a ministerial or judicial office. It agrees with Congregationalism in affirming the proper affiliation of contiguous churches, and the importance of a practical, administrative fellowship among these several households of faith. It agrees with Prelacy and Papacy in maintaining the doctrine of the unity of the whole Church of Christ on earth, but rejects entirely the papal and prelatic explanations and applications of this doctrine. It affiliates in general with the democratic or popular, rather than the hierarchal conception of the Church, yet emphasizes the kingly authority of Christ and His supreme headship, and exalts the ministry to a special place of honor as an order within the Church, and as being eminently His representatives in all church activities. It holds to the separate responsibility and even the full autonomy of the particular church, but maintains the right of every such organization to govern itself through elect representatives, or to associate itself with other like organizations in one system of judicial and general administration, adjusted with mutual obligations and mutual rights, for the better securing not merely of justice to individuals, but also of the highest welfare and growth of all. The eldership, or session, and the higher judicatories thus constituted, are not bodies existing in any sense independently of the Church, and having primary or independent authority: the primary source of authority is always the Church, and it is the Church which confers jurisdiction on the official representatives collectively. The immediate objects sought in the creation of these administrative bodies, beyond the expression of the general principle of unity among the churches thus affiliated, are the better preservation of soundness in doctrine, regularity in discipline, and purity in life, through such mutual counsel and assistance as may in these ways be secured. The more general objects contemplated are the promotion of knowledge and religion, the prevention of infidelity, error and immorality, and the furtherance of all great Christian interests. The action of these judicatories is ministerial or declarative only, and their power is altogether moral or spiritual.

Such in brief are the essential elements of the representative or Presbyterian polity. And for the system thus outlined it presents, if not as to minor features, which are largely left to human wisdom, still as to essential principles and general construction, ample warrant from the Word of God.[1]

In explaining and justifying this polity on scriptural grounds, nothing more than such general warrant will be affirmed. Presbyterianism, *jure divino*—a system directly prescribed and enjoined as to details in the New Testament—can no more be proven than a *jure divino* Prelacy or Independency. The attempt to find in the Bible a full, exact, invariable mode of government, adjusted to the needs of the Church in all varieties of condition, and so enjoined upon it that all departures or deviations become unscriptural and schismatical, has often been made in the interest of each of the three Protestant varieties of church polity, but has always been made in vain. And well will it be for Protestantism, if it surrenders this futile effort in future to the Papacy, and plants itself on the broad principle, that any polity is legitimate, which stands substantially on biblical foundations, and which justifies itself practically in the judgment and experience of the household of faith. That the Presbyterian or representative polity meets these tests in a high degree, and in the aggregate more fully than any other, will be apparent from the following considerations:

1. While the synagogue system, established among the Jews in the age of Christ, can not be urged by either Prelacy or Presbyterianism as an authoritative model for the Christian Church, it still is reasonable to presume that the churches formed among Jewish converts would spontaneously assume the structure of the synagogue, and would create offices which would be parallel to those found wherever a Jewish congregation was organized. That a body of official persons called elders, and elders of the people, and charged with the oversight of the spiritual interests of the synagogue, existed universally in the age of Christ; and that both He and his disciples were familiar with this ar-

---

[1] "Not that we think that any policie, and ane ordour in ceremonies, can be appoynted for al ages, times and places: for as ceremonies sik as men have devised, ar bot temporall, so may and aucht they to be changed, when they rather foster superstition then that they edifie the Kirk using the same." *Scotch Conf.*, Art. xx.

"There are some circumstances concerning the worship of God, and government of the Church, common to human actions and societies, which are to be ordered by the light of nature and Christian prudence, according to the general rules of the Word, which are always to be observed." *West. Conf.*, Chap. I.

"We believe the general platform of our government to be agreeable to the sacred Scriptures, but we do not believe that God has been pleased so to reveal and enjoin every minute circumstance of ecclesiastical government and discipline as not to leave room for orthodox churches of Christ, in these minutiæ, to differ with charity from one another." *Synod of N. Y. and Phila.*, 1786.

rangement, and recognized its historic validity and its religious value, as appears from various references, will not be questioned. It would naturally follow, under these conditions, that the Jewish converts at Jerusalem, in the absence of any divine instructions to the contrary, would organize themselves into what may be termed a Christian synagogue (James 2 : 2) with its presbytery or central group of elders, to whom, in conjunction with the apostles, the care of the organization should be entrusted. Such a process would not transpire immediately at the first assembling in Jerusalem after the ascension, or at once upon the extraordinary experiences of the Pentecost, but at the first moment when the necessity for closer organization became apparent. And as these converts met originally at the times already made sacred by religious use, and as their worship took on naturally the forms and the order familiar to the Hebrews, so it may be inferred that, when the moment of need arrived, they appropriated also that mode of organization for which their Hebrew training had so well prepared them.[1] The form of the special account given of the institution of the diaconate (Acts 6) implies that the process just described had already taken place, and that the diaconate was in fact an added office rendered needful by the unexampled combination of Jews and Gentiles within the one communion of saints.

2. Starting with this Hebraic germ at Jerusalem and elsewhere, it is not surprising that the apostles, guided by such venerated usage rather than by direct commandment, proceeded to ordain them elders in every city (Titus 1: 5), and in every church (Acts 14: 23) where like antecedent conditions existed, and the converts were chiefly of Jewish origin. It is not needful to suppose that exact, unvarying uniformity obtained in this process,—especially where churches were formed largely from Gentile converts, to whom a distinctively Jewish usage such as this would be both unfamiliar and unattractive. A large degree of freedom developed itself also in respect to the functions of both the elder and the deacon, as is apparent from the graphic sketches of both by Paul in the Pastoral Epistles. The Hebrew presbyter thus introduced became, by a natural change of name, the Gentile bishop; and in many cases was teacher and pastor as well as overseer of the church. Thus the process of organizing churches on

---

[1] "It is likely that several of the earliest Christian churches were converted synagogues, which became Christian churches as soon as the members, or as soon as the main part of their members, acknowledged Jesus as the Messiah. . . The apostles did not there so much form a Christian church, as make an existing congregation Christian by introducing the Christian sacraments and worship, and establishing whatever regulations were necessary for the newly adopted faith, leaving the machinery, if I may so speak, of government unchanged."— WHATELY, *Kingdom of Christ Delineated*, p. 84, seq.

this model obviously went on from year to year, with local variations, until the elder or bishop, invested with the right to govern and the function of teaching, became a characteristic official, if we may judge from the numerous references in the Acts and Epistles, in almost every region where the Gospel had gained foothold. At Lystra and Iconium and Antioch (Acts 14: 21–23), at Ephesus (Acts 20: 17, 28), at Philippi (Phil. 1: 1), and more generally (1 Peter 5: 1, James 5: 14), we find such ordained elders, bishops, overseers, pastors, several in each church apparently, engaged in teaching, in governing and in general oversight, under what had become, not merely a venerable usage, but a recognized and approved law of organization for the body of Christ. The passage (1 Tim. 5: 17), quoted to show that a distinction existed from the first between the teacher and the ruler, really exhibits no distinction in office, but simply a recognition of superiority in the primary function of instruction. The more general references bring to view but a single class, bearing these names indifferently, and doubtless varying widely in the scope and authoritativeness of their official functions.[1]

3. We may observe a like growth in the conception of government, as a distinct characteristic of the Church. At first the body of Christ appears as an unorganized company, taking on gradually the form of a household, and then the structure and character of a state, with a defined constitution and laws, and controlled by recognized authorities. As the necessity for government became evident, government itself appeared, first as a species of charism (1 Cor. 12: 28), but afterward more generally, as an ordinary office: Rom. 12: 8. At first the inspired leaders ruled largely in virtue of their inspiration; then came the charismatic ruling; finally each church, under apostolic or other like guidance, supplied itself with representative rulers as well as with adequate teachers. Supernatural government disappeared with prophecy and the gifts of healing and of tongues, yet government remained as an enduring feature of the Church. This is apparent from numerous references in the epistles to church authority and church administration. Nor is there any reference to such administration as exercised directly by the multitude of communicants: what we see habitually

---

[1] Gibbon, referring to the organization of the Church as late as the beginning of the fourth century, says:

"The public functions of religion were solely entrusted to the established ministers of the Church, bishops and the presbyters, two appellations which, in their first origin, appear to have distinguished the same office, and the same order of persons. The name of presbyter was expressive of their age, or rather of their gravity and wisdom. The title of bishop denoted their inspection over the faith and manners of the Christians who were committed to their pastoral care." *Decline and Fall of the Roman Empire*, Chap. XV.

is government through chosen representatives acting as a body. The autonomy of the Church is indeed preserved; these representatives are not imposed upon it, without its own consent, neither do they appear to rule as in their own right; it is the Church which rules in and through them. The ordinations of elders, bishops, overseers, by Paul and Barnabas, by Titus, and by the presbytery (1 Tim. 4: 14) indicate no assumed prelatical supremacy on their part, but only wise and right action in and for the churches which they thus supplied with proper official representatives. And what becomes thus apparent as the primitive process of church construction, stands forth as a rule which in all ordinary conditions ought still to be regarded as safe and wise, and in some real sense authoritative. Certainly, no inferior place can properly be assigned to government among the functions of a Christian church, nor is it likely that the representative principle thus introduced can wisely be altogether abandoned.

4. A fourth principle which the Presbyterian polity specially incorporates is the fellowship of the churches, and the unity of the Church, as well in government as in more general forms of administrative association. Against that false notion of unity, which destroys the autonomy of the particular church, and subjects all churches to the sway and domination of a priestly class, this polity is altogether opposed: the imperial unity of the papacy, the formal and political unity of prelacy, it strenuously resists as contrary to the supreme law of Christian liberty. In like manner, it opposes the antithetic idea that the unity of the Church inculcated in the New Testament, is rather an invisible, imperceptible ideal than a practical and useful fact, or at best an occasional and limited rather than a comprehensive, structural basis of church fellowship. It points to the Council at Jerusalem, not indeed as presenting an inspired model to be exactly followed in all coming time, but as indicating a great scriptural principle by which the churches of Christ were to be habitually guided in their organic association. Nothing could be stronger than the teachings of Paul respecting that unity of faith, order, constitution, which was so well exemplified in this primitive Council: Eph. 4: 1–16, Rom. 12: 4–9, 1 Cor. 12: 4–27. Traces of the actual recognition of this principle of fellowship, and even of confederation, appear in various passages in the Acts and in the Epistles. Nor can any just reason be urged why this unity should not express itself in governmental administration as well as in more general fellowship,—why church should not be associated with church, as well as saint with saint, in the exposition and applying of the law of Christ to the life and conduct of the disciple. What we actually see, in the way of discipline, involves the particular church only, 1 Cor. 5: 1–7: and it may be doubted whether any

instance occurred, during the first decade of organized Christianity, in which a case of discipline was carried beyond the individual congregation. Yet, the doctrine of church unity doubtless grew more and more into favor, under apostolic instruction, as the contribution of the churches of Macedonia and Achaia to the needy saints at Jerusalem beautifully shows, Rom. 15: 26; nor do we need to descend very far beyond the apostolic century to find this doctrine assuming even an unwarranted place and influence, and finally to see the autonomy and jurisdiction of the particular church wholly prostrate at the feet of an assuming hierarchy.

5. Such in outline are the scriptural foundations on which the Presbyterian polity claims to rest. In the aggregate they justify the conclusions, that the right of government like the right of organization was vested, not in the ministry as an order, but in the church,—that, in accordance with antecedent usage, the exercise of this right was committed by the church to representative men, who both ruled and taught within the household of faith,—that the administration of government passed by degrees into the hands of a specific class chosen for the purpose, but under final responsibility to the church itself,—and that under this general system, with many variations such as circumstances demanded, the Church at large came at length to be substantially Presbyterian, rather than either Prelatic or Independent in its structure and administration.—It is admitted that this type of polity, planted thus on the popular or democratic principle, did not long maintain its place against the imperialism which possessed the life of the times at all other points, and which even before the death of John, had invaded and infected the Church: 3 John 9–10. That imperialism found its incarnation first in prelacy, and then by a natural development in that papal usurpation which for twelve centuries, as a species of Antichrist, lorded it over the heritage of God. Yet the growth of this more primitive polity since the Reformation, and in close conjunction with the cardinal and scriptural doctrines then enunciated, and its extensive acceptance in all countries where those doctrines have been carried, furnish striking evidence both of its scriptural quality and of its practical worth. And to this might be added much convincing evidence derived from its historic career, from its affiliations with strong doctrine and with high religious culture, from its deep sympathy with human liberty and human rights, and from its vast propagative force as a missionary agency, both in Christian and in heathen lands.[1]

XII. CARDINAL PRINCIPLES IN ADMINISTRATION.—Turning at this

---

[1] BARNES, ALBERT, *Affinities of Presbyterianism;* HODGE, CHARLES, *What is Presbyterianism?*

point from these inquiries respecting the law of church organization, to the further question relating to the practical administration of church government, we may note at the outset certain regulative principles which are to be borne carefully in mind, in such administration:

First, Christ as the Divine Head of the Church is the supreme Judge and Lord in all ecclesiastical administration. Viewed in its relation to Him, the Church is essentially theocratic,—it is a sacred monarchy. In the Old Testament, the supremacy of the Jehovah was a cardinal fact; in the Gospel economy, the supremacy of the Messiah is no less cardinal. And with this divine headship there must be nothing in the constitution or administration of the Church to interfere; no person or collection of persons, no polity or government, can assume the place which rightfully belongs to Him. All human powers and prerogatives are to be wielded in loyal subservience to His will; final responsibility to Him is the bond by which both the Church, and they who rule within it, are to be held. Against all assumption of independent control, whether by pope or prelate or presbyter, or by the household of faith itself, His most solemn sentence is pronounced; 2 Thess. 2: 4–8.

Secondly: the Scriptures are the supreme and binding law. In the Mosaic dispensation, as in the Patriarchal, the divine Law was of necessity supplemented by miraculous manifestations—such as the Shekinah and the Urim and Thummim; but under the Gospel, the Written Word is sufficient and final. That Word is ample in its scope; no church has occasion to add any thing to its comprehensive requisitions. Whatever is appended to this divine constitution, in the way of requirement or prohibition, whether by individual authority or by the prescripts of councils, or in any other way, is in no sense obligatory upon the disciple. This Word is also plain in its directions, and is in little need of explanatory legislation by the Church. It is indeed left to the household of faith, to define the reach of its provisions, and to indicate specific applications of its generic precepts; but every such process must ever be conducted in the clear light shining immediately from the Scripture itself. This Word is also in the highest measure authoritative, and is entitled to the implicit respect and reverence of the Church, always and everywhere. It is the common law, the statutory volume, of Christianity; and as such remains perpetually the regulative guide in all ecclesiastical administration. Its place and seat in the Church are no less supreme or absolute, than those of Christ Himself. The guidance of the Spirit is indeed to be invoked in all exercise of church authority; but as an inspiring rule in such exercise, the Spirit and the Word will ever be one.

Thirdly: the limits of ecclesiastical administration are also divinely prescribed. One of the most serious errors in such administration, lies in the extension of church control beyond its legitimate boundaries,—the assumption of the right to rule in spheres into which it is not competent for the Church to enter. On the basis of the headship of Christ above all earthly authorities, and of the supremacy of the Scripture above all human laws or constitutions, the sway of the Church has often been carried intrusively, and even tyrannically, into the family and into the state, as well as into the life of the individual Christian. A spiritual despotism, thus usurping authority over man in every relation, has more than once made its appearance in Christendom, to the irreparable injury both of religion and of the souls of men. In like manner, the Church has often penetrated unjustifiably into the sphere of the individual conscience, either forbidding the believer to do what the Bible clearly allows, or commanding him to do what the Word of God does not require. Abundant illustrations of such error in administration will at once present themselves; the records of organized Christianity, under Protestant varieties in polity, as well as under the domination of the Papacy, continually reveal them.

The cardinal rule to be observed, is the strict limitation of church control within the sphere and under the conditions divinely prescribed. Christ is indeed the Lord of providence and of human life, as well as Lord over His own people: but His kingdom is not of this world, neither is His law to be asserted authoritatively, or His supremacy authoritatively maintained by the Church, over human kingdoms or authorities, as by a species of force. The State is as supreme within its own sphere as the Church is, and the attempt of the Church to control the State, through any other agency than that of spiritual influence, is a plain usurpation. Christ is also Lord of the believer, and the soul saved by His grace is bound to be loyal to Him in all its life; but there is a vast sphere of personal experience, privilege, duty, with which it would be sacrilege on the part ot the Church, as the appointed representative of Christ, to intermeddle. Its administrative functions must be limited chiefly to the outward life and actions of those who are associated in it; and to their life and actions mainly as these stand in some relation to the great ends for which the Church is constituted, and to its standing and efficiency as a representative of the Gospel among men. It ought also to be added that, within the limited sphere thus defined, the jurisdiction of the Church must ever be exercised under numerous limitations; and like other instrumentalities wielded by man, must often fail in practice to gain the high results at which it aims.

XIII. Practical Administration: Authority and Obedience.—One marked feature in the exercise of these church functions under the Gospel, should be noted at this point. In the Mosaic economy, though human instruments such as priests and prophets were always employed in this task of administration, the theocratic element was so constant, so conspicuous, and so controlling, as to leave little room for the play or exhibition of this human element. Jehovah Himself governed almost visibly; the authority was always His, and the obedience was always rendered directly to Him. Under the Gospel, while the Messiah sacrifices nothing in supremacy or authoritativeness, the human factors or agents appear much more prominent,—the part which man performs is much more distinct and more responsible. Hence the necessity for careful consideration of both the authority vested in those who rule, and the obedience required from those who are governed within the Church.

The authority vested in those who rule, as we have already seen in contemplating the ministerial office, is never inherent in the officer, but is delegated to him by the Church. It is true that this power is entrusted to the official by Christ Himself also, and is therefore to be wielded under a supreme sense of responsibility to him. Yet the assumption of any official power is justifiable only when the Church approves,—when the voice of the Master and the voice of His people are heard, in holy harmony one with the other, commissioning the person chosen. As delegated, such authority is never personal, but always functional—an adjunct of the office, rather than an endowment of the man. Although Christ and His people ordinarily associate the possession of appropriate gifts with the formal investiture with official prerogatives, yet it is never the gifted man, but the qualified official who rules. And as this authority is thus delegated and functional, it is of necessity limited in its scope within the scriptural and constitutional boundaries prescribed. It is limited first of all by the supreme authority of our Lord, and by the instructions clearly contained in His Word as the supreme law. It is limited further to the Church,—is never to be exercised outside of the Christian fold. And within this general sphere, it is limited still further to those specific duties and functions which the Church has assigned to the office. No church official is authorized to interfere either with the functions or prerogatives of any official of another class, or with the private life, the personal conscience, of the individual member. Exercised beyond its appointed boundaries, even the worthiest office becomes an usurpation and a curse, both to the holder and to the body over which he presides.

It is especially important to emphasize afresh at this point the doctrine of Scripture with regard to the spirit, the temper, in which all such authority is to be wielded. For it is evident that, far within the sphere assigned to him, and in the legitimate exercise of his powers, a church officer may rule in such a temper as makes him a tyrant rather than a servant. The best polity is no certain safeguard here. The disposition to enforce just law in a legalistic spirit is itself an infringement of the higher law of love. Cold indifference to the feelings or claims of those governed, ambitious desire to control where control is not demanded, the disposition to make or to carry issues which are personal rather than generic or abstract, are all at variance with the biblical injunctions to those who rule within the household of faith. The spirit of service, the temper of charity, the mood of meekness and unselfish consecration, the supreme sense of allegiance to the Gospel law, and loyalty to Him who is Lord over all, are indispensable here. If the church officer possesses not these traits in high degree— if he be not free essentially from these faults and defects, he can only offend the little ones whom he aspires to govern and train for the Master: and better were it for him that a millstone were hanged about his neck, and he were drowned in the depths of the sea.

But church administration presupposes obedience as well as authority. The mood of disobedience, the spirit of transgression, the manifestation of revolt and rebellion, are all alien to the conception of the Church as a divine kingdom. Where there are rulers appointed of God, there must be subjects in whom appropriate submission, fidelity in conforming to law, fealty to the body of Christ, should find a just manifestation. Such obedience must, first of all, be intelligent,— based upon proper recognition by the subject of the nature of the Church as an organism, of the constitution and laws to be obeyed, and of the authority exercised over him. A blind or thoughtless submission are not sufficient: the sway of Christ in His Church has its foundation in the educated intelligence of His people. This obedience must also be cordial,—carrying with it the heart and the will, as truly as the understanding. As the household of faith rests essentially on the voluntary principle, no one entering it or remaining in it except by choice, so all force, compulsion, obedience secured by severities or constraints, are at variance with the nature of the connection assumed. Nor is it mere surrendery of the will, a passive obedience such as Romanism requires, that is demanded here: the loving soul must cordially acquiesce both in the law and in the authority that enforces it.

Church obedience, by the nature of the case, should be both complete and perpetual. It implies more than an observance of some requisitions to the exclusion of others,—the judgment or wish of the subject overruling, wherever it is inclined, the will and law of the body. It implies more than an occasional observance, followed by neglect or by transgression, at the option of the disciple. True obedience submits to every demand of rightful authority, and submits at all times, and amid whatever difficulties. The vital figure which Paul employs in his first letter to the Corinthians—the figure of the body made up of many living members, each filling its own office, and making its beneficent contribution to the efficiency and welfare of the whole structure—beautifully illustrates that great duty of spiritual obedience on which the Apostle in other passages so frequently dwells; Rom. 12: 5–6. Such biblical obedience properly culminates in that noble loyalty to the Church, which in the list of Christian virtues may well rank next to loyalty to Christ Himself;—not merely personal submission, however hearty or complete, but positive fealty which stands fearlessly by the church authority, however imperilled in the discharge of its legitimate functions, and which defends and supports the Church at all hazards with knightly ardor, as the true Bride of Christ among men.

XIV. DISCIPLINE AS A CHURCH FUNCTION.—It only remains, under the general topic here considered, to sketch briefly the discipline which the Church of Christ is constrained to administer to those who may prove to be disobedient.[1] In the broadest sense, discipline implies training, regulation, culture of those who are loyal at heart, as well as the correction of transgressors. More specifically, the term relates to the latter process in its various forms and stages. In this sense, it has been well defined as the exercise of that authority, and the application of that system of laws, which the Lord Jesus Christ hath appointed in His Church, with reference to all visible departures from the principle of loyalty. Discipline was recognized in the Protestant Symbols generally, as a legitimate and necessary function of the Church, though in practice the Protestant bodies of the sixteenth and seventeenth centuries often departed very widely from their own doctrine as to the obligation of the churches to exercise such discipline. While the right to such exercise was theoretically maintained, on the general ground that the household of faith is also a divine and authoritative kingdom, the duty was, as Calvin confesses, far too widely neglected. The right itself was also in many instances sadly perverted,—especially where the civil authorities were, as in Geneva, admitted as administrative functionaries within the Church, and discipline was

---

[1] References on Church Discipline; General Principles: CALVIN, *Institutes*, Book IV: 12; DWIGHT, *Sermon* 162; DICK, *Theol.*, Lect. 101; WATSON, *Theol. Inst.*, Part IV, Chap. II; VAN OOSTERZEE, *Practical Theol.*—Practical Rules: Scotch First and Second Books of Discipline; Presbyt. Book of Discipline, and other denominational Manuals.

enforced by civil as well as ecclesiastical penalties. Lutheran princes in like manner commanded their subjects to attend religious service three times on the Sabbath, and for failure punished the rich with fines, and the poor with scourging and imprisonment. It was not strange that a function thus perverted should fall, as it did in most continental communions, into general disrepute. The revival in more recent times, of both the doctrine and the practice, may be regarded as one of the pleasing indications of progress in both spirituality and effectiveness, among the Protestant churches. Under the papal conception of the Church, discipline can only be an occasional punitive process, conducted by the priesthood, and of comparatively little significance, excepting where it may be invoked as an infliction upon civil rulers or heretical bodies, whom the Church seeks to coerce.

Protestantism differs from the Church of Rome in regarding discipline as a power vested, not in the priesthood, but in the church as a Christian body. Both the injunction of our Lord (Matt. 18: 17), and the historic example recorded in the epistles to the Corinthian church, show that the collective group of believers, and they only, possess disciplinary power. It has sometimes been argued on doubtful grounds, that this power is vested solely in the male members of the particular church—in fact, it pertains to the body in its totality. Yet, as we have seen, it is consistent with ancient Jewish usage, and with sound principle, to commit the administration of this trust to persons specially competent to discharge it,—not merely to those who may fill the office of instruction, but also to others chosen for their fitness to act for the body, in this delicate relation.

Protestantism differs also from Romanism in its general definition of disciplinable offences. An offence has been very broadly defined as anything in the principles or practice of a church member which is contrary to the Word of God, or which, if it be not in its own nature sinful, may tempt others to sin, or mar their spiritual edification: Presbyt. Book of Discipline, Chap. I. More specifically, such offences may be classified as follows: overt, and especially, flagrant sins, 1 Cor. 5: 1-5; gross indulgences, inconsistent with the Christian life, 1 Cor. 5: 11; maintaining, and especially, inculcating, heretical or mischievous doctrines, Titus 3: 10-11, Gal. 1: 8-9; serious neglect of clear personal duty, to the dishonor of Christ and His Church, 1 Tim. 5: 7-8; plain violation of the precepts of Christian brotherhood, Matt. 18: 15; leading others astray from the path of obedience, 2 Thess. 3: 6, 14; exciting divisions and schism in the Church, Rom. 16: 17-19. The primary and main tests of an offence are always to be found in the Scripture: whatever is not directly or by clear implication condemned in the Word of God, can not expose the disciple to just discipline. Subordinate tests may appear, as in the definition given, in the demonstrated relations of an act to other disciples, or to the church as a body. It is also requisite, as a rule of equity and of prudence, that the alleged offence should be carefully estimated both in the light of the Bible, and in view of what may be known of its flagrancy or its mischievous influence. The evils which discipline is divinely designed to prevent, must be obvious, and all milder preliminary processes must have been tried, before the offender can be scripturally arraigned.

The ends to be sought in church discipline are, in general, the vindication of the honor of Christ, and the promotion of the purity and edification of the Church;—more specifically, the removal of offences which are injurious to the church life, and to the social influence of Christianity. The benefit of the offender himself is to be sought, so far as this is consistent with these more general ends. A disciplinary process may sometimes avail to bring such a person to repentance and return to duty, when all milder measures have failed. Discipline is often of value in deterring those who might be misled by evil example, or who if unwarned would be liable to fall into like evil courses.— The spirit in which discipline is to be administered is sufficiently indicated in the strong apostolic cautions respecting it; Gal. 6: 1-2, 1 Cor. 4: 21, 1 Thess. 3: 15, and others. The offending disciple is not to be counted as an enemy, but admonished as a brother: it is not the rod, as a symbol of authority, but the temper of love and of meekness, that is to govern. It is not so much the function of the Church to punish, as to correct and to improve and edify; the restoration of the wanderer is to be sought, from love to Christ and to the souls of men. In the royal passage, Matt. 18: 15-18, our Lord has Himself indicated the spirit as well as the method to be pursued, in all cases of offence. Unquestionably there is great need for most careful recognition of such injunctions, since no function of the Church or of its officers carries with it greater exposures, or subjects the sanctified character to severer tests.

Respecting the modes of instituting discipline, and the extent to which disciplinary processes may be carried, the Scriptures lay down none but general rules, leaving particular steps and measures to the judgment of the household of faith. The law of Christ, just referred to, is regarded by all Protestant communions as the prescribed basis of all judicial procedure. It is also recognized by them, that all church action is ministerial and declarative only,—that the imposition of penalties bearing upon the person or property, or on the social or civil position of an offender, does not belong to the Church. Most Protestant churches admit that the civil power can not properly be in any way invoked, to assist in the enforcement of ecclesiastical jurisdiction or infliction. The Church prescribes its own penalties, which may end in private confession and proper reparation to a party aggrieved, or in public confession or admonition; or may proceed to a suspension of the offender, for a period more or less prolonged, from the enjoyment of church privileges, or to an actual and open excommunication of the guilty party from the household of faith. This right is vested in every church organization, and no external power, civil or otherwise, can justly arrest its exercise. The right of restoring offending persons to fellowship, upon adequate evidence of repentance and return to Christian duty, is also vested in the Church: its doors should be no more closed against a penitent backslider, than against the repenting sinner for the first time consecrating himself to Christ.

CHAPTER V.

THE CHURCH IN HUMAN SOCIETY

ITS UNITY, ITS GROWTH, ITS RELATIONS.

The Church has thus far been contemplated as an institution, standing at the outset in the divine plan of salvation, and historically manifested in accordance with that plan,— an institution composed of certain constituents, impersonal and personal, and organized permanently under a definite constitution, as a divine structure or kingdom, endowed with every requisite to complete organization and to enduring efficiency. But this may be regarded as wholly an interior view; it portrays the Church as it exists inwardly, but does not indicate the character of this unique institution as a spiritual agency acting extensively and vitally on the world of humanity. These external aspects and services will now be considered. Three general topics successively demand attention; the question of Church Unity, the Laws of Church Growth, and the generic Relations sustained by the Church in Human Life.

I. PRESENT CHURCH DIVISIONS: FORMS AND CAUSES.—In the preceding discussions, the Church has always been contemplated as essentially one. In the three great epochs of its history, it has indeed presented itself in three corresponding forms: but these have appeared only as successive stages in the development of one and the same divine organism. Extensive divisions of view have also become apparent, in respect to creeds and sacraments and ordinances, to the doctrine of membership and of offices and officers, and to the modes of polity upon which the Church should be constructed. But these divisions, however extensive or serious, have not furnished decisive proof that the Church is not in essence and substance one. We have found rather that this principle of unity is in fact as essential to the very conception of the Church, notwithstanding such divisions, as it is to the conception of the human body with which the Church is so often compared in Scripture; we have found that if the Church is not, beneath all varieties and antagonisms, thus one and single, no adequate account can be given, either of its existence, or of its place and offices in the scheme of salvation.

Yet ecclesiastical history is a record of innumerable conflicts, diversities, separations, schisms, within this holy and gracious organism. The one Church of God presents itself before us in fact as an extensive series of churches, widely unlike in faith and order and worship, and often in the attitude of distrust or aversion, or of open antagonism. Nominal Christendom is divided into the three great sections: the Greek, the Roman, and the Protestant. The Roman communion, and in great degree the Greek communion also, have each maintained an external unity, in the presence of many inward differences and conflicts. Protestantism exists in a large number of sects, divided not merely by geographic lines, but by multiplied differences in construction, method and faith. Within its main divisions, we discover an extensive array of minor organizations, whose differences are apparently more influential in practice than their agreements, and whose real unity in Christ hardly finds any distinct form of expression. Even within the domain of particular denominations, we further discover schools, parties, tendencies, often actively at war with each other, and struggling for supremacy at whatever cost to the common faith. The actual attitude of the Christian Church is thus one of multiplicity, division, antagonism, rather than of that unity which the apostles so steadfastly enjoined; and the pathetic prayer of Christ that His people might all be one, suggests to the student of the Church only a remote, apparently an unattainable, ideal.

Turning to consider briefly the causes of such multiplicity, we discover first of all the simple and just law of geographic division, consequent upon the distribution of the Church in many lands, and among widely varying nations. It is indeed a recognizable fact of Scripture, that the disciples at Jerusalem, and in other cities also, however great their numbers grew to be, were associated habitually in what was termed the one local church : at least, no evidence of local separation, as to organization, appears in the record; Acts 11 : 22, 13: 1, 1 Cor. 1: 2. It is also probable that the plural term, churches, was employed only in describing groups composed of the local organizations of a given region, more or less extensive; and that the law of unity still predominated, even under the sense of separation thus occasioned by distance; Rom. 16: 1–2: and the apostolic letters to churches. But at length the growth of the common Christianity in Western Asia and in Eastern Europe compelled a completer separation. The believers in each locality formed a church for themselves; churches thus formed were largely independent of one another; and steadily extending division on the geographic basis became the general law.—This law is still active, and still both legitimate and universal. Wherever the number of believers becomes too great for convenience in assembling together for worship, or wherever they are too widely scattered to assemble in any given place, the establishment of another center of religious life and work becomes a duty as well as a necessity. It is no schism, to multiply churches on this basis: either geographic distribution or numerical magnitude amply justifies the process. It is on this general ground that a large proportion of the divisions of Protestantism, in both Europe and America, are to be explained. It was natural and just, that the churches in any given province or state should associate themselves in a form of unity, bounded by the courses of rivers or the lines of civil government. And, had the taunt of Bossuet had no other foundation than this, the Reformers might have smiled at its impotency, even though their provincial organizations exhibited less of prestige and power than the Church of Rome, scattered through many lands, yet preserving through all distribution its formal unity. It needs only to be noted here that such a principle suggests its own limitations: and that any excessive multiplication of churches along such lines, either local or provincial, is a schismatical departure from the proper unity of the Gospel.

But at this point another law of distribution comes in,—the law of diversity. Three general types of such diversity appear, in connection with polity, with modes of worship, and with systems of doctrine. Thus, each of the four varieties of ecclesiastical organization has its advocates and adherents; and Christendom is consequently divided into four great classes of churches, existing under these several schemes of organization. The Greek Christian and the Romanist agree in their conception of a hierarchal administration, but differ as to its proper center and its rightful head. The prelatical communions agree with both in locating authority in the hands of the clergy, but strenuously resist both the patriarchal and the papal assumptions of supremacy. Popular varieties of government differ from all of these in locating church power in the people, but also differ widely among themselves as to the extent in which such power may be entrusted by the people to certain representative rulers, and as to the proper relations of church to church in judicial administration.—Modes of worship furnish a second ground of diversity. Two great classes of churches here come into view. Those which adhere rigidly to liturgical forms, or to a prescribed administration of the sacraments, or to certain modes of praise, and which compel church organization on their specific basis, constitute the first class: and those which regard written liturgies with disfavor, rebel against formal limitations in worship, and allow variations in sacramental usage, constitute the second. A third class of denominations might be described as occupying an intermediate position, or possibly one of indifference, to such liturgical issues, and as being organized rather on the basis of distinctions which are either governmental or doctrinal.—Varieties in belief constitute a still deeper ground of church division. Each of the main types of theology—the Lutheran, the Arminian, the Calvinistic—furnishes a general basis for denominational distribution: and within these general lines there is room, as the history of Protestant theology has abundantly shown, for still further distribution of the same class. While all are agreed in the essential facts of faith, and for the most part in the central aspects of the truth believed, theories and explanations differ widely; certain aspects of the truth are emphasized, while others are retired; historical contentions and controversies arise, and organic divisions are created. It is hardly needful to mention here the segregations of this class which serious heresies, such as the denial of the deity of Christ, have occasioned: these are rather separations from the common Christianity, than organized forms of belief within it. In many ways, this law of distribution on the basis of doctrine makes itself apparent in history: Christendom is in fact almost as widely separate and disparted here, as in respect to worship or to polity.

II. CHURCH DIVISIONS: GOOD AND EVIL FRUITS.—The general fact is thus confessed, that the Church of God on earth exists under wide varieties of name and organization. The main causes, and the more conspicuous forms of such variety, have just been noted. Of the issues, good and evil, of such a complex process of distribution, there is much to be said:

Postponing for the moment the question of organic unity among all believers throughout the world, we may note here the suggestive fact that, while Judaism was struggling to preserve an external unity even though it was perishing spiritually, the Christian Church planted itself from the first on the broader platform,—the platform of spiritual unity, notwithstanding local distribution and geographic expansion. Even wide variety, such as appeared between Jewish and Gentile converts, or between the schools of Apollos and Cephas at Corinth, was not destructive of this fundamental sense of spiritual unity. And, were the multiplication of churches to be conducted in our time as it was in the apostolic age, with no characteristic lines of separation in belief or order, there would be nothing in the process in any degree adverse to the most complete fellowship on the part of contiguous organizations. The law of spiritual unity would still hold the Church together as one, though its congregations were counted by millions.

Nor is segregation on the basis of recognized differences, such as have been named, necessarily a departure from this cardinal law. If as Protestants, we agree for example in the position that there is no complete form of polity absolutely imposed in Scripture, and that Christian congregations, organized on the basis of either of the existing types of polity, are true churches of Christ, we may then peaceably divide according to our individual belief as to the degree of scripturalness, or of general value and desirableness in any one of these admissible types. If we agree that liturgical worship is Christian worship, and that the less formal worship of most Protestant communions is also Christian worship, we may, without being schismatical, follow individual preferences, and legitimately seek fellowship with those in any Christian community who hold like preferences in the matter of devotion. If we are agreed that the Lutheran, the Arminian, and the Calvinistic varieties of theology are alike evangelical—that they contain, amid many circumstantial differences in arrangement and emphasis and real teaching, the essential doctrines of grace, we violate no law of the Gospel if we choose one rather than the others, or associate ourselves ecclesiastically with those who make the same choice. The existence of such tendencies to difference is an unquestionable fact, and decided justification of these tendencies may be found in the very nature of Christianity; and it is therefore no schism if such differences are allowed, within proper limits, to affect Christian fellowship or church organization.

There are indeed some advantages naturally suggesting themselves to our thought, which may result to the general cause from such distribution. The principle of spiritual unity, for example, may receive one of its most impressive exemplifications in immediate conjunction with the organizing of churches and denominations on these subsidiary bases. While the Calvinist and the Arminian strongly emphasize their respective conceptions of doctrine, and enter into organization with other Calvinists or other Arminians in order to defend, exalt, promulgate their several systems, they may not be crowding out of sight the underlying verities in which as Christians they are agreed, but may rather be bringing out even the more fully, in and through their theologic contrasts, the one blessed Gospel which is the foundation of their belief and of their hope of salvation. In many directions it might be shown that denominational divisions, in their true place and office, are not injurious, but are even beneficial to the common cause of Christ. The popular comparison of these distributed varieties of Christianity to the divisions of an army, moving by diverse processes, and under different array, toward a common consummation, is accurate as well as trite.

Schism thus enters into these segregating processes, not in every stage or form, but simply at the point where division changes into antagonism,—where the devotion to a specific theology, or polity, or mode of worship, brings in deviation from that cardinal law of love which binds all such divisions together in holy oneness, within the single and indivisible Household of Faith.[1] No one can be blind to the existence of this liability, in various forms. It is discernible in the disposition to insist on some given denominational peculiarity, such as the episcopate, or baptism by immersion, or the singing of psalms only, as indispensable to the constitution of a Christian church, and consequently to refuse the name of a church to any Christian body organized on a different basis. It is hardly less discernible in the sectarian temper which emphasizes unduly any such peculiarity, and is inclined to enter into active hostility in its behalf, or to look coldly or contemptuously on those brethren in Christ who refuse to receive it. It is discernible also in the inclination to multiply sects upon comparatively trivial issues, or to build up higher walls of separation around existing sects, or to oppose such movements as the body of Christ is more or less consciously making toward closer visible union. And, while a temperate, generous denominationalism may be justified at the high tribunal of Christian love, all true disciples of Christ are bound to resist, in whatever form it may appear, this schismatical and sectarian spirit, as essentially contrary to the common Gospel. Certain it is that the Church can never assume its proper place, or wield its full measure of influence in human society, while such a spirit prevails in Christendom.

III. ORGANIC ONENESS: THE PAPAL VIEW.—The Church of Rome

---

[1] See the two impressive sermons of JOHN HOWE on the *Carnality of Religious Contention:* and also that on the question, appropriate to the present age, *What may most hopefully be attempted among Protestants, that our Divisions may not be our Ruin.*

claims to have found a solution of this perplexing problem of unity in its doctrine of organic oneness,—in a unification of Christendom which is formal and external, rather than inward or vital. The elements of this organic oneness are, first, a uniform polity, with its fixed orders of clergy, with its pontifical head, with its established rules and canons, to be accepted as authoritative in all Christian congregations throughout the world : secondly, a uniform liturgy, with like fixedness and elaborateness in detail, to be followed exactly, and according to pontifical regulation, by all believers in all lands: and thirdly, a uniform creed, clear and full, and invested with authoritative sacredness, to which every assembly of disciples, wherever located, should give implicit credence. In order to the securing of such threefold uniformity, the Church of Rome maintains that there must be to this one Church a geographic center, a continuous history, and a single supreme head, in whose person the unity of Christendom is represented. Such in brief is the papal dogma, and such is the papal scheme of Christian unification. It is at least conceivable that such a scheme and doctrine should be carried out in history, and that the Church of Christ, on the basis of such unity in polity, worship and faith, should attach itself universally and loyally to the Roman see, as its proper center and representative. The dream is a grand one, though it be a dream.

The attempt at realization has been far from successful. On external grounds, relating to the geographic location and the papal headship, the Greek Church, and certain Prelatic communions also, have refused the formal union proposed. On internal grounds, Protestantism generally has broken away from the Romish fellowship, and sought unification on a deeper principle, a broader basis. The proposal of uniformity in government, worship, belief, has not commended itself to Protestant thought. The Papal polity has exhibited too slight biblical warrant, and has proven itself in practice to be too fraught with peril to Christian liberty. The liturgy of Rome has diverged too far from the teaching and models of Scripture, and is too heavily overloaded with sensuous and corrupting accretions, to be accepted as a guide and rule in devotion. The Romish creed, though containing much that is biblical, falls away from sound doctrine at too many points, and is too much infected with human elements, to be believed by all Christian men, as the final canon and norm of faith. Moreover, it is manifest historically that the oneness secured in this external way, has been formal, ecclesiastical, and partial, rather than spiritual or complete. The uniform polity proposed, has tended steadily to hierarchy, and to religious despotism : the uniform worship has resulted in the grossest formalism and superstition : and the uniformity in creed has issued extensively in the destruction of rational faith, and in much positive unbelief, even within the bosom of the Church. With such results in full view, Protestantism can never accept the solution of the problem of Christian unity which Romanism has proposed.

Nor is there just reason for belief, that any present efforts at organic union among Protestants would bring a larger measure of success. Illustrations of such effort may be seen on one side in those struggles after one comprehensive state church, which have appeared so conspicuously in the history of Protestantism in Europe, and on the other in the earnest endeavors of those earnest souls who see in such organic oneness the proper cure for the current evils of denominational division. But history bears steadily increasing testimony to the futility of the attempt to make the church in any country coterminous with the state. Nor does history encourage the hope of universal agreement through moral influence, on any given basis of organic union. No uniform mode of organization or worship could be proposed at present, without creating new and fiercer divisions; no uniform standard of belief, without developing larger, intenser diversities. Protestants may amicably agree to regard their differences in these respects as relatively indifferent; but amicable agreement of this sort is not union, nor would union on the basis of such indifferentism possess any high degree of worth or of effectiveness. A temperate denominationalism, with all its exposures, is a better practical basis than indifferent unionism, or a dead uniformity. It may well be maintained that, wherever the followers of Christ are few in number, and remote in position, the organization of a single church on whatever evangelical basis and under whatever rulings, is to be sought as the best attainable expression of the holy tie which draws such disciples together. But wherever other conditions exist, such an obligation loses much of its force; the influence of secondary considerations enters in legitimately to modify the primary law, and churches which represent the varieties as well as the unities of the common faith, come justly into existence. Nor is there sufficient reason to believe that such varieties will cease to exist, or to affect ecclesiastical organization, and denominational development, even down to millennial times.

IV. SPIRITUAL UNITY: THE PROTESTANT VIEW.—Setting aside as impracticable the dream of organic union, whether in the form of a state church, or as the expression of a controlling Christian charity, Protestantism still strongly emphasizes, as a cardinal element, the underlying principle of spiritual unity. The invisible Church in whose existence all Protestants believe, is always one and indivisible; and all visible churches, built on evangelical doctrine, and however organized, have a legitimate place within that one divine household. That household can not indeed be said to include these various churches corporeally, since there are members in them who are Christians in form only; nor is it limited by them, since it doubtless contains some who belong to no visible church. Yet Protestantism places this sublime conception over against the papal dogma of organic oneness, and affirms that, in the spiritual sense here indicated, all believers, however far apart geographically or denominationally, have a place and name within this one holy family—the *Cœtus Fidelium*, which indeed includes no less the heavenly than the earthly disciples of the Messiah. This was the response of the Reformers to the claim of Rome, and also their fraternal response and greeting to one another, in view of the external divisions which were holding them asunder. It is indeed a matter of history that many leading minds among them longed for some closer bond; the conception of a great confederation, in which all the Protestant communions might in some way be visibly joined together, found many earnest advocates, especially in the Reformed circles. But events proved such a confederation impracticable; and all rested at last in the incorporation in their Confessions of the broad Christian principle, that the Church of God on earth, despite all varieties, is forever and indissolubly One.[1]

It must be confessed that Prosestantism has witnessed many serious departures from its avowed doctrine. It has seen sect springing up after sect, on the basis of slight diversities in belief or order or mode of devotion, in strange indifference to this fundamental law. It has seen the spirit of sect inciting these divided communions not merely to seclusion from one another, or to suspicion or alienation, but even to bitter rivalries and strenuous warfare. It has seen denominations, Prelatic and Presbyterian and Independent, striving after political supremacy, and as state churches making intolerant assaults upon the Christian rights of other churches. For two centuries or more after Protestantism had gained its position in the northern half of Europe, we find it still failing to carry out even the negative principle of toleration; and even yet, after more than three centuries of experience, we see the positive principle of brotherhood in Christ struggling in vain for adequate recognition. The history of Protestant Christianity contains many a sad chapter, illustrative of such failures to put into practice what all have agreed to hold as cardinal doctrine. And the taunt of the papist and the jeer of the unbeliever

---

[1] DURY, JOHN, *Earnest Plea for Gospel Communion*, A. D. 1654. Also, his Petition to the British Parliament for the calling of a "General Synod of Protestants in due time, for the better settling of weighty matters in the Church which now trouble not only the consciences of most men, but disturb the tranquillity of publick states, and divide the churches one from another, to the great hindrance of Christianity, and the dishonor of Religion." See also Correspondence on the subject between Cranmer, Calvin, and others: *Zurich Letters*.

are still sharp as arrows, in the breast of its disunited and fragmentary communions.

Can it be questioned that one of the primal duties of Protestantism in our time is to seek after the deeper, purer unity which belongs essentially, according to the scriptural delineation, to the Household of Faith? The apparent arrest of the tendency toward segregation around minor issues, and the movements toward organic union on the part of denominations separated by only slight differences, are encouraging indications that this obligation is coming to be more largely realized. Such also is the closer confederation of bodies essentially alike in faith and order, but widely separated in locality and in respect to their particular mission.[1] The multiplied forms of practical fellowship and union in Christian service, are further indications in the same direction. The spirit of unity, as inculcated in the New Testament, has at least begun to manifest itself effectively along such lines,—as if in introductory answer to the intercession of the Redeemer. But these are preliminary indications merely: their value lies largely in the suggestion they convey of possibilities incomparably greater. How much these possibilities may yet include, a thoughtful student of that mediatorial prayer would find it difficult to define. Certain it is that the unification of evangelical Protestantism, in essence if not in organic form, to such an extent that the deepest impression it shall make upon all its members and on the world at large will be one, not of diversity, but of true union, is a result not only possible in itself, but intrinsically of incalculable moment to the common Christianity,—a result for which all true disciples, in imitation of Christ, should ever pray.

V. THE CHRISTIAN CHURCH A GROWTH: GENERAL CONCEPTION.—
In his letter to the Ephesian Church, Paul introduces, and skillfully blends together, two familiar images, alike descriptive of the Church of Christ: Eph. 2: 21. The first represents that Church as a building in process of construction,—a building resting on divine foundations, and fitly framed together, gradually rising stage by stage into the magnificent proportions of an holy temple in the Lord. The second describes it rather as a vital growth, a living tree, starting from a divine germ, and developing by healthful processes, until it reaches finally its consummation as a matured and fruitful organism of grace.

---

[1] "In forming this Alliance, the Presbyterian Churches do not mean to change their fraternal relations to other Churches, but will be ready, as heretofore, to join with them in Christian fellowship, and in advancing the cause of the Redeemer, on the general principle, maintained and taught in the Reformed Confessions, *that the Church of God on earth, though composed of many members, is one body in the communion of the Holy Ghost, of which body Christ is the Supreme Head, and the Scriptures alone are the infallible law.*" Const. *Presbyterian Alliance;* Preamble.

The truth common to both metaphors, and one often inculcated elsewhere in the New Testament, is that the Church is not something accidentally thrown together, or spontaneously produced, or shaped by no organizing principles, but is rather, as truly as a tree or a temple, a structural growth—the living issue of a divine process of development, according to laws and principles divinely prescribed. The Pauline description of the Church as a body, the Body of Christ, with parts and members each in place, and all instinct with one and the same gracious life, conveys essentially the same conception.

It is specially to be noted that the Church as thus contemplated, is not a human, but a divine construction. All attempts to explain the existence and growth of this gracious organism on natural principles, after the manner of Gibbon, are signal failures. Human elements have indeed been blended with the divine at many points in the development of the Church: we see society, general and civil, philosophies of various types, human usages and sentiments, and multiplied other earthly influences, flowing in to affect both its outward manifestations and its inward life. But the Church is not an evolution from such germs; they have affected, but they did not create it. Higher forces than the religious sentiment in man, or the impulse to fellowship which this sentiment gives, or the agency of fashions or tendencies in life, must be introduced in order to explain either its existence or its growth. God is as truly the Creator of the Church, as He was the Creator of nature: back of forces, laws, germs, atoms, we find Him in the former process as truly as in the latter. His fiat made the worlds and man: His fiat gave form and life to the Church.

As a divine rather than human construction, the Church throughout its long history reveals a sublime process of development, stage after stage, dispensation after dispensation. While its essential principles never change, and many of its institutions and provisions stand from epoch to epoch unaltered, the Church is still in many other aspects a living, growing organism. Even the revelation on which it reposes as a sure foundation, rose by long gradations into its final form: so the plan of redemption required many centuries of preparation, before it could announce its culminating provisions. In like manner, the beliefs, the creeds and theologies, of the Church reveal a process of both intellectual and spiritual development: its experience and its capacities expand with the ages: and its mission to humanity steadily widens in both extent and significance. The history of other institutions, the rise and progress of empires, the upspringing even of the great natural faiths of the world, furnish no parallel to this gracious development. Nor can the result be accounted for on any other hypothesis than that God is in the Church,—that the Holy Ghost is its animating principle, and that its growth is as supernatural as was its first creation. The crowning fact is that the God of providence is also here, as in the experience of the individual believer, the God of grace, Lord and Giver of life.

Hence arises an interesting inquiry respecting what may be termed the laws, the regulative principles, the divinely ordained methods, of church growth. For, while we may not know just how the divine vitality flows in upon this spiritual organism, producing such vigor and development as have been described, we may reverently study those laws, principles, methods, according to which the gracious result is made to appear. In such directions the growth of the Church in its totality, or the growth of any particular church, may be as readily apprehended as the process of erecting a temple, or the broad and grand outspreading of an oak.

VI. THE INTERNAL LAW OF CHURCH GROWTH: SPIRITUAL PROPAGATION.—What is contemplated here is an increase and enlargement from within, resembling that through which the family broadens into the tribe, or the tribe is multiplied into the state or the nation. We may find a primary illustration of this in the Christian household, viewed as a divinely ordained instrumentality for the perpetuation and diffusion of religion. God has in all dispensations utilized the pious family in this way, availing Himself of all its wondrous potencies as aids in preserving and multiplying among men the influence of His truth and grace. Three times, says Luther, did Jehovah introduce His scheme of mercy in and with a single family,—as if one such household, thoroughly sanctified by the indwelling presence of religion, would become an expanding germ through whose holy vitalities all the families of the earth should be blessed. What has been aptly described as the outpropagating power of the Christian stock,[1] has thus abundantly verified itself at all periods in the experience of the people of God. By parental instruction and nurture, by the careful training of children in divine truth and law, by faithful observance of the appointed sacraments and ordinances of the Gospel, the pious household has ever proven itself thus the primary agency employed of God in extending the sphere and influence of piety in the world. It is indeed in this view of the spiritual capabilities embodied in the Christian home, that we find one of the supreme reasons for that ordinance of nature which setteth the solitary in families: Ps. 68: 6, Mal. 2: 15.

On a broader scale, each Christian church is thus a family, brought

---

[1] BUSHNELL, H., *Christian Nurture:* p. 195. "God is from the first looking for a godly seed; or, what is nowise different, inserting such laws of population, that piety itself shall finally overpopulate the world."

together by spiritual attractions, and welded and unified through love, in order that it may become, in the spiritual sense, a propagative agency in the interest of religion,—an agency not merely preserving, as if it were an inherited estate, the grace it has received, but also by more active processes diffusing and perpetuating that grace among men. In the economy of the Gospel it seems not only a fixed, but also a primary principle, that vital religion should be spread abroad through this unique instrumentality. To this end such a sacrament as infant baptism is introduced into the constitution of the church, to be a visible emblem and pledge of spiritual life yet to be imparted. To this end various methods of instruction and culture are provided, in order that from the outset youthful minds may be habituated, within the household of faith, to the teachings and the tempers of religion. To this end the children of believing parents are even counted as constructively within the church from their birth, and at proper age are invited to contemplate it as their privilege to enter into full communion, by participation in that interior sacrament whose office it is to express in most affecting form the unity of each and all believers in the one family of Christ. In such ways, every Christian Church is thus set upon the task of providing from age to age for its own permanence and expansion, by the training within its own hallowed circle of successive generations of disciples. It was chiefly by this process that the Abrahamic was expanded into the Jewish, and this again into the Christian Church. It was largely by these methods that the church of the Pentecost at Jerusalem has, by its outpropagating power, become the church of humanity,—represented by tens of thousands of particular churches, inheriting its mission and spirit, and continuing the same gracious development in many lands.

On a scale still broader, the Church of Christ on the earth is to increase primarily by the same inward process to the end of time. It is worthy of note that the Papal Church has availed itself of this grand principle of development, in a grosser form: steadily aiming to perpetuate itself not so much by aggression upon the outer world of unbelief, as by the careful infolding within its ever broadening circle, of each new generation of adherents,—claiming as its own every child born within its pale, and on which its baptismal consecration has been bestowed. It is also to be noted that the churches of the Reformation were administered largely on this principle, growing and expecting to grow, not so much by captures from the world, as by the introduction of each successive generation of children into the experience and the inheritance of grace. Many of the Protestant Confessions, and eminently the Symbols of Westminster, are strongly characterized by this principle: and so far as the communions planted on such Confessions have been true to their own doctrinal affirmations, they have enjoyed a large degree of growth along these interior lines. May it not be regarded as one of the most propitious facts of our time that evangelical Protestantism, of every variety, is becoming so extensively imbued with a sense of the values of this inward mode of development;—that the hearts of the fathers are turning so tenderly toward the children in the spiritual household,—that instrumentalities and methods aiming at the instruction and conversion of the young are so remarkably multiplying,—and that the increase of particular churches from year to year is coming to be measured chiefly by the fidelity with which they thus believe in, and thus employ this primary law of church growth?

The biblical basis for this view of church development by interior propagation, may be briefly stated. Its germs clearly lie in the provisions of the Abrahamic economy and covenant; Gen. 18: 18–19. Illustrations of it appear at various points in the Hebraic dispensation; Deut. 6: 7, Ps. 78: 4–8. Nor did it belong to the seclusive stages or eras of the true religion only. It is suggestive that our Lord lays down in so many ways His view of the relations of children to the kingdom of heaven, and of their right to the recognition and aid of His Church. It is suggestive also that, at the outset of the new dispensation, Peter at the Pentecost should lay such stress on the fullness of the promise both to believers and to their children; Acts 2: 39. The duties of parents and children respectively are often urged in the Pauline Epistles, Col. 3: 20–21; and especially the obligation of devout parents to train up their offspring in the nurture and admonition of the Lord; Eph. 6: 1–4. So also, the descriptions of the Church as a family, and of Christianity as the religion of the household and the home, inculcate forcibly the same lesson,—that the largest and richest growth of this divine organism, will be enjoyed when this domestic type of religion is most fully appreciated and put into practice.

A single remark is needful here respecting the specific peril involved in the application of this law. The Christian Church is not national like the Jewish, or formal and ceremonial like the Papal communion. It must therefore guard itself against the Jewish and Romish error of supposing that true membership in the Church can be obtained by birth or inheritance, or by submission to outward rites or the observance of Christian ordinances. Some forms of Protestantism have fallen into this error by accepting, under certain outward conditions, as actual members those who at best are only constructively such,—multiplying numbers without sufficient regard for regenerate character as the only adequate qualification. Regenerative baptisms, catechetical admissions, half-way covenants, and other like processes, may increase the numerical aggregate of the Church, but can only diminish its true strength, its spiritual efficiency. Such methods can only Judaize our Christianity. It is in such directions that this primary law of church development confronts its gravest peril: formalism does its most destructive work at just this point. The growth we are contemplating must be spiritual throughout, or it will prove corrupting and fatal. And the only adequate protection lies in loyal adherence to the scriptural principle that saving faith in Christ, is the sole, universal, essential and perpetual condition of complete church membership,—as truly in the child nurtured within the Christian home and in the family of grace, as in the adult transgressor, convicted and penitent before the Lord.

VII. THE EXTERNAL LAW OF CHURCH GROWTH: SPIRITUAL CONQUEST.—Here we pass beyond the conception of the Church as a divine household, growing and multiplying from within, to contemplate that Church rather as a grand missionary agency, sent forth to conquer and possess the world of humanity for Christ. Among the primary Christian beliefs stands the belief in the possibility of converting the world to Christianity. This belief rests on the revealed plan and will of the Father, on the direct commands and assurances of our Lord, and on the pledged and verified gift and presence of the Holy Spirit. It is confirmed by what we have seen and known of the inherent efficiencies of Gospel truth, of the vital power of religion in the human heart, of the potential influences exerted by the Church, and of the glorious triumphs already won by spiritual Christianity among the most enlightened nations and races of men. To reject this cardinal belief,—to rest rather in the opinion that the Christian religion is merely local or temporal in its range—a type of faith incapable of being carried into all lands, or of subduing unto Christ the entire world of humanity—would be equivalent to a confession that the Gospel itself is an illusion, most disappointing at the point where its capabilities were to be most fully tested, and where its promises appeared to be brightest: Ps. 72, Isa. 40: 3–5, Matt. 28: 18–20, Acts 3: 19–26.

As the agent of God in the execution of this sublime purpose, the Church becomes of necessity a missionary organization, endowed and authorized to bear this Gospel to every creature. The world is its field, and the entire race are the objects of its thought and labor. Into all the earth it is sent, to subdue all the earth unto Christ, John 1: 9–10, Rom. 1: 16. And each particular church, in its own measure, is thus a missionary body as well as a consecrated household,— designed under the divine economy to grow as well by drawing into its hallowed circle those who are without, as by nurturing unto holiness those who are within its fold. Every such church has a specific mission to humanity,—it is a messenger of glad tidings to every sinner, however far astray, whom it can by any means invite into the marriage supper of the Lamb, Luke 14: 15-24. This is a cardinal obligation, wrought into the constitution of the Christian Church at large, and of each particular organization; and any deviation from it, even in thought, is infidelity to the great commission given to His earthly body by the ascended Head.

It should also be borne in mind, that the one, sole, universal method of fulfilling that commission, must be found in the instruction, the persuasion, the conviction and conversion of individual souls. Not baptismal rites, or formal professions, or merely external memberships of any sort, are to be sought, in this sublime process of conquering the world for our Immanuel. The warnings against reliance on such methods,—against attempting to secure increase rather than growth, by enrollment rather than through regeneration, stand in Scripture side by side with the great commission itself. The conversion of souls is the one and only process by which the Church is to win and save lost humanity. What does conversion involve? It involves intelligent acquaintance with the truth and grace of the Gospel: it involves honest recognition of personal sin and guilt and need: it involves true repentance and true faith in the divine Christ as a perfect Redeemer. In a word, conversion is nothing else than the instant, hearty, complete turning of the sinner, under divine influence and with the aid of the Spirit, away from all sin, unto Christ as his personal Savior, with absolute recognition of His claims, and with irrevocable purpose to serve Him, cordially, supremely and forever. For such conversion there can be in the scheme of grace no possible substitute. And should the Church come to depend on any merely outward adherence, any formal or ceremonial enrollment, in lieu of this spiritual experience, the inevitable result would be an increase which bore with it no true enlargement,—an organization in which ceremony had supplanted piety, and in which external show and glitter had both obscured the proper glory of inward holiness, and induced indifference to all effectual outward activities.

Growth by spiritual conquest, through the instruction and conversion of the outlying world of humanity, is therefore the great external law or method in all church development. It has been the peculiar privilege of Protestantism, even from the period of the Reformation, but more distinctly in these later times, to see and utilize this law, as the Church of Rome, both mediæval and modern, has failed to do. Though Protestant communions have adhered too closely to the papal theory of church growth—though the formal conception of the Church as an external society, or an organization coterminous with the state, into which men may come as an outward privilege, apart from the matter of conversion, has too largely pervaded Protestant thought, yet in the main evangelical Protestantism has cordially seen and accepted the higher, more scriptural view. The full discovery through Luther of the doctrine of justification by faith was hardly more important than this consequent discovery of the sublime commission of the Church to save the world. It is at this point that Protestant have shown their vast superiority to Papal missions,—in the fact that they have aimed primarily, not at church enlargement through ceremonial enrollments, but at the conversion and ingathering of souls. And it is a most suggestive fact that those Christian bodies which have seen this primary obligation most distinctly, and have given themselves most zealously to its fulfillment, are precisely those which are increasing most rapidly, and whose future seems brightest with spiritual promise.

It may be anticipated that this method of growth will reveal its worth more and more distinctly as the great process of subduing the world unto Christ draws nearer to its culmination. Thus far, the task of pushing the lines of Christian occupation into hostile territory, has been carried on with incessant difficulty: in the apprehension of many, the result, if not doubtful, is very remote. But God often hurries on His gracious processes, especially in their maturing stages,—the fields of salvation whiten rapidly at the last. Nor is it unlikely that a time will come when, instead of the toilsome effort of the present, a nation shall be born as in a day—when an impenitent world will come flocking into the Church, as doves to their windows: Isa. 60. While the household of faith illustrates inwardly the principle of family development, and at a steadily increasing ratio adds to its volume through the nurture of its own offspring, we may expect that its function as an army of conquest will exhibit like advance in efficiency, and in the measure of success. To this high end its powers and resources will be more and more fully consecrated: its methods will be improved, and its influence widened, and its courage increased, until its adequacy to the task will be no longer questioned. Then, with startling rapidity, the great harvest of humanity will ripen, and will be triumphantly gathered: Rev. 5: 13.

VIII. ILLICIT PROCESSES OF CHURCH GROWTH.—These two laws or methods of church growth, by spiritual propagation and spiritual conquest, indicate the only and the sufficient modes whereby the consummation of the Church and Kingdom of God on earth is to be reached. Nothing more is needful than the diligent application of these divine methods, in their multiplied varieties of form and action, to secure the final enthronement of spiritual Christianity as the religion of mankind. It remains to note the fact that illicit processes have often been introduced in apparent conjunction with, or in open opposition to, these gracious modes of growth. Human ambitions, unsanctified zeal, impatience in view of the slow developments of grace, and other earthly influences, are constantly breaking in at many points upon this divine unfolding. A glimpse at some of these unauthorized methods, born of the wish of man rather than of the revealed will of God, may be of service here.

Passing by the obvious mistakes of the Papacy, and of ritualistic Christianity already adverted to, we shall find within the circle of positive Protestantism a series of such illicit processes, against which the Church of Christ should ever be carefully protected. The first of these is the substitution of false and narrowing notions of the Church itself in the place of the broad biblical conception,—especially the regarding of the Church as an external, material, political or social organization, rather than such a spiritual organism as it is divinely intended to be. A second error may be seen in the disposition to compromise the divine foundations of doctrine on which the Church is builded,—especially at the points where such doctrine is most unpalatable to unbelieving minds, or awakens the greatest opposition in human society. A third appears in the inclination to lower the standard or the terms of admission, so as to make access to the Church less offensive or trying to those who are not thoroughly surrendered to the claim and sway of Christ. Kindred to this is the still more serious error of reducing the standard of character and attainment in those who are already members within this divine household,—such as allowing extensive conformity with the world, failing to forbid doubtful or pernicious practices, loosening the avowed bonds of discipleship or fellowship, or accepting as sufficient a low grade of spiritual manhood or womanhood. Still another illicit process appears in the disposition to secure growth by spectacular arrangements, such as attract the natural interest of men merely,—splendor in architecture, pompous ceremonies, official dignities and display, artistic music, and other like instrumentalities, whose object is rather to draw and please, than to awaken or convict or edify. These may be taken as the more obvious illustrations of an insidious tendency to allure the mind of believers away from those great primal conditions of growth on which the Church is in fact dependent,—a tendency revealed in a thousand ways, but fraught in every form with irreparable mischiefs.

Is it not manifest that the introduction of such methods can, at the best, only interrupt the action of those diviner modes of growth which have been already considered? Is it not obvious that these lower modes, though they may apparently succeed in filling the Church with numbers, will tend steadily to produce just such a pitiful result as the church in Laodicea presented? Rich and increased in goods and having need of nothing, in an external sense, that church was to the vision of faith, wretched, miserable, poor, blind, naked indeed; splendid in its visibilities, but weak and fruitless and decaying at the heart. The warning to Laodicea, conveyed by John (Rev. 3: 17), is of universal application. Growth unlawfully secured is not true growth; it may appear as increase, expansion, outward success, but inwardly it is always corrupting, if not fatal. The teaching of the Scripture is clear, solemn, conclusive here. There must be no compromising of essential truth—there must be no abjuring of the vital principle of conversion—there must be no lowering of the Gospel standard of holiness —there must be no surrender at any point of any thing that belongs to the Church as a supernatural, spiritual organization, planted on Christ as the sure foundation, and vivified and moulded throughout by His Spirit and His grace. There may be value in wealth, learning, position—in architecture or music or official dignity, as mere accessories: but no church truly grows through such helps, or can live by them. From every experiment of this class, thoughtful minds will ever return to the two simple, spiritual methods of growth divinely indicated, to find in these rather than in any and all inventions of men, the means by which the Church of Christ, fitly framed together, groweth unto an holy temple in the Lord. And well will it be for spiritual Protestantism, and especially for the more wealthy and cultured and conspicuous sections of that Protestantism, if they abjure all papal or ritualistic or formal dreams of advancement, and act upon the high principle that the Church liveth not by bread alone, but by the word of God, the spirit of God, and the methods of God only.

IX. THE CHURCH IN HUMAN SOCIETY: GENERAL VIEW.—Thus far, the Church has been contemplated as an institution, divinely planted, developing historically, and justifying itself by its perceived relations to the nature of man as a religious being, and to religion as a divine force in human life;—an institution having certain impersonal constituents such as doctrines, sacraments, ordinances, and composed of persons sustaining various connections with it as members and as officers;—an institution planted on the general basis of government, and taking on the form of a gracious kingdom, with some definite type of constitution and polity, and revealing its quality as such in administration and in discipline. We have seen the Church, separated widely in form and usage, and existing in a state of division, yet holding to the fundamental conception of unity, and presenting itself before the world notwithstanding such diversities as in essence and substance One Church of God among men. We have also beheld this one Church as a living growth—the vital Body of Christ, developing steadily from age to age, under certain authoritative laws, by certain fixed processes, toward a future as extensive as humanity—a future of gracious and glorious supremacy in all the earth. It now remains to inquire more specifically, in brief, respecting the position of the Church in human society, the place it properly holds or should seek to hold in human life, the relations it sustains or should sustain to the other great institutions and interests of men.

Two false impressions should be noted at the outset. On one side, it is affirmed that the Church is an artificial and abnormal institute in the world—the creation of priests or enthusiasts, or at best the architectural efflorescence of a type of religion, which is living out its brief day in the career of humanity, and which, as it is outgrown and dies out of life, will carry the Church with it into decay and oblivion. It is true, it is said, that Christianity differs from the other natural faiths, in the fact that, wherever it goes, it expresses or embodies itself in this peculiar institution: but when this faith declines, as other faiths have declined in history, the institution will crumble and perish with it. The relations of the Church to human society are therefore but casual, temporary, unimportant.—On another side, the Church is viewed as an institution wholly divine in structure, aiming at ends peculiar to itself, planted in the world but in no sense of the world—a temporary tabernacle for the ingathering of the elect, and a place wherein religion may be sheltered from the influences of life, but standing in no divinely ordered relationship to humanity as a whole, or to human society as a surrounding element. In the former view, the Church is simply a temporary construction or institute framed by the religious nature: in this it is an organization wholly supernatural in structure and mission—as widely separate from ordinary life or experience, as was that mystical sheet which Peter beheld in sacred vision only.

Clearly such is far from being the biblical conception. While the Church is not of the world as to its origin, its faith, its spirit and tendency—while in such aspects it is as widely separated from all other institutions and interests and movements of our fallen humanity as if it were organized on another planet, yet it is as truly sent into the world as were the Apostles for whom the Savior prayed before His passion—as was that Savior Himself. It has a mission, as distinctively as they severally had a mission: it inherits their mission, and finds one of the primal reasons for its existence in the gracious relations which it is thus called to sustain to the world of humanity. The Church is in human society in order that it may instruct, awaken, spiritualize, regenerate society, in virtue of its own diviner life. While it is at many points affected, sometimes disastrously, by these social connections which its great commission constrains it to assume—while human society reacts upon it at a thousand points, shaping its organization, influencing its teaching, determining even the quality and measure of its religious vitalities, still the Church is the embodied presence of Christ in the world—the representative of His grace, and His chief agent in the restoration of lost men to Himself. Considered apart from this redemptive mission, which is consequent upon and analogous to the mediatorial mission of our Lord, the Church would become as great an enigma to us, as a vessel would be to one who had never known what the ocean is. If we comprehend what human society is, in its varied institutions and laws and interests—in its grand controlling forces and tendencies, and especially in its myriad phases of sin and need, we may also know why God created, endowed, and commissioned His Church as He did; and why He set it up in the world, to stand through all the ages, as the one indestructible thing, the one dominating institution, in human life.

It is true that we at first behold the Church secluded within the family, hidden as a treasure within the tribe, holden strictly within the domain of a single nation, as if it sustained no such œcumenical office or relations. But the reasons for such preparatory discipline through seclusion have already been noted; the seclusion itself was a prophecy of the universality in connection and mission, that was to follow it. Even in the Old Testament, as in the Messianic Psalms, and in the culminating predictions of Isaiah and Daniel, this world-wide relationship was clearly foretold. The stone cut without hands out of the mountain was to roll on irresistibly, until it had crushed down all oppositions; the kingdom which Daniel foresaw, established in narrowness and privacy, was to overthrow all hostile dominions, and to rule in majesty from the rising to the setting of the sun. In the New Testament, while our Lord and the apostles were first of all engaged in planting the kingdom of heaven in human hearts, and in establishing Christian churches wherever converts could be found, still Christ Himself clearly contemplated a time when the growing mustard seed should fill the lands with its verdure, and the apostles looked forward to a day when Jew and Gentile, men of all nations and all nations of men, should be folded within the circle of this outspreading, beneficent faith.

X. THE CHURCH AND HUMAN SIN.—Contemplating this relationship of the Church to human society, first in more generic, than in more specific forms, we are confronted at the outset by that which constitutes the central feature in the position of the Church in the world—its mission to human sin.—Here, as at many other points in the

Christian scheme of doctrine, the one Church is sadly divided in its faith and teaching; and one of the sorest hindrances to its success in this universal mission is revealed in such divisions. Yet on many of the essential elements in the scriptural doctrine of sin, the Church is already substantially one. That sin exists in man, and exists universally,—that it is more than a mere conflict between matter and spirit, or between the body and the soul, and more than a trivial incident or accident in human experience,—that it lies deeper than action, and in some sense possesses the nature, and flows in a turbid current through the entire life,—that it involves responsibility at every stage in its dark development, and brings guilt and condemnation, and the possibility of spiritual and even everlasting death, on every sinning soul; these are propositions in which evangelical churches may be said to be essentially agreed. It is also a fact of great significance, that the profoundest movements of Christian thought in our time are toward closer unity around the more fundamental elements in this doctrine; and it may be anticipated that, as the Church thus reaches deeper agreement in conviction, and consequently in feeling, its sublime mission to the sin of the world will become more grandly significant, more transcendently glorious.

As sin is universal, this mission is a mission to humanity; and as sin is multiplex in manifestation and profound in influence, revealing itself in ten thousand subtle ways in the individual life, and permeating and controlling society in every moral aspect, this restorative mission must assume like variety, penetrativeness, efficiency. As the representative of Christ in the world, it is the high task of the Church to take the sin of the world in its heart, as did the Savior Himself; and to minister to it in all its deformities and corruptions, in His spirit, and by the complex methods which His Gospel supplies. Here we are led at once to contemplate the multiplicity of this mission, and the vastness as well as variety of the services which the Church is called, in the name of Christ, to render to a sinful world. Human methods of improvement which contemplate only the cultivation of some single virtue, specific reforms which aim at the correction of some single vice, philanthropic movements looking toward the advancement of mankind in some particular social interest, grow trivial in comparison with the gigantic task to which the Church of God addresses itself. In like manner do the organizations and machineries of men, designed to secure such ends through joint endeavor, fade into insignificance when compared with that array of resources, agencies, powers, which are divinely concentrated in the Christian Church. And surely no commission that man could obtain from his own convictions, or from the combined sympathies of his fellows, can equal in impressiveness the commandment of the Lord to bear His saving message to every creature;—as no fervors of benevolence, no inspirations of just wrath against evil, can equal the gracious potencies that flow into the soul of the commissioned Church, through the indwelling Spirit of God.

The temper in which this redemptive mission is to be prosecuted, is sufficiently indicated in the career of Him from whom the commission came. On the one side, the Church of Christ is to set itself in irrevocable opposition to sin, in every form, of every grade. Not only is it to grant no countenance to sin within its own circle: it is to be the unyielding foe of sin in human life. History reveals the pregnant fact, that the times of signal peril to the Church—the times when its work and influence among men were least productive, and when corruption most easily crept like miasma into the secret sources and currents of its own life, were those in which low views of sin, compromises with sin, wicked yielding to sin, were widely prevalent. On the contrary, it has always been the fact that deepened convictions concerning sin, both within the Church and without, and especially an unswerving hatred of all sin in the world, have invariably been the harbinger of augmented power, of more glorious fruitage. The wicked world itself despises a compromising, but fears and admires, and even yields to, a resolute and holy Church. The testimony of Christianity against sin is never so powerful as when it finds expression through the Church: compared with its deep, reverberating protests, the eloquence of the most effective preacher, the earnest endeavor of the private believer, seem insignificant.

On the other side, the temper of the Church must ever be one of Christlike love. Righteous hostility to sin and tender compassion for the sinner are convertible terms in Christian experience. The happy paradox reveals itself supremely in the heart and life of our Lord Himself; it is verified abundantly in apostolic instructions and example. And in this respect, as in the former, it is the peculiar function of this spiritual organization to express to the world the pitying compassion of the Father, the redemptive mercy of the Son, the consummating grace of the Spirit. For, nothing but the revelation of this triune Love can ever draw humanity away from sin, into the true life of responsive love and holiness. A Church itself unmoved by such transcendent emotions, is a Church without power; it may hold orthodox views respecting sin, and may be stirred up to resistance to sin, but it can not overcome sin. Hence the value of a ministry suffused in all its purpose and effort with holy love: hence the value of churches, organized under the inspirations of brotherhood, and filled with tender yearnings for the spiritual welfare of all within their reach: hence the value of benevolent institutions, evangelical charities, beneficent movements in society, designed to express church feeling, and to win all classes and conditions of men into church fellowship. Until the world is thus made to see and believe that the Church of God is a loving Church,—that while it hates and resists the sin, it ever pities and tries to help the sinner, the great mission of the Church as a savior of humanity from sin, must remain essentially unfulfilled.

Such in brief is the most generic relation of the Christian Church to humanity—a relation resting on the demonstrated basis of universal sin, and on the primal function of the Church as the commissioned agent of God in the deliverance of humanity from sin. No narrower view of its commission,—contemplating that commission as elective and partial rather than universal, or regarding it as confined to testimony against sin, or to witnessing against the world as evil,—can be admitted here. Christ for the world, and the world for Christ, is rather at once the broad and tender teaching of the Word, and the inspiring motto of all who truly apprehend the Gospel.

XI. THE CHURCH AND HUMAN INSTITUTIONS: CHURCH AND STATE.—Two coördinate institutions, both of divine appointment in their respective spheres, both universal as mankind and alike essential to the well-being of men, stand side by side with the Christian Church, wherever it is established,—the Family and the State. What are the relations of the Church, and what is its mission, to these two primordial institutions?

The relations of the Church to the Family have already been noted in substance. We have seen how large a place the sanctified household has always held in the developing economy of redemption, and what peculiar ties forever bind in one the Christian Home and the Christian Church. We have noted the tender responsibilities sustained by the household of faith toward the children of believers, and recognized the gracious and beautiful ministries due from the larger to this smaller family circle, in virtue of the divine covenant with both. It remains only to note the obligation of the Church of God to emphasize the biblical doctrine of the family, and to protect this divine institution against the insidious influences combining on many sides to corrupt and destroy it. The Church is bound to enforce by every available method the scriptural doctrine, even against civil usages, in the matter of divorce.[1] It is bound also to utter its most solemn condemnation upon all sins against the purity, the peacefulness, the holy unity of the household, contemplated as first among the beneficent gifts of God to men. It is bound, further, to bring the

---

[1] WOOLSEY: *Divorce and Divorce Legislation.* HOVEY, A., *Scriptural Law*, etc.

light and the sanctifying grace of the Gospel into every home which it can penetrate, and to do whatever it may toward making every such home itself a veritable house of God—a true gate of heaven to all who dwell beneath its roof. For the Christianized Home is at once the most impressive witness to the saving efficacy of the Gospel, and the most effective adjunct which spiritual Christianity can command, in the discharge of its gracious mission to mankind.

The question respecting the relations of the Church to the State is much more complex, and in many aspects more difficult. A few suggestions pointing towards a comprehensive answer, may here be introduced; the answer itself would require an extensive survey of theories, and a complicated discussion of the nature and functions of each of these closely affiliated and related, yet widely differing institutions.[1] The peculiar blending of the church, first with the family, then with the tribe and the nation, prior to the Christian dispensation, and later the progressive unifying of the Church with the Roman State under the Papacy, and still later the varieties of combination established between the Church and the civil powers in Europe, Protestant as well as Papal, at and after the Reformation, have already been briefly mentioned. We have also noted certain evil influences of such combinations upon the spiritual vigor of the Church, upon its doctrine of membership and its conception of religious character, and upon its voluntary and missionary zeal, as a regenerative force in human life. History suggests, if it does not clearly prove, the conclusion that the greatest mistake of Protestantism after the Reformation appears in its illusive theories respecting the union of Church and State, and in the embarrassing and weakening complications which everywhere attended the attempts to turn such theories into practice. These attempts have, in numberless instances, resulted in strenuous conflicts between civil and ecclesiastical powers, in which the state has sometimes been prostrated at the feet of an assuming church, and the church has more often been constrained to submit to the jurisdiction of an ambitious and unsanctified state. They have also borne their natural fruitage in many intestinal disturbances within the household of faith, and in division after division among those who on all other questions were essentially one in belief and purpose. Nor is there a more painful chapter in the history of modern Christianity than that which describes the jealousies, the antagonisms, the scheming of differ-

---

[1] References: PALMER, *Church of Christ*, Part V; CUNNINGHAM, *Church Principles*, Chap. VI-VIII; HODGE, *Church Polity*, Chap. VII; BAIRD. R., *Religion in America;* THOMPSON, J. P., *Church and State in the United States:* SPEAR, S. T., *Religion and the State*. Also HOOKER, *Eccl. Polity*, Book VIII,, Chap. IV, and WARBURTON, *Works*, Alliance of Church and State.

ent Protestant bodies to secure for themselves the endorsement and the patronage of civil power.[1]

Dorner (II : 469) describes what he regards as a better tendency, in the recent effort in Germany, "to separate the law of the Protestant Church from canon law, by the development and realization of Protestant ideas concerning the form and government of the Church in its intrinsic independence of the state." Still he maintains that this must be accomplished "in unison with the spirit of a national or congregational church." But the question at once arises whether the Church can assert such intrinsic independence, and develop without hindrance its own free conceptions of law, while retaining the illusion of a national organization—while resting for support on civil patronage, and looking to the state for endorsement and position. The only broad and permanent answer to this question, must be found ultimately in the abandonment of all direct state connection. The only law with which the Church of Christ has any occasion to conform itself, is His law given in His own Word, and standing forth in entire independence of political endorsement. And the only support on which the Church can rely, or has any clear right to rely, is the free and loving support of those who voluntarily seek its shelter, and enjoy the life and fellowship which it embodies. Civil establishments, in which the bestowment of patronage carries necessarily with it a correlative right to control, have proven in the past, and can prove in the future, only a hindrance to a spiritual, aggressive Protestantism. It is certainly both a significant and a hopeful fact, that this view is coming to be recognized by more thoughtful leaders in Church and State, and that the problem of disestablishment is already urging itself upon European Protestantism as one of the vital issues in a rapidly advancing future.

Such formal separation would by no means result in setting these two divine institutions in an attitude of entire independence or isolation. For, while their spheres are almost wholly separate, and while the heavenly kingdom has laws, purposes, a spirit and life, with which the earthly kingdom may not intermeddle, yet as alike divine in origin, both institutions are sacredly pledged to each other in the support of those great interests of humanity which they are alike ordained of God to subserve. The Church on the one side is bound to uphold just law, to sustain constituted authority, to throw the whole weight of its influence in support of right government. It can not justly assume an attitude of indifference in the presence of threatened anarchy: it can not refuse to stand by the State, in the exercise of its legitimate

---

[1] See the histories of the conflicts and disruptions in British Presbyterianism: NEAL, STOUGHTON, McCRIE, HETHERINGTON, and others. DORNER, *Hist. Prot. Theology*, II : 50—60; COLERIDGE, *Constitution of Church and State*.

powers. To do otherwise, would not only be a consent to the reckless imperilling of the interests of human society; it would also involve dangerous exposure of the Church itself, since pure Christianity thrives only or thrives best in times of civil peace. The value of this position is abundantly attested by the history of modern governments wherever such Christianity prevails. At this moment, the strongest influence anywhere upholding rightful and beneficent government, is the influence flowing silently but pervasively forth from the Christian Church: and this influence, it may be noted, is most powerful and most effectual in those lands where the Church exists in completest independence of the civil power.

On the other hand, there are services of vast significance which the State may render, and is bound to render, to the Church. Regarding that Church as a beneficent organization merely, founded in an unselfish temper for the inculcation of sound morals and the enforcement of mutual duties among men, the State may properly grant it those immunities and privileges which all wise governments accede to charitable associations and enterprises. Viewing the Church as a vast educational agency only, accumulating immense resources and instrumentalities for the instruction of those who are to be citizens, the State should openly protect and foster this agency, so far as this is consistent with its own relations to the human society for whose welfare the Church is thus laboring. And in the discharge of its more distinctive mission to the spiritual life in man, the Church may legitimately ask for the protecting sympathy of the State, so far as this may insure its peaceable assembling and fellowship, and the support of law in sustaining before men its religious position and office. Civil government can not regard Christianity and atheism with equal favor, as is sometimes claimed, since Christianity is the sure ally of good government, while atheism tends always to anarchy, and to the destruction of human society. In the light of these general propositions, many subordinate questions, such as the obligation of oaths, the enforcement of the Christian Sabbath, the repression of profanity, the taxation of church property, the civil support of ecclesiastical discipline, may be at least approximately settled.[1]

XII. THE CHURCH AND EDUCATION: CHURCH AND CULTURE.—As the Church sustains direct relations to the other two primordial institutions of humanity, the family and the state, so it carries on two specific and adjunctive ministries to humanity itself, in conjunction

---

[1] See LUTHARDT, *Moral Truths of Christianity*, Lecture VII, and notes, for valuable suggestions respecting the moral ties binding the State and Church in unity, and the reciprocal duties of the two institutions. WHEWELL, *Elements of Morality:* Book V: Ch. XVI–XVII.

with its chief central ministration to the soul. These adjunctive ministries may be broadly classified as the intellectual and the ethical: to each of these some passing reference should be made.

The dogma that ignorance is the mother of devotion, attributed to an eminent Roman pontiff, is entirely at variance with both the genius and the history of the Christian religion. Looking back upon the intellectual life, even of the Hebrew, we discover at once the suggestive fact that the Church, with its laws, its ordinances, its constituted teachers, its household training, was in reality the divinely ordained school in which the Israelitic mind gained that remarkable development which gave it, even on natural grounds, such prominence in ancient history. If we contemplate Christianity as an educating force—if we consider the Church of Christ as a school, in which knowledge is to be conveyed, the intellect of men quickened, the capacity to apprehend and utilize all other truth developed into effective vigor, we see the same lesson inculcated in far higher, grander form. Thus, when Guizot styles the Reformation a great insurrection of human intelligence,[1] he simply expresses a sublime fact respecting the effective ministries of the Gospel and the Church, even from the twelfth century onward, through the entire period of the revival of learning, to the awakened mind of Europe. For it was not an intelligence lying back of Christianity and sustaining it, but an intelligence which Christianity had itself brought into activity, which in that supreme hour rose up against the attempts even of a tyrannizing Church to repress free thought, and in a mighty insurrection gave to the world at once a purer purpose and a broadened mind. So the world owes first to Luther, then to Calvin, the suggestion of the common school; but both Calvin and Luther derived the conception from their own Christianized intelligence, and from the doctrine and usage of the Church long before the Reformation, and the schools which they planted stood always, by a natural law, in an adjunctive relation to the churches which they organized.

Nor is this connection between the Church and the intellectual life in man limited to a specific era such as the sixteenth century, or to the development of mind which accompanied that great spiritual and social as well as mental insurrection, which we style the Reformation. Wherever Protestantism in later times has gone, it has carried with it like improvement in the intellectual, no less than the religious experience of mankind. Using the term, education, in the broadest sense, as the intelligent development of the community rather than the technical training of a class, we see it originating largely in the Christian Church, or at least receiving from the Church its chief

---

[1] *History of Civilization in Europe*, Lect. XII; also elsewhere.

protection and invigoration. If it be not literally true that where there are no churches, there are no schools, it still is true that the school and the church prosper most when standing side by side,—the church planting and endowing and utilizing the school, and in turn receiving from the school that strengthened support which an improved intellectual life supplies to rational faith. Many specific questions arise at this point,—such as the relation between the religious and the secular elements in education, the respective provinces of the church and the state, the place of the Bible and of religious teaching in the school—which may be solved in the light of the general principle just defined.—In respect to the higher forms of education, the law thus stated receives still finer illustration. It is a suggestive fact of history that, as it was the Church that preserved classical learning during the long medieval obscuration, so it was the Church which finally gave back the treasure it had held in trust, and which laid the foundations of those great universities where art and learning and science have found for centuries their safe and enduring home. What the Church during the past four hundred years, and especially since the Reformation, has done for art in the specific sense,—for sculpture and painting and music;—what the Church has done for higher learning, for classic scholarship, for literature in its varieties, for poetry and eloquence and history;—what the Church has done for philosophy and ethics, for law, for medicine, and even for those physical sciences whose advocates now so often repudiate the historic relationship, it would require volumes adequately to describe. If from these multiplex forms of higher education, as they now stand forth among the chief glories of our modern life, all that the Christian Church has been instrumental in contributing, were obliterated, the residuum would be too small for measurement: the breadth, the sweetness, the dignity of our culture would be almost wholly lost.[1]

It constitutes no adequate objection to this position, that the world has seen true intellectual life, as in Greece, where neither the Church nor Christianity was present as a producing force: or that there have been, and now are, intelligent and cultivated minds who reject Christianity, and despise the Church. Nor is it an adequate objection, though one often urged, that Christianity as a system of truth seems sometimes to fetter the mind rather than to expand or broaden it: or further that the Church has sometimes, as during the fifteenth century, proven rather to be a prison-house in which free thought has been confined—a prejudiced and tyrannical court where the intellect has been savagely condemned to the rack and the stake. These must be confessed to be exceptional or abnormal conditions rather than a general

---

[1] Brace. C. L., *Gesta Christi—Humane Progress under Christianity.*

state. May it not be that the culture of Greece was so powerless to affect practical life, and so evanescent, because it never received such added scope and volume, such moral stimulations, as the Christian faith and the Christian Church would have supplied? May it not also be, that those educated minds who in time past have rejected, or who are now rejecting the Church and the Gospel, owe their mental development, their scientific bias and capability, and the very knowledge in which they rest, to that organized Christianity which surrounds them as a quickening atmosphere whithersoever they go in the prosecution of their scientific investigations? Is it not true, furthermore, that the Christian faith is in its nature stimulating and expanding rather than repressive; and that it indicates certain boundaries which the human mind may not traverse, only because the laws of that mind, as well as the nature of religion, require just such limitations? And certainly it is not a departure from candid reasoning to draw a line between Jesuitism and Christianity—to claim a distinction between the Inquisition and the Christian Church, and to protest against the arraignment of the latter for the stupidities, the malevolence, the cruelties of the former. If fearful mistakes, horrid crimes, have been committed in the name of liberty, mistakes much more fearful, crimes more horrid and inexcusable by far, have been wrought by wicked men in the name of the Church and of religion.

Nor do the questions now under discussion in the realm of the physical sciences, or of philosophy or sociology or ethics, furnish any just ground of objection to this asserted relation between the Church of Christ and the intellectual life of Christendom. The apprehensions of Christian men lest the facts or the doctrines of Revelation should be undermined as the result of such debate, and the hopeful boastings of unbelief in view of some apparent antagonisms between these facts and doctrines and the deductions of science, are alike without foundation. We have seen such antagonisms too often disappearing in the light of broader, deeper unities; we have too often witnessed such assaults coming to naught, and foiled unbelief confessing its failure. It is true that the oppositions between Christianity and such unbelief were never more broad or vital than during the present age; and also that unbelief, like faith, exists under a continuous law of progress, and may therefore be expected to assume darker, deadlier forms in coming ages, even to the end. But as Christianity has withstood all past assault, and is withstanding triumphantly all present assault, so we may expect it to triumph more and more gloriously, from age to age. And the Church, as the representative of the intellectual influences incorporated in the Christian faith, may be expected, so long as it remains true to its own nature and its beneficent mission, to stand forth in human society, through all the future as "the superlative educational force of the world."[1]

XIII. THE CHURCH AND MORALITY: CHURCH AND REFORMS.— These ministries of Christianity to the intellectual life in man, precious though they are, become incidental when compared with its contributions to his moral life. And as in the former direction, so here the Church, next to the Bible itself, is the ordained seat and source of these moral ministrations.

The question whether scriptural is superior to natural morality, may readily be answered. The argument in the negative, urged by English Deists from Herbert and Shaftesbury to Toland and Matthew Tindal, though conducted with great skill, has signally failed. Not only has the objection to the morality of the Bible, based on certain Old Testament facts and injunctions, been abundantly met: the position that nature supplies a sufficient basis for sound morality, and that the moral precepts of Scripture are consequently needless, has been fully shown to be invalid.[2] While it is true that natural and biblical morality are essentially one and the same, as to principle, it is also true that the latter goes far beyond the former in the extent of its range, and in the spiritual thoroughness of its applications. While natural morality concerns itself chiefly with external relations, and with outward acts, the morality of the Bible deals more with purposes, feelings, and even the transient impulses of the soul. Especially is it true that the latter excels in the type and measure of authority with which its precepts are enforced. When the calm demands of reason, the pleadings of conscience, the discovered relations of action as right or wrong, and the judgment of human society, and the will of God as seen in nature, have all been invoked to enforce the claim of duty, the potency of natural morality to secure obedience is wholly exhausted. It can go no further in urging its own right to rule the soul; and if the will be not affected by these incentives, it can do nothing but give way at last to the furious impulses of passion, or to the fierce clamors of selfish interest.

But scriptural morality, just at this point, brings to bear upon the soul a far higher range of incentives. It reveals the God of nature

---

[1] STORRS, R. S., *Divine Origin of Christianity*, Lect. VII. "Skeptics themselves, with whatever learning, eloquence or wit, appear to me but involuntary witnesses to the underlying and impenetrating influence of this religion, which has given possibility to even their hostile culture and force." See also SHAIRP, *Culture and Religion*; LUTHARDT, *Moral Truths*, Lect. IX.

[2] LELAND, *View of the Principal Deistical Writers*; FARRAR, *History of Free Thought*; CAIRNS, *Unbelief in the Eighteenth Century*. Also, on the deistic side, HERBERT, *De Religione Gentilium*; SHAFTESBURY, *Characteristics*, etc.; TINDAL, *Christianity as old as the Creation*.

in more impressive form, as the moral Governor and final Judge of all mankind. It reveals this Divine Being in Christ, as a perfect example of pure ethical living, and as an inspiring stimulus toward righteous action. It reveals the same Being in the Holy Spirit, making the moral law manifest in the heart, spiritualizing its every precept, and at the same time encouraging and enabling the soul to obey. In like manner, it reveals in the Gospel a vast series of invitations, promises, warnings, hopes, all teaching men to estimate their actions in the light of eternity—with supreme reference to the ultimate and everlasting issues of their conduct. In a word, the morality of the Scripture concentrates around the ethical life of man the entire force of the Divine Personality and of the Divine Relations, in a way which is wholly impracticable to the morality of nature; and by this higher method aims to make, and actually does make, the best moralist a better man by making him a Christian. It both develops more extensively the ethical capabilities, and works out a far higher class of results in the practical life. A completer manhood, with broadened views of duty, and with more vigorous and effective impulses toward spiritual obedience,—with stricter discipline of self, with a loftier type of nature and life, and with closer affiliation with God and all divine things, must be the certain and the blessed outcome.

But the Christian Church is by its very nature an ordained teacher of biblical morality, and within its appointed sphere it is the most effective instrument of God in enthroning such morality in the heart and in the life of mankind. All attempts to separate the ethical element of Scripture from its scheme of grace—all attempts to emphasize the inculcation of doctrine, or submission to ceremonies, or the exercise of faith in Christ as an atoning Savior, as if these constituted the whole of the plan of salvation, apart from the faithful and loving observance of the law of God revealed in His Word, are fraught with error, and with peril to the soul. It is indeed the function of the Church to proclaim the essential doctrines of the Gospel, and to invite all men to believe the truth which God has spoken; it is its function to exalt the sacraments, and commend to men the Christian ordinances and the appointed means of grace; it is eminently its function to lift up the Cross, and to magnify the atoning love thereon exhibited, and to invite a burdened and sinful world to the great Redeemer. But it is no less the function of the Church to exalt the divine law, to set forth the moral precepts of the Scripture, to press the claims of duty upon the conscience, to present Christ as an example in righteous living, and to control the world by all the forces inherent in true biblical morality. The Church is as truly a teacher of ethics as of doctrine— as truly a messenger of holiness as a messenger of grace. Love and duty, acceptance and obedience, faith and righteousness, are the kindred obligations with which it is ever to deal.

This general view of the ministry of the Church to the moral life of humanity brings out its special mission with respect to human sin, and to the specific sins of any given man or period. If a church which contents itself with announcing doctrines, offering the sacraments, or holding up the Cross in an abstract way, is insufficient and culpable, hardly less so is that church which merely enunciates morality in general, but never applies moral rules to the actual life of the world. The Church of any age must have courage enough to see and deal with the sins of that age,—to hold up before the times, with utmost plainness and fidelity, the law of God for the times. What the world needs to know is the claim of righteousness, in order that it may the better heed that call to grace, which is in essence a summons to salvation in and through regenerate, sanctified character. The blood of Christ is effectual in salvation only in so far as it also cleanseth from all sin; and they only are saved, who are thus rescued from their sins, through those purifying processes which the gracious morality of Scripture undertakes. Hence the peculiar mission of the Church of Christ to the moral life;—a mission which is not to be carried out by the right living of the private member, or by occasional proclamations from the pulpit, but by a grand movement of the Church itself as a sanctified organization along the loftiest lines of biblical morality—a holy host leading the world, through the efficacies of sacred precept and holy example upward steadfastly toward right and godly living. It can hardly be questioned that such was the vision of His Church which filled the mind of Christ, as He saw that Church moving onward through the ages toward its predestined place at the head of humanity. That glimpses of such a comprehensive ethical as well as spiritual mission, lingered as a holy dream in the mind of Paul, some of his epistles seem distinctly to suggest. The consummation of our humanity of which the apostle dreams, is one in which morality and holiness, duty and grace, obedience and love, are indissolubly blended.

XIV. THE CHURCH AND CIVILIZATION.—Such in brief are the specific relations of the Church to the intellectual and to the moral nature of man respectively. It now remains to inquire finally respecting its comprehensive relation and ministry to our aggregated human life, as indicated in the term, civilization.

Even in the narrowest sense of that term, as including the interchange of graceful civilities, the prevalence of social order, the refinements of education, and the like, it remains true that, in the phrase of Burke, these results have flowed in upon society mainly through the action of two influences, the spirit of a gentleman and the spirit of religion. In the full sense the latter term embraces the former; religion is ever the source and fount of true gentlemanliness. Guizot defines civilization more broadly as the progress of both society and the individual in all that goes to constitute comfort and elevation in human existence; yet Guizot regards the spirit of religion, or Christianity, as first among the social forces through whose agency such progress comes. In the broadest sense, civilization may be described as the sum total of human development in any given age,—the vast aggregate of those material, social, political and religious conditions in any specified land and period, on which this progressive maturing of individuals and of society is found to depend. A proper comprehension of the term must include not merely the specific state of things, with all of comfort, blessing, advance included in it, but also the causes of which that social state is the perceived effect. Nor can the definition be restricted, after the manner of Buckle and his school, to physical or material conditions, or even to mental aptitudes, or political organization, or ethical bias. It is impossible to account for the existence of any high and enduring type of civilization, without admitting the presence and influence of what Burke styles the spirit of religion, and eminently in modern life of the presence and influence of the Christian religion. No theory of civilization can be truly comprehensive which does not fitly recognize the agency of this supreme factor,—which does not find, back of and beneath all other influences, the truth and temper of vital Christianity, and the effective ministrations of the Christian Church.

The ministry of the Church to modern civilization may be said to commence with its enforcement of the doctrine of human progress— the capabilities of humanity in the direction of progress, and the grounds of hope that such progress is to be realized. Against the pessimism of Schopenhauer—against the dark notion that the career of the human race is to be downward rather than upward, and that the final issue of life will be a catastrophe rather than a consummation, the Church of God, surviving and growing with the centuries, and steadily becoming more and more beneficent in teaching and influence, is a perpetual and a convincing protest. In like manner, over against all dreams of a civilization, perfected through soil and climate, through machineries, through political constitutions, through education and art and culture only, the Church stands as a steadfast witness,—lifting up the sublime antithesis of a civilization to be gained through character, character regenerated by the power of God, and perfected through grace and faith in Christ Jesus. It is a sound proposition, that the progress of society in respect to merely material conditions or physical comforts, must always be limited by its equal progress along those higher ranges of experience and advantage which the term, civilization, most centrally represents. It is a proposition no less sound, that this higher social progress is vitally dependent on the progress of the individuals who compose such society, in all the elements of true manhood, and eminently in those elements which appertain to elevated, sanctified character. But Christianity aims to advance society by just this inward process upon individual personality and manhood; and the outward and general advances which the civilized world is making, are found historically to be turning more and more upon the success of the Gospel in thus renovating, restoring human character. Christianity is thus the supreme factor in all true, enduring civilization: and the Church as its representative is, therefore, even more than all inventions, all industries, all education and art and civil policy, the great civilizer of men. In a word, the progress which the world most needs, is progress which Christianity, which the Church, alone supplies.

More specifically, it is one of the functions of the Christian Church to correct the strong tendencies of civilization itself toward wrong or false developments,—to protest, for example, against the materialism which, in the midst of specious appearances of advance, is surely leading humanity down to lower experiences, and ultimately to a barbaric condition,—to strive against the illusive sway of a merely intellectual or esthetic theory of progress, since education without morality and culture without religion, as modern history abundantly shows, can give no guarantee of healthful and permanent advance, against the deterioration and corruptions of universal sin. The Church is rather steadfastly to turn the eyes of men toward the true secret of advance, and to exhort humanity to make progress first of all and above all by becoming holy. It is also the blessed function of the Church, to associate the idea of civilization with righteousness, with benevolence, with the sense of brotherhood, with the consciousness of the supreme accountability of both men and society to God,—thus suffusing and dignifying all movements in the interest of civilization, with Christian graces and Christian virtues. It is also one of its functions to supply right incentives, adequate inspirations, in the direction of social advancement. The ordinary impulses that move men on in such civilizing processes often prove inadequate. Selfishness, seeking merely the advantage of the individual, is not a motive on which society can permanently rely as a force to raise it, age after age, into better conditions. Nor will the sense of need, the craving of awakened desires, the demands of taste, prove any more reliable: these may engender spontaneous and strong movements for a time, but when the day of gratification comes, the impulse dies away, and lethargy and decadence surely follow. Neither can mankind rely on the incentives of benevolence, the impulses of patriotism or of philanthropy, however true or pure, to sustain enduringly the civilization of the world: such forces have too often revealed their inadequacy in the presence of the clamors of interest, the seductions of passion, the downward drift of human nature. It is Christianity alone which can supply the incentives essential to sound advance: it is the Christian Church alone which preserves in the heart of humanity those finer, those divine inspirations which alone can either enable man to appreciate true progress, or qualify him to strive after and to gain it.[1]

The position of the Church with reference to current social questions and issues, is therefore one of vital interest. No graver mistake can be made than that of supposing that the Church is to stand aloof from such practical concerns, and to content itself with the positive proclamation of the Gospel. For the Gospel itself is a fire in the earth; and there is no living interest of humanity which that Gospel is not designed to reach and benefit. No true reform, as we have seen, can be carried forward successfully on other than Christian principles; and the Church of God owes it both to the Master whom it represents and to the humanity whom it is sent to save, to be in the very center of all wise and pure reform—its regulator and its inspiration. In like manner, all movements in the direction of charity—all institutions for the benefit of suffering classes, and all efforts to supply special need in any part of the world, may justly claim the support of the Church. Most of these institutions and efforts are indeed the offspring of Christianity; their presence in Christianized rather than heathen lands is proof of their origin. And one of the most convincing evidences of its divine quality which the Church can supply, will be found in its steadfast maintenance of every agency, every movement, which has the temper of humanity as its indwelling impulse. Nor can the Church be indifferent to any of those numerous questions respecting the rights of property, the claims of labor and capital, the needs and demands of the laboring classes, the distribution of political power, the organization of society in the interest of the poor rather than the rich, which lie at the basis of so much political and social agitation in this age. For, is it not already apparent that no proposition of capitalists or laborers as classes, no merely political scheme of adjustment, no

---

[1] "Religion controls the forces which mould and refine the soul and society. It is the main-spring or the governing wheel which gives motion, and it also regulates and harmonizes all movements. * * Its glory lies in making all things new, not without other agencies, but through its control over them, and through its sway over the individual soul." WOOLSEY, *Religion of the Future*, p. 397–400.

philanthropic plan of amelioration, can really solve the grave problems here suggested? And is it not the growing conviction that no voice but the voice of Christ, uttered through His Church, can speak the word which will calm these social agitations, and give to society adequate guarantee of a civilization in which the rights of all and the interests of all shall be harmoniously blended in one?

It is thus the peculiar privilege of the Church of Christ to take the great interests of humanity, of the world, on its heart, and to apply the Gospel whose messenger it is, to every human need, in order to the ultimate production of a truly Christian civilization. Not only is the Church to solve the spiritual problems of human life; it is to minister, as an angel of mercy, to that life in even its lowest forms of need, and by the power of love to lift it out of every degradation, every deformity, every antagonism, into the strength, beauty, peace, which spiritual Christianity imparts. The Bible is the Book of the Future—the future of earth as well as the future of heaven; and the Church of the Bible, one in spirit and beautified by grace, has the future of the earth, the future of mankind, in its hands. The Bible reveals, and the Church believes in, a glorious consummation for humanity, and for the earth—a consummation to be secured through the Gospel. No other forces than truth and love, and the Holy Ghost, are requisite to that consummation: no other agent than the Church is needful to bring it to pass. And as the Church grows inwardly in character, and is multiplied outwardly from continent to continent, civilization will surely follow, in grander and still grander forms, until in the completed development of the Church, humanity shall reach its glorious maturity. Then will come to pass the ancient prophecy, that the Mountain of the Lord shall be established in the top of the mountains, and it shall be exalted above the hills; AND ALL NATIONS SHALL FLOW UNTO IT.

www.ingramcontent.com/pod-product-compliance
Lightning Source LLC
Chambersburg PA
CBHW020846160426
43192CB00007B/802